THE MACRAMÉ BOOK

Fig. 1 Space Divider. Wool 18″ x 36″. *Joan Michaels Paque*. Photo, *Hank Paque*.

THE MACRAMÉ BOOK

HELENE BRESS

CHARLES SCRIBNER'S SONS   NEW YORK

CREDITS

Photographs—Allen Bress
Knot diagrams—Seymour Bress
Illustrations—Trudy Nicholson
Illustration on page 117—Doramay Keasbey

A-10.72[MZ]

Printed in the United States of America
Library of Congress Catalog Card Number 79-37222
SBN 684-12756-3 (Trade cloth)

For
Seymour

Fig. 2   Flower. *Margie Thurman.*

LINES FROM A MACRAMANIAC

I contemplate with some chagrin
the unexpected state I'm in:

When any graduate of Vassar
prefers to make an antimacassar
instead of, say, an antitoxin,
she doubtless has a head with rocks in.

My tastes had always run to yachting,
modern dance and Greek—not knotting;
I thought that Macramé was not
a piece of handwork, but a Scot.

A clod I was, a duffer whose
infrequent stabs at tying shoes
would end, with constancy uncanny,
in knots irrevocably granny.

When suddenly, with little warning,
I woke to find myself, one morning,
struck with pangs of macramania,
and growing, with each moment, zania.

I entered on a knotting binge
by ravaging my bathrobe fringe
with beaded knot and Josephine.
(It seems to me it should demean

an empress of such fame to lend
her handle to a carrick bend.)
From there I seized a clothesline, which is
now reduced to single hitches.

All things on which my hands were laid
were in an instant macraméd.
For diamond rings and furs I care not;
I ask for nothing but a square knot.

And now, in keeping with this format,
my doorstep has a knotted doormat;
my shower has a knotted curtain;
a knotted waistband keeps my shirt in.

My hair, when recently shampooed,
is settled in a knotted snood;
my knees are warmed with knotted shawls;
a knotted hanging decks the halls.

My floors are laid with knotted rugs;
my arms are wrapped in knotted shrugs;
the tassels on my shades consist
of head of Turk and monkey's fist.

I covered up the baby grand
with bullion knot and overhand.
(What other handicraft or hobby
provides one with a knotted Knabe?)

I'm hoping that in time the tide'll
change and leave my fingers idle.
Perhaps some day with luck I'll find
a man who's macramé-inclined.

And then the tie I conjure up shall
be a knot that's strictly nuptial.

SYLVIA CASSEDY

Acknowledgments

What is it that makes craftsmen—as a group—the great people they are? Is it their involvement in something in which they find great fulfillment?

The copious amount of cooperation, confidence, and trust that I encountered while writing this book was extraordinary. It has made it a particularly pleasant adventure for me.

Before I had written down even one word, Claribel Rathke offered to type my manuscript for me—and that was no idle offer. A pleasant, willing typist, well versed in the crafts—a perfect combination.

Thoughtfulness and helpfulness abounded. Thank you, Ellen Bennett, for the many kind things you did—so freely and cordially. Dear Martha and Dear Jeanne—I could always count on you. Whether it was encouragement, technical advice, a sounding board, or—whatever, Martha Hoering and Jeanne Vernon were always there. Among those other free spirits who saw a challenge, accepted it willingly, and solved it magnificently were Doramay Keasbey, Mary Belle Frey, and Trudy Nicholson.

A very special thank you to all of those whose work is shown in the book—and to all of those who sent photographs or lent work for us to photograph, and—alas—there was no room to show it. Your cooperation cannot be overstated.

Behind the cold, stone façades of our nation's museums are some very warm people. Those I have come in contact with are very knowlegeable as well, and very willing to share their knowledge with you. Particular thanks to Doris Bowman of the Smithsonian Institution in Washington, D.C. Thanks, too, to Grace Cooper and my other Smithsonian friends. At the Cooper-Hewitt Museum of Decorative Arts and Design, N.Y., my thanks go to Milton Sonday and Sandra Shaffer for their kind assistance even before their collection was properly housed in their new headquarters.

Because of her kindness and calm confidence, my editor, Elinor Parker, made this book a pleasure to write. There are many people behind the scenes at Charles Scribner's Sons. They have treated me well.

I have a very dear family—and each helped in his own way.

My son Allen was my photographer. With great pride, I say that his work speaks for itself. How nice to have had a photographer on the premises. How nice to have had such a dependable and easy to work with photographer who used much good judgment and who respected the work of others—as well as his own.

My son Steven helped directly when he could and his efforts can be found in many places in this book. What can't be shown are all the very important, indirect ways in which he helped—such as apprenticing in the darkroom and respecting my need to work uninterruptedly.

My son Dan was away at college. The vibrations he sent home were of encouragement and pride.

And as for my husband, Seymour, I'm afraid words won't adequately express the contributions he made and my appreciation of them. In between his very many responsibilities, he made time to draw up all the knot diagrams, was substitute typist, substitute photographer, and full-time hand-holder. When I said "I can't," he looked at me with such sincere, utter disbelief that I began to believe "I could." He constantly supplied me with a very liberal sprinkling of that most important, undefinable something we usually refer to—as love.

Contents

THE MACRAMÉ BOOK

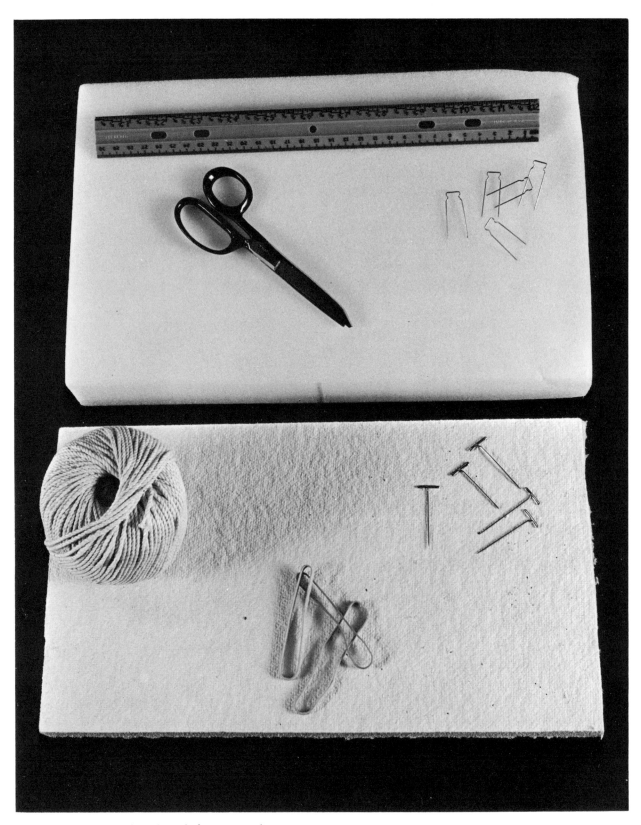

Fig. 3 Basic Materials and Tools for Macramé.

1

IN THE BEGINNING

Macramé is fun to do—and easy to learn. If you are a beginner, follow the first two chapters through from beginning to end and you will learn the basics, unravel the mysteries of macramé, and complete several projects as well.

Happy Knotting!

MATERIALS NEEDED TO BEGIN

The materials pictured are good to start with.
1. *Knotting Board.* The knotting board should be firm, yet allow pins to penetrate. The two pictured are readily available and work very successfully.
    —Polyurethane (plastic foam) Kneeling Pad, Pillow or Pillow Form. A convenient size is about 12″ x 16″. The kneeling pad is available in hardware stores; the pillow or pillow form wherever pillows are sold: dime stores, department stores, fabric stores, etc.
    —Insulating Board. Available from lumberyards. Sometimes scraps are sold; often a large sheet must be bought and cut to size.

If the above are not available, look in Chapter 3, pages 85 to 87 for some substitutes.
2. *Sturdy Pins.* Have on hand about two dozen.
    —"T" pins or "Wig" pins are good for use with either type of knotting board. If you can't find them with sewing supplies, try the department where hair accessories are sold.
    —"U" pins or "Tidy" pins work very well with plastic foam knotting boards. These are most often found on sewing and notions counters.
3. *Cord or twine.* For the first few projects seine twine #18 or #21 is most desirable and most readily available. It's generally obtainable in hardware stores and hardware departments of department stores. Other sizes work well, too. If you cannot get seine twine, some good substitutes are jute, cotton and rayon rug yarn, or any strong, hard twisted cord you may have.
4. *Rubber Bands.*
5. *Scissors.*
6. *Yardstick or Ruler.*
7. *Tracing Paper.*

TO BEGIN—OVERHAND KNOT

A very useful knot to know is the overhand knot. You've probably tied it hundreds of times before for various purposes.

Let's begin by practicing this simple knot.

The only material you need in order to learn and practice this is one 18-inch cord made of any material.

To make the overhand knot:

    Near one end, make a loop over the cord.

    Bring the end under the cord, and through the loop.

    Pull taut.

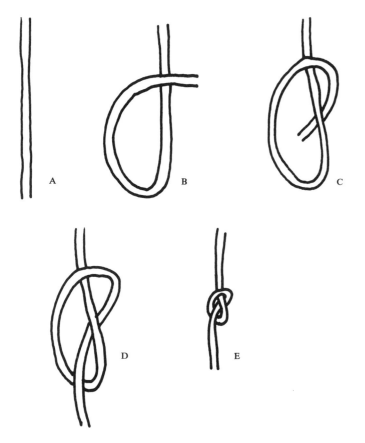

One overhand knot is completed. It's not a thing of beauty in itself, but will have many uses.

For practice, repeat the knot all along the cord. Spacing, at this time, is not important.

SQUARE KNOT

One of the very basic knots in macramé is the square knot. Let's learn this knot by making a little sample.

Materials needed: Seine twine #18 or #21, or jute. Cut 4 cords 2 feet long.

    Tie an overhand knot in each cord about 1½ inches from one end.

    Put a pin through each overhand knot and pin each cord onto your knotting board. The knots should be touching each other.

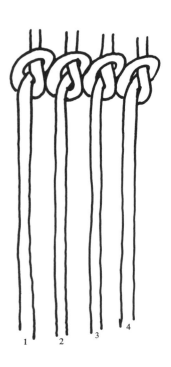

The two central cords are stationary core cords. They may be pinned down near the bottom of the knotting board, if desired.

To do the square knot:

Take the cord on the right (cord 4) and place it over and to the left of the two central cords. Drop cord 4.

Bring cord 1 under the two central cords and through the loop on the right.

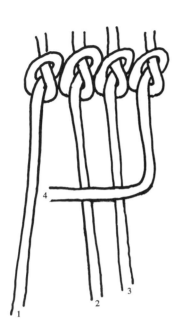

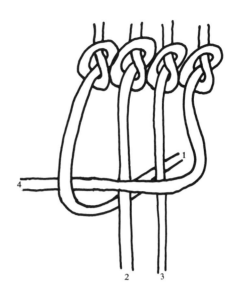

Tighten by pulling on cords 1 and 4.

Pull firmly—but not with all your strength. The first half of the square knot is completed and should be just below the overhand knots.

Take the cord on the left (cord 1) and place it on top of cord 4. (The figure you have now made resembles a backwards 4.)

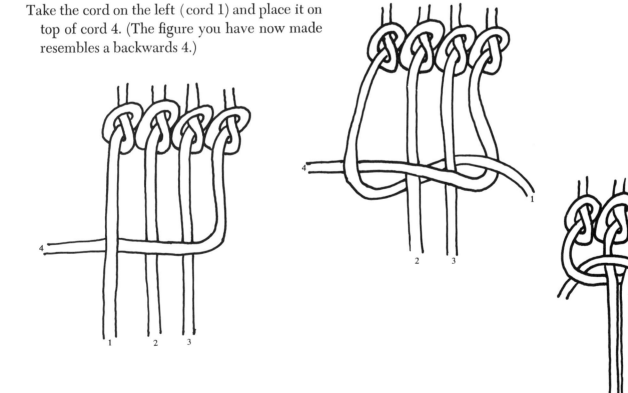

The second half of the square knot is the same as the first, but in reverse.

Cord 4 is now on the left. Bring it over and to the right of the two central cords. Drop cord 4.

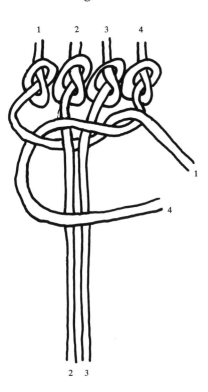

Bring cord 1 under the two central cords, and through the loop on the left.

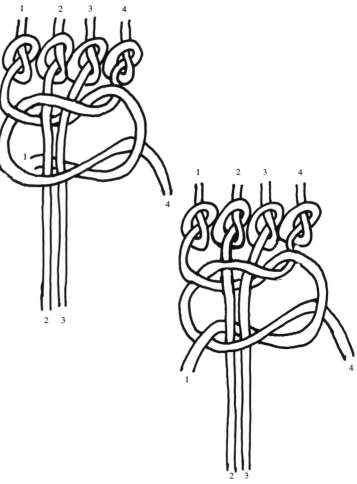

Place cord 1 on top of cord 4.

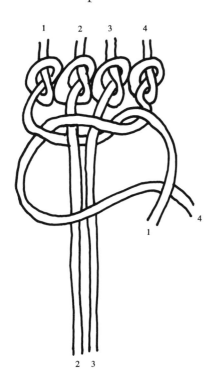

Tighten with cords 1 and 4.
One square knot is now completed.

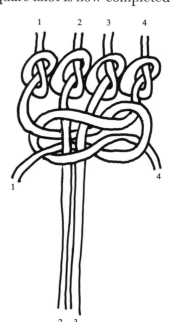

After making several knots, a rhythm will begin to emerge.

First half:
Start with the right cord—

Right	OVER	central cords
Left	OVER	cord 4
	UNDER	central cords
and	THRU	loop

Second half:
Start with the left cord—

Left	OVER	central cords
Right	OVER	cord 1
	UNDER	central cords
and	THRU	loop.

Briefly: Over, Over, Under and Through
Over, Over, Under and Through

Continue making square knots until the knotting cords become too short to handle easily. You will now have a row, or sennit,* of square knots measuring about 4 inches. The knotting cords will be quite short, and the two central cords quite long. There is a great deal of take-up in knotting cords, and practically none with the core cords.

For more practice, mount some more cords or continue by making the belt on the next page.

SQUARE KNOT PROJECT #1

Sash with Square Knots

Materials needed: Seine twine #18 or #21, or jute. Amount needed: 17 yards. Beads are optional for this project. If used, 12 are needed. Holes must be large enough for the cords to go through.

To prepare:
Cut 4 cords 2 yards long.
Cut 2 cords 4½ yards long.

---

* A sennit is a vertical series of like knots—for example, a square knot sennit.

7

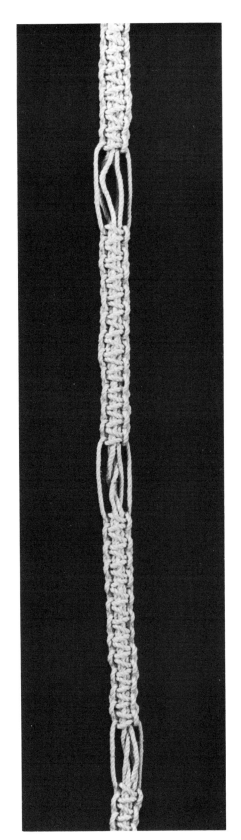

Fig. 4 Project #1. Square Knot Belt. *Steven Bress.*

Make an overhand knot in each cord—about 20 inches from one end.

Pin the cords onto the board as follows:

Pin the shorter cords onto the board first. Then pin the long cords on either side of the shorter cords. The overhand knots should be touching.

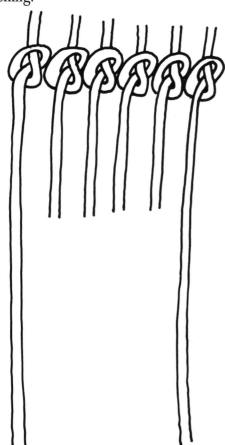

You will be knotting with the two outer cords ONLY. Shorten them and secure with a rubber band. To shorten:

Starting from about 18 inches below the overhand knot, wind the cord around your palm, always placing the cord *alongside* the previous cord and working out toward your fingertips. When you have completely wound the cord, slip it off your hand and place a rubber band around the center. If the winding was done carefully, the cord will release easily as the knotting progresses. If done sloppily, you'll have to undo it occasionally and rewrap.

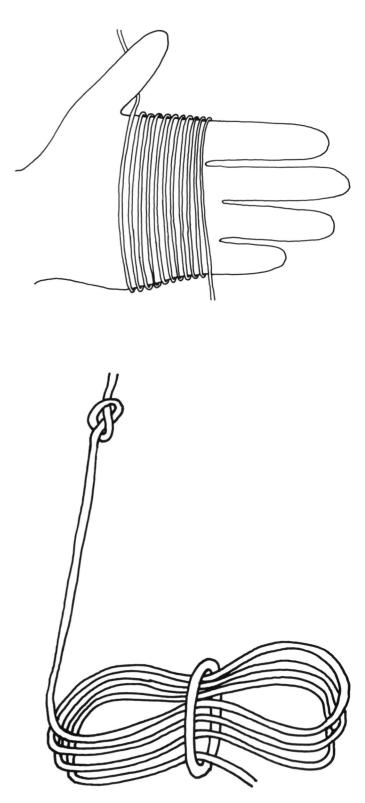

8

Leave the four central core cords dangling straight down, or pin them to the bottom of the knotting board. You will *not* be knotting with these. You'll be knotting *around* these core cords. In the sampler, you knotted around two core cords. In this project, you'll knot around four core cords.

Knotting:

Take the two outside cords and make a square knot.

Continue making square knots, one below the other until the sennit measures four inches.

Put a pin 1½ inches below the last square knot.

Make a square knot and tighten it just below the pin.

Continue making square knots until four inches are completed.

Skip a space of 1½ inches as before.

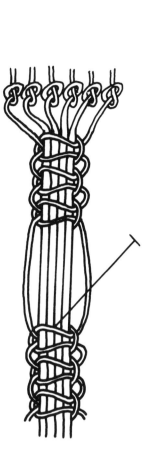

Note: When the knotting nears the bottom of the board, unpin it and move it up to a more comfortable knotting height.

Repeat the above directions until the square knot sections just about circle your waist.

Make overhand knots on each cord, including the core cords, just below the last square knot.

Trim the cords until they all measure 20 inches from the overhand knots.

To finish:

If you are not using beads

Make overhand knots near the end of each cord.

If you are using beads

Slip a bead onto the end of one of the 20 inch strands.

Make an overhand knot below the bead to keep it from falling off.

Repeat the above two steps for each 20 inch strand on both ends of your belt.

One project completed! Different spacings, different yarns, and more or fewer beads will give you a belt that is quite distinct from this one.

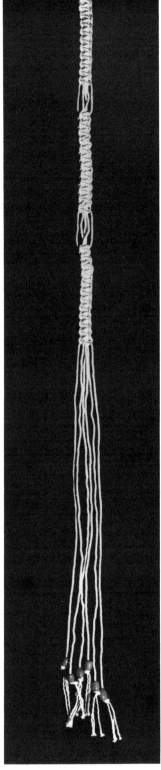

Fig. 5   End of Square Knot Sash. A bead is slipped onto the end of the cord and an overhand knot is made below it to keep it in place. *Steven Bress.*

9

Alternating Square Knot Sash

Materials needed: Seine twine #18 or #21, or jute. Amount needed: 48 yards. Substitute yarns are listed on page 3. Beads are optional. If used, 24 are needed. Holes must be large enough for the cord to go through.

To prepare:
Cut twelve cords 4 yards long.
Tie an overhand knot about 20 inches from the end of each cord.
Pin each cord to the knotting board and have each knot touching the next.
Shorten each cord and secure it with a rubber band.

This belt will be worked using groups of four cords throughout. The two outer cords of each group will be used to knot around the two core cords of that group.

Knotting:
Take the first four cords—1, 2, 3, 4.
Using these cords, make a sennit of five square knots.
Repeat this with the next four cords—5, 6, 7, 8.
Same with the last four cords—9, 10, 11, 12.

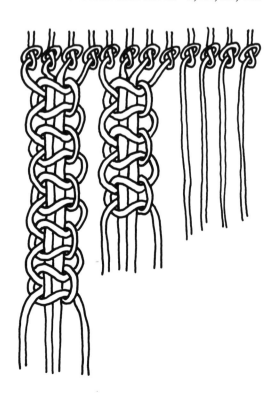

Fig. 6 Project #2. Alternating Square Knot Sash. *Steven Bress.*

Now we'll join the three rows.

Put aside the first two cords—cords 1 and 2.

Take the next four cords—3, 4, 5, 6.

Using these four cords, tie two square knots one below the other.

Take the next four cords—7, 8, 9, 10.

Using those cords, tie two square knots. There will be two cords left over on the right side —11, 12.

Now to regroup:

Pick up cords 1, 2, 3, 4.

Make a sennit of five square knots with those four cords.

Do the same with cords 5, 6, 7, and 8.

Same with cords 9, 10, 11, and 12.

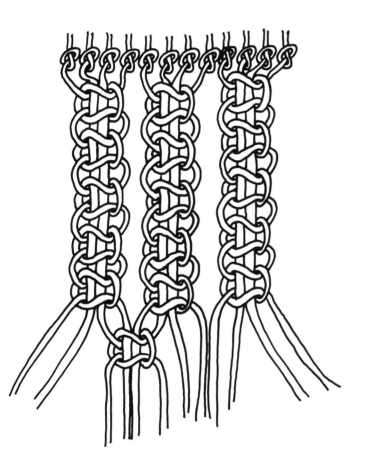

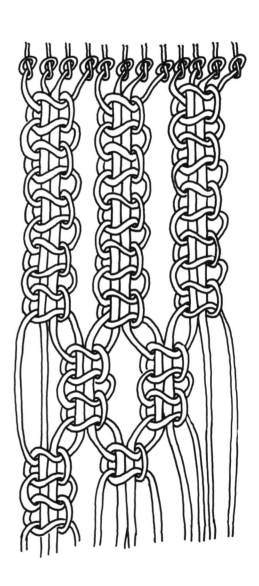

11

Keep alternating the square knot sections until the knotted portion fits almost completely around your waist.

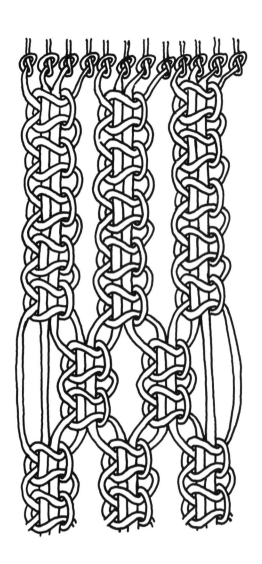

To finish:
Tie an overhand knot on each cord just below the last square knot, then finish as in Square Knot Project #1.

DOUBLE HALF HITCH

The two knots most basic to macramé are the square knot, which you now know, and the double half hitch. The double half hitch can be made horizontally, vertically, diagonally, and in a straight or curved line. To learn the double half hitch, let's make another sample.

Materials needed: Seine twine #18 or #21, or jute. Substitute yarns are listed on page 3.

To prepare:
Cut eight cords—each cord 2 feet long.
Make an overhand knot in each cord, about 1½ inches from one end.
Pin the cords to your knotting board side by side. Put one pin through the center of each overhand knot and pin them to the board so that the knots are touching each other.

To knot:
Place a pin between cord 1 and cord 2.
Bring cord 1 on top of all the other cords and place it just below the line of overhand knots. Cord 1 will now be used as a knot bearer.

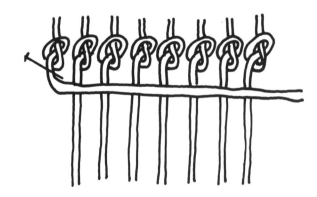

Hold the knot bearer (cord 1) horizontally with
  your right hand.
With your left hand, pick up cord 2.
**Bring cord 2 up, and on top of the knot bearer.

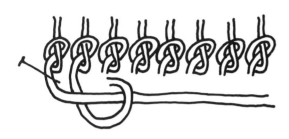

(Keep the knotting cord well over to the right to
avoid getting tangled in the pins.)
  Bring it under the knot bearer and
  Through the loop it formed.

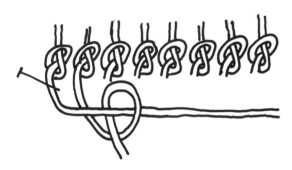

  Pull cord 2 taut while pushing it close to the
  pins.**

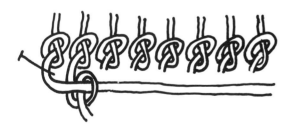

Half the knot has been formed.
  With the same cord (cord 2) repeat the steps
  between the asterisks.

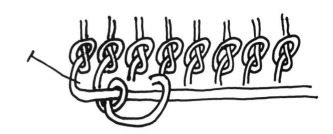

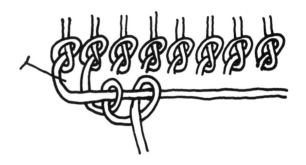

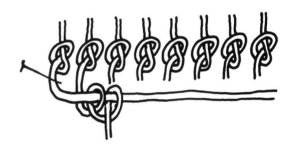

Be sure the knots are standing vertically and are
pushed close to the overhand knots before tightening the cord. One complete double half hitch
has been made.
  Continue knotting this way with the rest of the
  cords across the row.

To return—double half hitch from right to left
Cord 1 will still be used as your knot bearer.
Put a pin between cord 8 and your knot bearer.
Bring the knot bearer over to the left and on top of all the other cords.

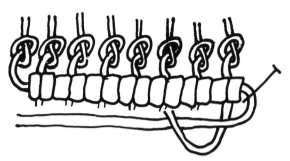

Hold knot bearer with your left hand. Keep it close to and parallel to the previous row of knots.

With your right hand pick up cord 8.

**Bring it on top of knot bearer. (Keep the knotting cord well over to the left to avoid getting tangled in the pins.)

Take cord 8 under the knot bearer and through the loop you've formed.

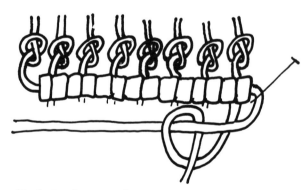

Push it close to the previous row of knots and pull it taut.**

With the same cord (cord 8) repeat the steps between the asterisks.

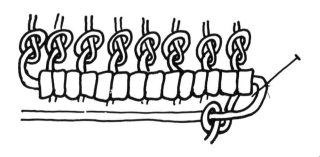

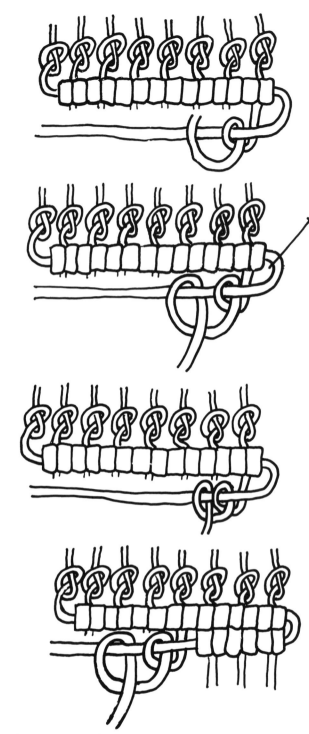

Continue in this manner across the row, using cords 7 through 2 in turn.

Repeat rows 1 and 2.

When you have completed four rows, you will begin to be comfortable with the double half hitch. Now we're going to use this same knot in a slightly different way—and will form an angle.

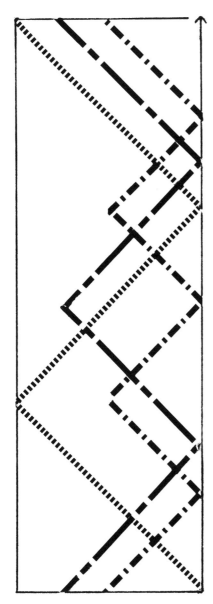

PATTERN FOR ANGLES

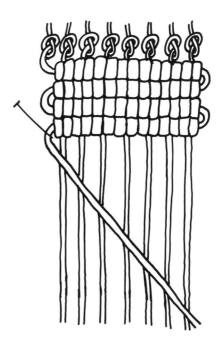

Hold the knot bearer firmly with your right hand, remembering to keep the knot bearer at the proper angle.

Trace the pattern for angles onto a piece of paper. Pin the paper pattern onto your knotting board so that the arrow touches the bottom right corner of your knotting. Choose as your guide for angling the line on the pattern which is closest to cord 1. Cord 1 will be your knot bearer again.

Place a pin between cords 1 and 2.

Bring cord 1 on top of all the other cords and place it at an angle this time. Choose as your guide the line on the paper pattern which is closest to cord 1.

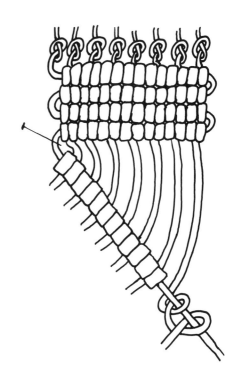

Double half hitch as before, with cord 2 through 8, keeping the knot bearer at an angle.

15

To return, place a pin between cord 8 and the knot bearer.

Bring the knot bearer to the left and on top of all the other cords.

Hold the knot bearer with your left hand along the same pattern line you have been following.

Double half hitch along the knot bearer, using cords 8 through 2.

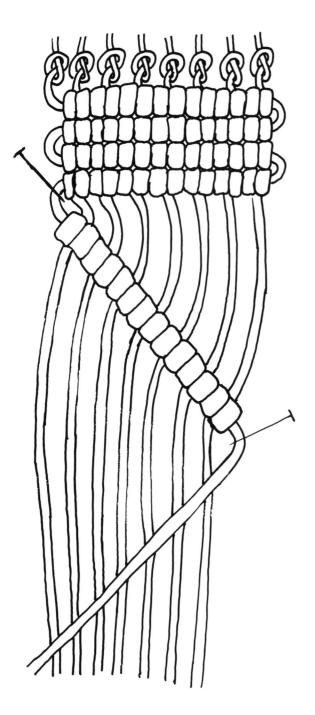

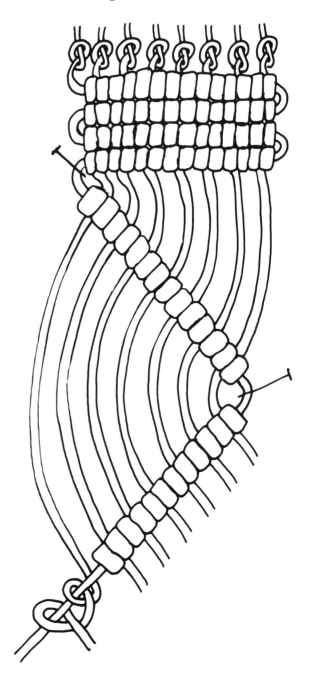

Continue as above one or two more times.
The sash on the next page uses this technique.

SASH USING DOUBLE HALF HITCH
PROJECT #3

Materials needed: Seine twine #18 or #21, or jute. Amount needed: 30 yards. Substitute yarns are listed on page 3.

To prepare:
Cut ten cords, each cord three yards long. Place each cord in a separate pile so that they won't tangle.
Take one cord and tie an overhand knot about 20 inches from one end.
Put a pin through the overhand knot and pin it to the knotting board.
Shorten the cord.

Repeat the same steps for each of the remaining cords.
Pin the cords side by side, as on the sampler.

Cord 1 will be your knot bearer throughout this project.

To knot:
Start by making two rows of horizontal double half hitches, as in the sample.

Pin the paper pattern you used for your sample under your knotting as before. This will again be used as a guide for angling.
Bring the knot bearer on top of the other cords and place it at an angle. Use as your guide the line on the paper pattern which is closest to cord 1.
Double half hitch with cords 2 through 10.
Place a pin between cord 10 and the knot bearer.
Angle knot bearer to the left, on top of the other cords.
Double half hitch with cords 10 through 2.
Continue to angle to the right and left until the sash just about meets around your waist.

Now make two more rows of horizontal double half hitches.

To finish:
Remove the overhand knots from the beginning of the sash. The sash will now have ten strands hanging at each end. On each strand make

17

about four or five overhand knots at irregular intervals, as in the picture.

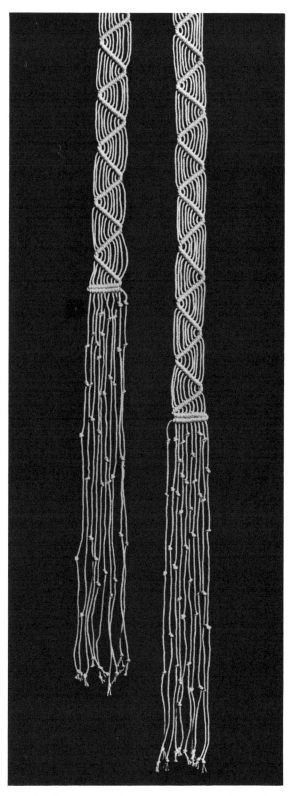

Fig. 7 Project #3. Sash using double half stitches. Overhand knots at irregular intervals form the ending of this sash.

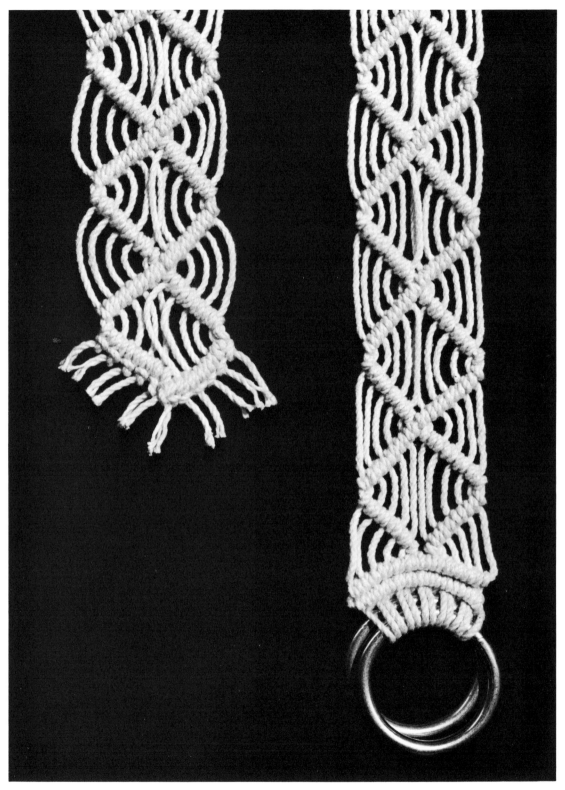

Fig. 8 Project #4. Beginning and ending of the Diamond Belt.

18

DIAMOND BELT PROJECT #4

Materials needed: Seine twine #18 or #21, or
jute. Amount needed: 36 yards. Two rings—"O"
or "D" rings—about 1½ inches in size. (See page
116.) Substitute yarns are listed on page 3. If
heavier yarns are used, larger rings may be
needed.

To prepare:
Pin the two rings to the board.
Cut one cord six yards long.
Fold that cord in half.
Place the folded half—the end with the loop—on
    top of, around, and behind the rings.

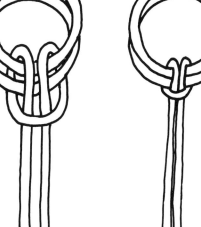

Take the cut ends of the cord and slip them
    through the loop in the cord.
Pull the ends tight.
Detailed drawings of this on page 63.
Shorten each end of the cords separately.

Repeat the above with five more cords.
You now have 12 working cords on your rings and
each cord is three yards long.
Do two rows of double half hitches, as in the
    previous project, but keep the knots close to
    the rings. This will keep the rings firmly in
    place.

Trace the diamond pattern onto a piece of paper.
Pin this pattern to the board so that the point of
the diamond is between cords 6 and 7.

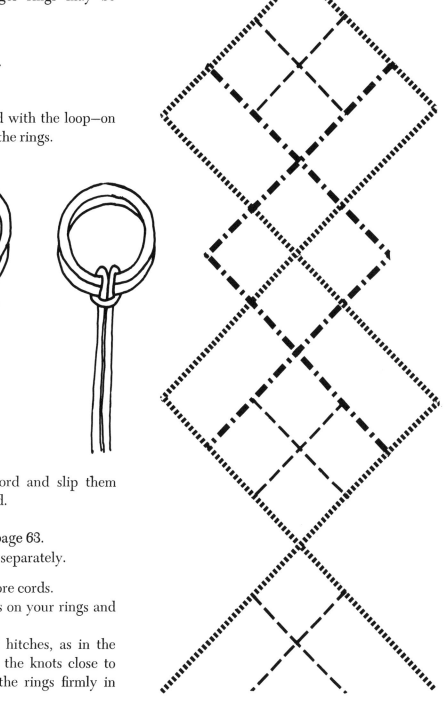

Divide your cords in half. Put the first six cords
   aside to the left, and work with the six cords
   on the right.
Cord 7 will be your knot bearer for this part.
Angle to the right using cords 8 through 12 in
   order.

Now put these cords aside and let's go back to
those you set aside before. Cord 6 will be your
knot bearer for this side.

   Angle to the left, using cords 5 through 1 in
   order.

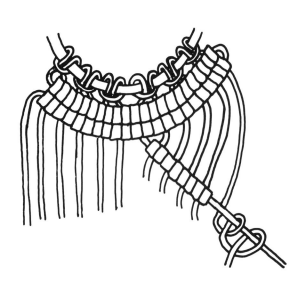

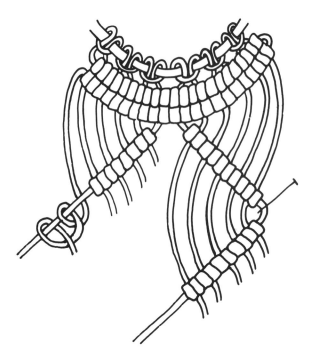

Place a pin between the knot bearer (cord 7)
   and cord 12. Angle back, using cords 12
   through 8 in order. Use as your guide that
   line on the pattern closest to cord 7 where it
   begins to angle back.

Place a pin between the knot bearer (cord 6) and
   cord 1. Angle back to the right, using cords 1
   through 5 in order.

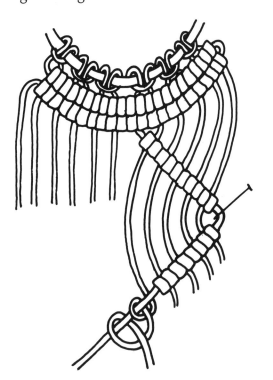

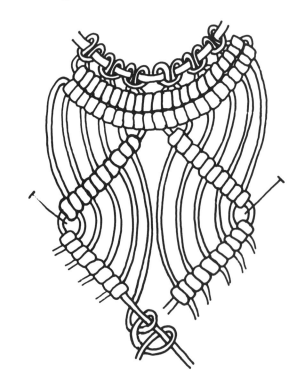

Both knot-bearing cords are now back in the center. To close the diamond they form:

Take cord 7 and place it on top of cord 6.

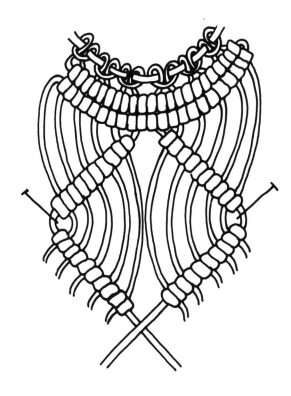

With cord 6, double half hitch over cord 7.

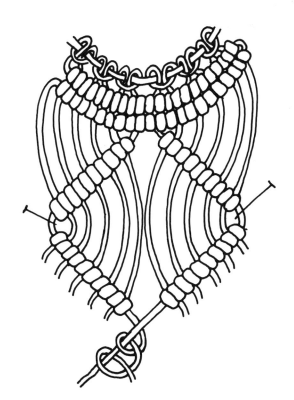

Cord 7 now becomes the holding cord for the left part of the diamond, and cord 6 now becomes the holding cord for the right part of the diamond.

Continue making diamonds as above until the belt is a few inches longer than your waist.

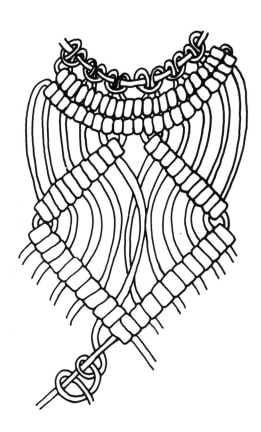

To finish: Make overhand knots just below the last row of double half hitches. Trim the cords so that they're about half an inch long.

21

Fig. 9 Project #5. Belt. Diamonds with Variations. The beginning and ending of the belt are shown.

BELT: DIAMONDS WITH VARIATIONS
PROJECT #5

Materials needed: Seine twine #18 or #21, or jute. Amount needed: 56 yards. Buckle 1½ inches-2 inches wide. Substitute yarns are listed on page 3. If using other yarns, use any buckle that will hold 14 cords comfortably.

To prepare:

Cut seven cords, each cord 8 yards long.

Fold each cord in half and mount it onto your buckle the same way you mounted cords on the rings in the previous project.

You will now have 14 cords and each cord will be four yards long. Use the paper pattern you made for the previous project. Pin it to your board with the point of the diamond between cords 7 and 8. Your middle cords, cords 7 and 8, are knot bearers.

Diamond #1

Make one complete diamond as in the previous project.

Diamond #2

Continue by making a second diamond, but make only the top half of it.

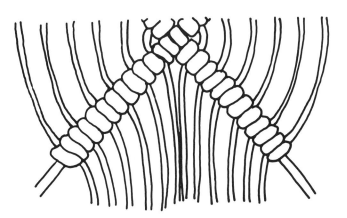

We will now work with the four central cords (5, 6, 9, 10). Cords 5 and 10 will be the knotting cords; cords 6 and 9 will be the stationary core cords.

Using the four central cords, make a sennit of square knots. When you reach the center of the diamond, count the number of knots needed to get to that point. Make the same number for the bottom half of the sennit.

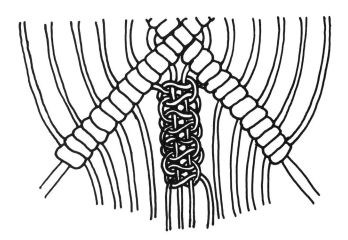

Finish the bottom of the diamond.

Diamond #3

Make the top half of diamond #3.

Put the two knot-bearing cords aside.

Make a square knot, using cords 1 and 14. Knot these cords around all the remaining cords.

Do not draw the square knot in too tightly; do not tighten it so much that the diamond draws in.

Make the bottom half of the diamond, using the cords in the same order as they come from the top half of the diamond.

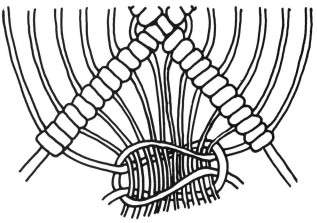

Diamond #4—Alternating Square Knots

Make the top half of the next diamond.

Row 1—Make a square knot with the four central cord (cords 5, 6, 9, and 10).

Row 2—Alternate the square knots and make two square knots in this row—one with cords 3, 4, 5, 6, the other with cords 9, 10, 11, and 12.

Row 3—Alternate again. Three square knots will be made in this row: one with cords 1, 2, 3, 4, one with cords 5, 6, 9, 10, and one with cords 11, 12, 13, and 14.

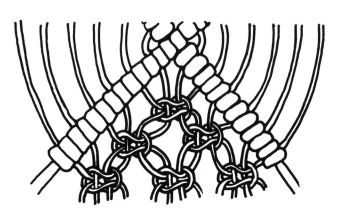

The two knot-bearing cords will not be used for making any square knots.

Row 4—Knot the same as you did row 2.

Row 5—Knot the same as you did row 1.

Make the bottom half of the diamond.

Repeat these four diamonds until the belt goes almost completely around your waist. Then do a few more diamonds with alternating square knots so that the buckle "tongue" will have a hole to go through.

To finish:

Work on the back side of the belt. With a crochet hook or a large-eyed embroidery needle, pull each end through two knots. Make an overhand knot as close to the belt as possible. Clip the end short. If desired, glue the ends down, and if the belt will be washed, use a glue that is not water soluble.

Variations of the previous belts are easy to design. Different materials, the use of color, different spacings, using the knots in a different order, are all ways of varying the original theme.

The chart on pp. 100–106 will be a helpful guide for cord selections.

Once you feel secure with the basic knots and the variations presented in this chapter, you have graduated from the beginner stage.

The following chapters of this book are intended to present new material, answer questions and, most hopefully, to inspire.

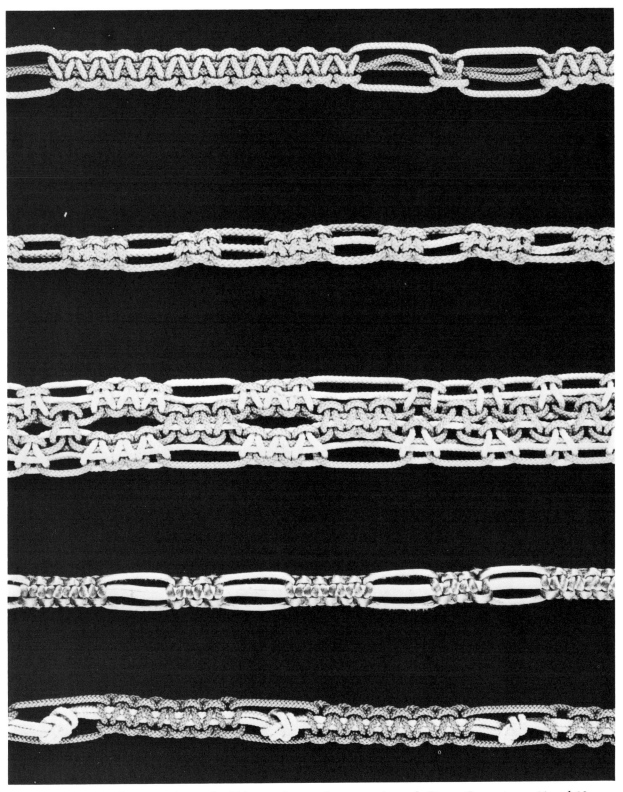

Fig. 10 Variations of Square Knot Belts. Polypropylene and rayon satin cord. *Steven Bress at ages 11 and 12.*

25

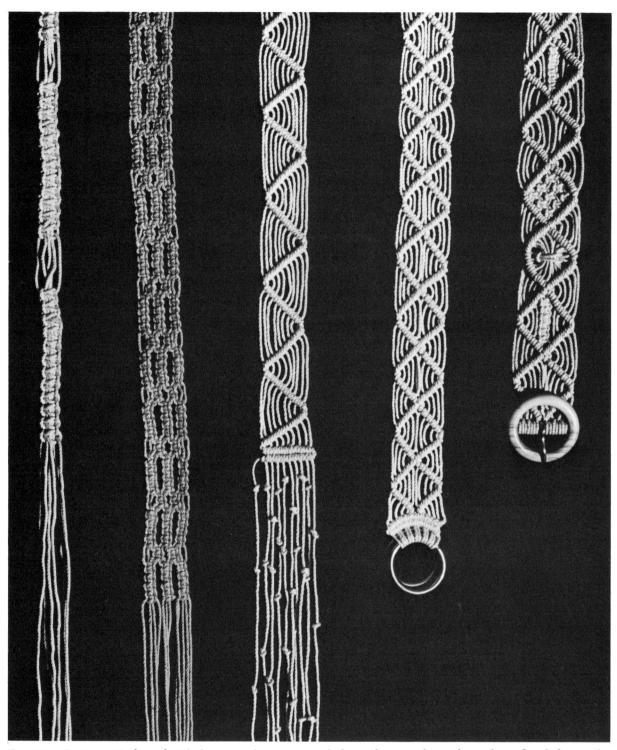

Fig. 11   Projects #1 through #5. Once you have mastered the techniques for making these five belts, you're well into the art of macramé.

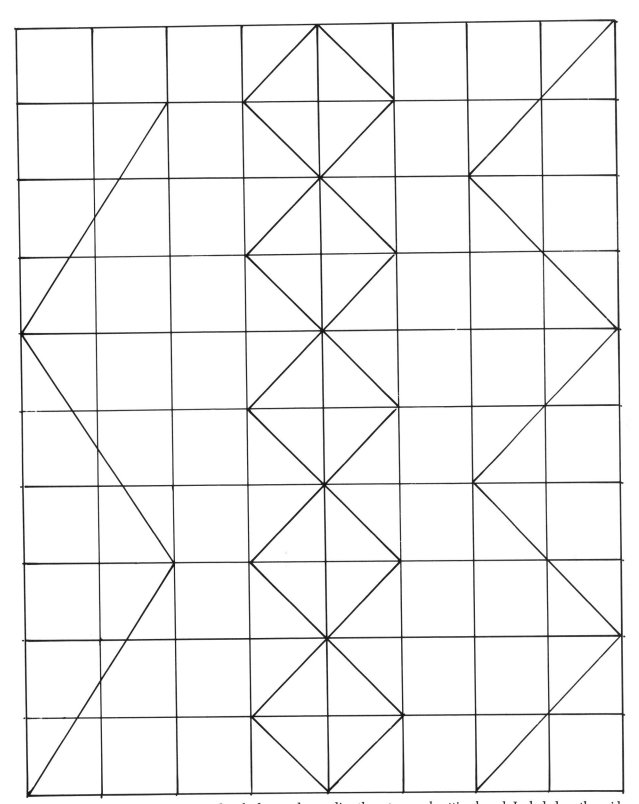

Grid. It's very helpful to have a grid tacked to or drawn directly onto your knotting board. Included on the grid on this page are some of the angles most commonly used in macramé. The straight lines and angles help you to keep your knotting straight.

2
THEMES AND VARIATIONS

Now that you know the basics of macramé, the door is wide open. You can close the door on the first chapter, and just refer to the remaining chapters from now on. The basic knots are reviewed; some new ones are added for you to learn at your convenience. We'll try to help you resolve your problems and free you to create your own projects.

TERMS USED IN MACRAMÉ

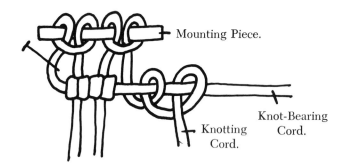

Mounting Piece.

Knot-Bearing Cord.

Knotting Cord.

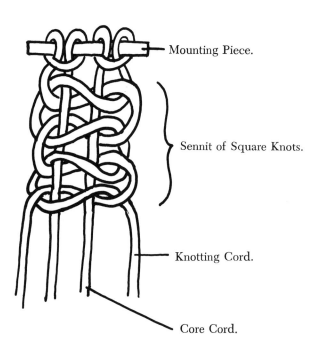

Mounting Piece.

Sennit of Square Knots.

Knotting Cord.

Core Cord.

I A. *Sennit of Square Knots*
One square knot is made directly below the next.

I B. *Sennit of Square Knots Using One Light-Colored Knotting Cord and One Dark Knotting Cord*
The colors are reversed on the other side of the sennit.

28

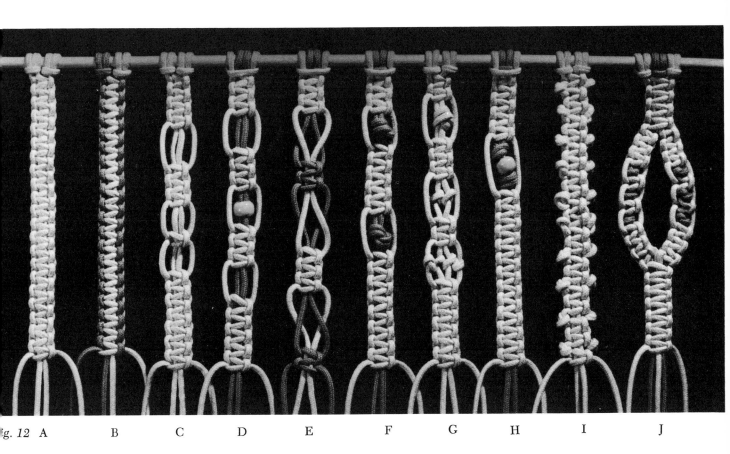

Fig. 12 A   B   C   D   E   F   G   H   I   J

I C. *Square Knot Sennit with Spaces*

A sennit of four square knots was made. A pin was placed below the fourth knot. A square knot was made below the pin and tightened right beneath the pin.

I D. *Two-Color Square Knot Sennit with Bead*

The bead was slipped onto the two core cords and pushed up into place. More knots were made below it.

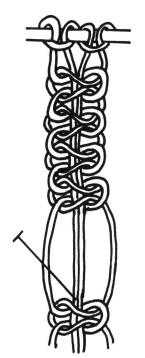

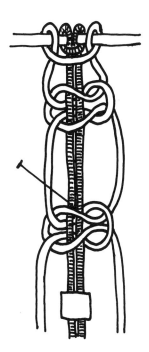

29

I E. *Square Knot Sennit with Knotting Cords and Core Cords Switching Positions for an Interesting Color and Design Effect*

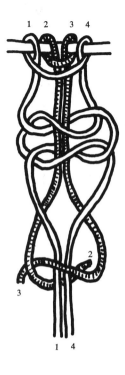

I G. *Square Knot Sennit with Overhand Knot Variations*

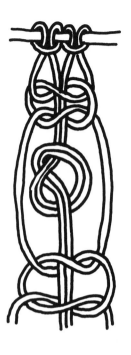

I F. *Two-Color Square Knot Sennit with Overhand Knots*

As in this sennit, a second color can be hidden within a sennit and brought to the surface at will. In this case, an overhand knot accentuates the second color.

I H. *Two-Color Square Knot Sennit with Overhand Knot and Bead*
The bead adds a third color to this sennit.

I I. *Square Knot Sennit with Overhand Knots at the Edges of Every Other Square Knot*

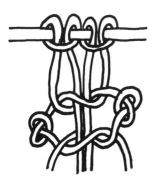

I J. *Two-Color, Six-Strand Square Knot Sennit*
Four square knots were made, using the two outside cords as knotting cords, and the remaining four cords as core cords. The sennit was then split into two parts, with two light-colored cords and one dark-colored cord in each part. Using the light cords as knotting cords, three more square knots were formed with each group. The darker cord was then used to make an overhand knot.

II *Spirals*

A spiral is made by repeating the first half of the square knot over, and over, and over again—until the desired length is made. The only trick is this: after you have made a few half square knots (about four or five), you will notice that the sennit has begun to twist and is almost facing your knotting board.

Allow the knotting cords to continue going in the direction in which they are headed and help them along. Bring the top knotting cord over to the side to which it is pointing. Bring the bottom knotting cord under the core cords and to the opposite side. Now continue making half square knots exactly as you had been before. After a few more half knots have been made, the spiraling action will repeat itself.

II A. *Spiral Sennit of Half Square Knots*
The first half of the square knot (as described on page 5) was made over and over again.

II B. *Spiral Sennit of Half Square Knots*
This sennit twists in the direction opposite to the first one because it is made with the

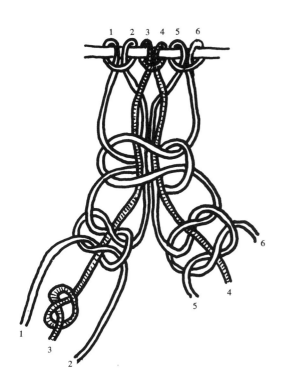

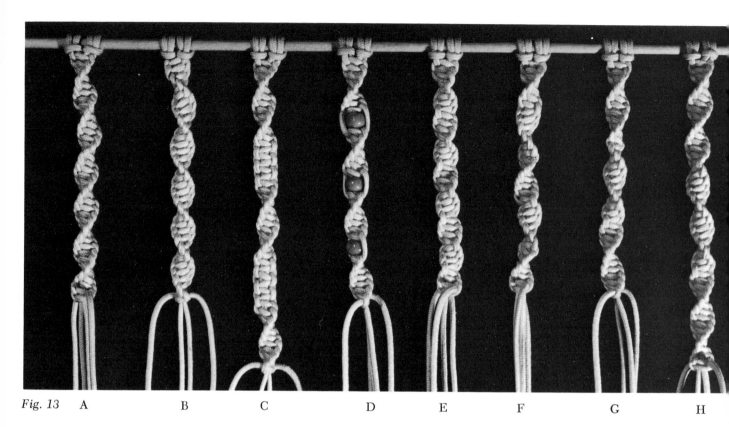

Fig. 13   A   B   C   D   E   F   G   H

II C. *Spiral Sennit Interrupted with Bands of Whole Square Knot Sennits*

II D. *Spiral Sennit with Beads*

II E. *Spiral Sennit with Direction of Twist Changing After Four Half Square Knots*
Four half square knots were made using the first half of the square knot, then four were made using the second half of the square knot. This was repeated throughout.

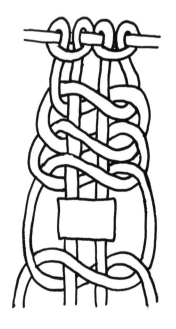

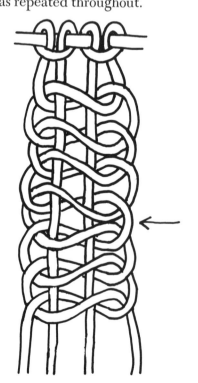

32

II F. *Spiral Sennit with Direction of the Twist Changing After Seven Half Square Knots*

II G. *Spiral Sennit with Direction of the Twist Changing After Eleven Half Square Knots*

II H. *Spiral Sennit with Direction of Twist Changing After Fifteen Half Square Knots*

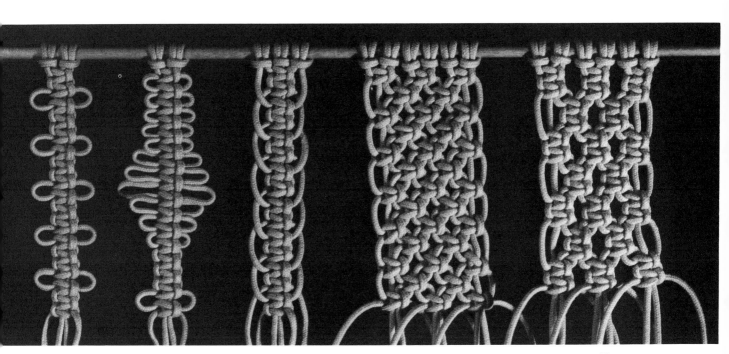

Fig. 14   A   B   C   D   E

III A. *Square Knot Sennit with Picots*

Place a pin a distance below the second square knot of the sennit. Make a square knot or two below the pin. Remove the pin, and slide the square knots close to the previous knots. The slack cords between the square knots will now bow out. If several picots are to be made, graph paper will be a helpful guide for spacing the pins.

III B. *Square Knot Sennit with Picots of Graduated Sizes*

Increase or decrease the distance of the pin beneath the square knots to get picots of varying sizes.

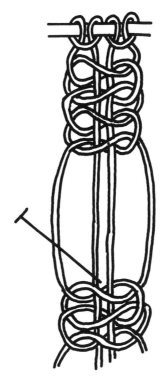

33

III C. *Six-Strand Square Knot Sennit Using Only Two Core Cords and Two Knotting Cords at One Time*

First, cords 2 and 5 were used as knotting cords and two square knots were made. Then, cords 1 and 6 were used and two square knots were made.

III D. *Alternating Square Knot Band—One and One*

Four cords, two knotting cords and two core cords, were used for each square knot throughout this sample.

Row 1—One square knot was made with each group of four cords:

Cords 1, 2, 3, and 4 were used for the first square knot;

Cords 5, 6, 7, and 8 were used for the second square knot;

Cords 9, 10, 11, and 12 were used for the third square knot.

Row 2—The first two cords were put aside. The next four cords (cords 3, 4, 5, and

6) were used to make a square knot. Then, the next four cords (cords 7, 8, 9, and 10) were used to make a square knot. The last two cords were not used in this row.

Row 3—Same as Row 1.
Row 4—Same as Row 2.

The same pattern was repeated throughout.

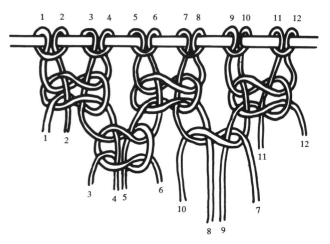

III E. *Alternating Square Knot Band—Two and Two*

The same groupings of the cords were used in this sample, but two square knots were made with each set of cords instead of one. Many more variations of this sort are possible.

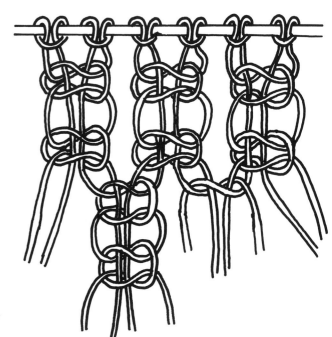

34

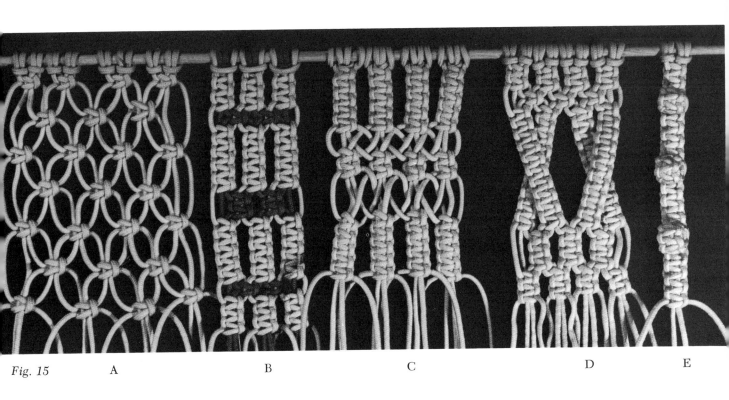

Fig. 15   A   B   C   D   E

IV A. *Alternating Square Knots with an Open, Net-like Effect*

The same technique is used as in the previous samples, but spaces are left between the knots. To keep the spaces even, graph paper can be pinned to your knotting board and pins placed just above the point where the knots are to be made. The knots are then made below the pins. Or, the knots can be formed around an appropriately sized implement, such as a dowel or a ruler.

IV B. *A Pattern of Alternating Square Knots Using Two Colors*

IV D. *Alternating Square Knots and a Cross-over of Square Knot Sennits*

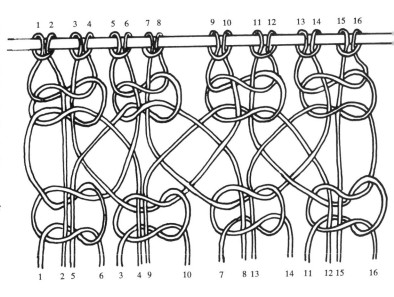

IV C. *Alternating Square Knots with Knotting and Core Cords Changing Places*

IV E. *Square Knot Sennit with Raised Picots*
A sennit of square knots was made. A little space was left and four more square knots were made. Each core cord was threaded onto a large-eyed yarn needle. The core cords were brought up and then put through the space left between the square knots. The core cords were pulled tight and a raised picot was formed. More square knots were made directly below the raised picot.

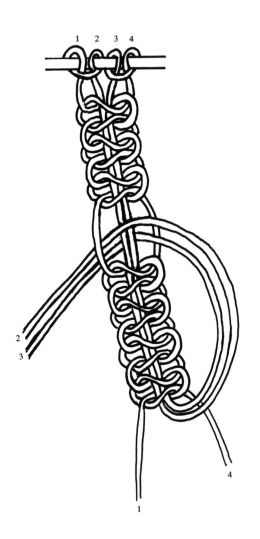

V A. *Rows of Horizontal Double Half Hitches*

V B. *Rows of Horizontal Double Half Hitches with Spaces In Between*

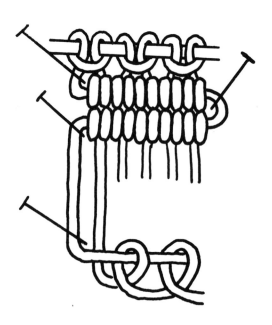

V C. *Diagonal Double Half Hitches*
The holding cord is held at an angle and double half hitches are knotted onto it. It's helpful to pin guide lines to your knotting board so that the angles you form will be even. (There is a more complete description in Chapter 1.)

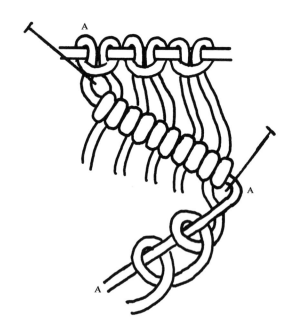

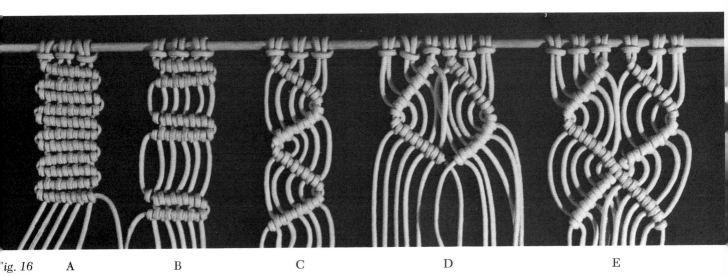

Fig. 16   A   B   C   D   E

V D. *Diagonal Double Half Hitches to Form a Diamond*

The two center cords (cords A and B) are the knot-bearing cords.

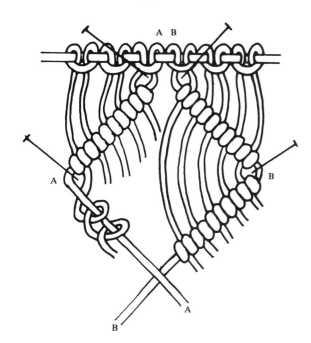

V E. *One Diamond Completed and Another Started*

The point at which the diamonds cross is flat and neat. When the two knot-bearing cords have both reached the center of the diamond, place cord A OVER cord B. Take cord B and make a double half hitch onto cord A.

Cord A now becomes the knot bearer for the right side of the next diamond and cord B becomes the knot bearer for the left side of the next diamond.

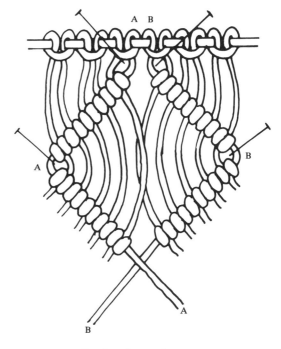

Continued on next page

37

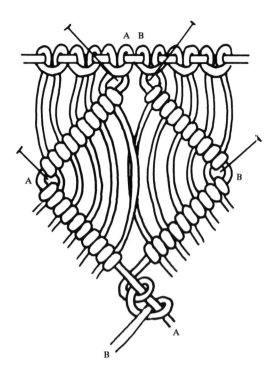

VI A. *X's Made with Double Half Hitches*
For X's, the first and last cord are the knot bearers.

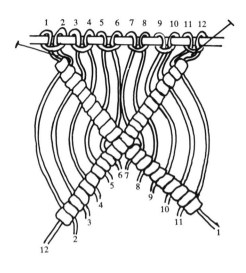

VI B. *Double Diamonds with Double Half Hitches*
The two center cords (6 and 7) are the knot bearers for the first row of the diamond. The cords on either side of this (cords 5 and 8) become the knot bearers for the second row of the diamond. These same cords (cords 5 and 8) remain the knot bearers for the next row. Cords 6 and 7 then become the knot bearers for the fourth row, which completes the double diamond.

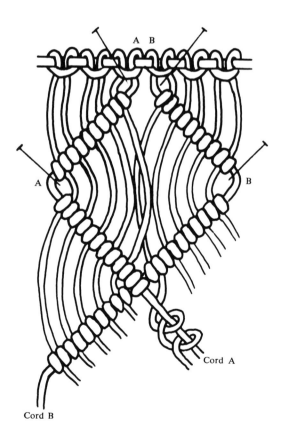

Cord A

Cord B

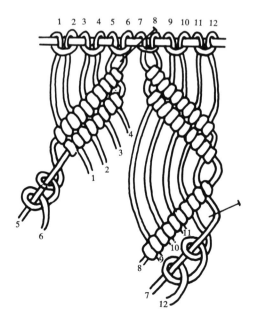

38

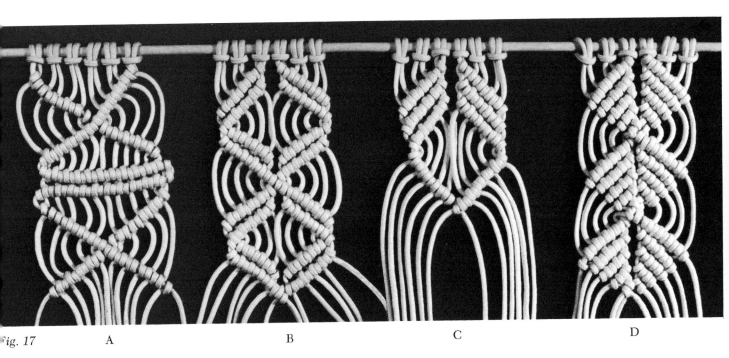

Fig. 17   A   B   C   D

VI C. *Diamond Variation*

The two center cords (6 and 7) are knot bearers for the first row; 5 and 8 for the second row; 4 and 9 for the third row. Cords 4 and 9 continue as knot bearers to complete the diamond.

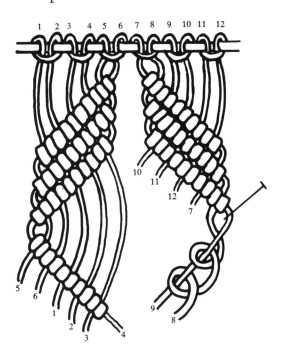

VI D. *Double Half Hitch Variation*

Row 1—Cords 6 and 7 are knot bearers and all the other cords are hitched onto them. The knot bearers are now set aside and not used for the rest of the motif.

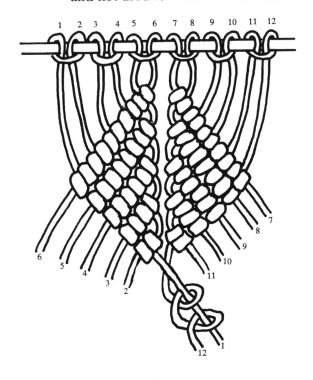

Continued on next page

39

Row 2—Cords 5 and 8 are knot bearers and all the cords, except 6 and 7 are hitched onto them. The knot bearers are set aside and not used for the rest of the motif.

Row 3—Cords 4 and 9 are knot bearers, and all the cords, except 5, 6, 7, and 8, are knotted onto it. The knot bearers are set aside and not used for the rest of the motif.

Row 4—Cords 3 and 10 are knot bearers, and the same knotting pattern as above is followed.

Row 5—Cords 2 and 11 are knot bearers. The same knotting pattern as above is followed.

VII A. *Diamond with Square Knot Acting as a Gathering Knot*
The top half of the diamond is formed in the usual manner. The two knot-bearing cords (cords 6 and 7) are now put aside and are not used while the square knot is

being made. The two outside cords (cords 1 and 12) are picked up and are used to make a square knot using the cords remaining within the diamond as core cords. So as not to distort the diamond shape, the square knot is not pulled in too taut.

The bottom half of the diamond is now made in the usual manner. For a graceful effect, hitch the cords onto the bottom half in the same order as they come from the top part of the diamond.

VII B. *Diamond with Alternating Square Knots*
The top half of the diamond is formed in the usual manner. The two knot-bearing cords are put aside, and are not used to make the center pattern. Starting with the four center cords, a square knot is made. The pattern of alternating square knots is continued:

> 2 knots in the second row
> 3 knots in the third row
> 2 knots in the fourth row
> 1 knot in the fifth row

Then the knot-bearing cords are angled back to the center, and the diamond is completed.

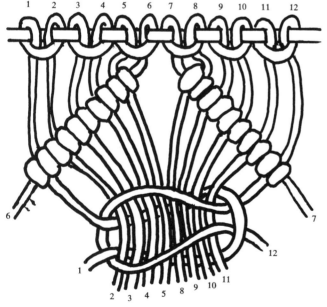

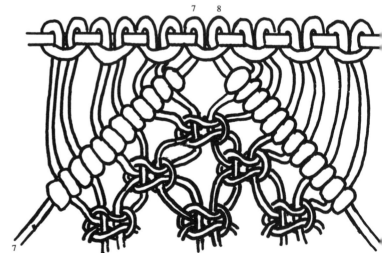

40

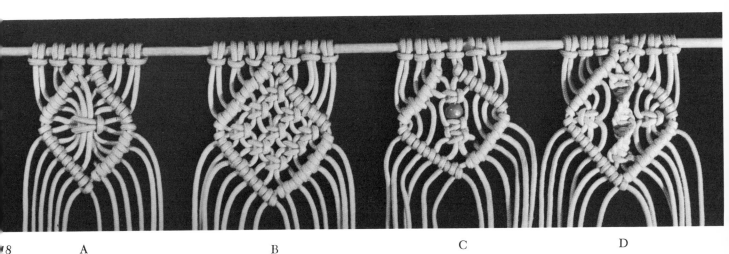

A   B   C   D

VII C. *Diamond with Square Knot Sennit and Bead*

The top half of the diamond is made in the usual manner. With the four central cords, a square knot sennit with a bead is made. The bottom half of the diamond is then completed.

VII D. *Diamond with a Spiral and Square Knots*

Fourteen cords are used this time, and the top half of the diamond is completed in the usual manner. The two knot-bearing cords are put aside. A spiral of half knots is made down the center and one square knot is made on either side of it. Notice that the two square knots are mirror images of one another. One is made in the conventional way. In the other the knotting sequence is reversed.

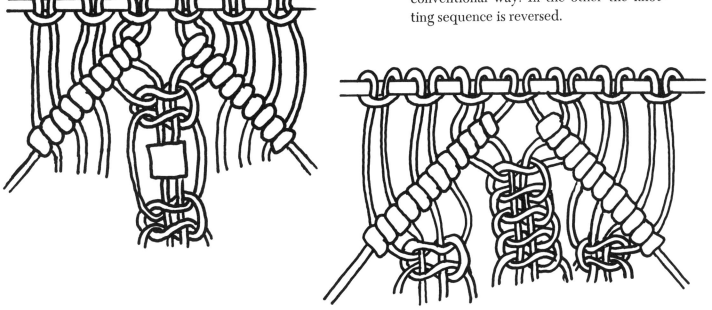

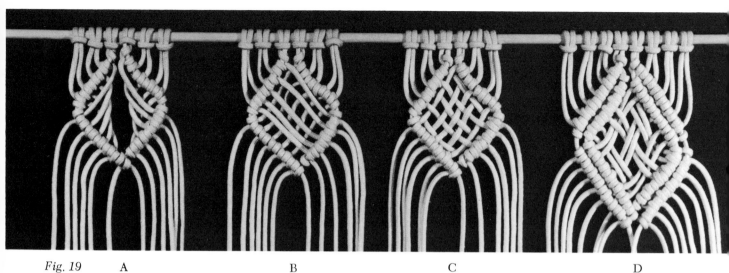

Fig. 19   A   B   C   D

VIII A. *Diamond Variation*

The top half of the diamond is formed in the usual manner. Then the knot-bearing cord on the right (cord 7) is angled back to the center and the knotting cords are hitched on in this order: cord 8 first, 9 next, then 10, 11, and 12. The knot bearing cord on the left (cord 6) is then angled back to the center, and the knotting cords are hitched on in this order: 5, 4, 3, 2, and 1.

VIII B. *Diamond Variation*

The top half of the diamond is formed in the usual manner. The knot-bearing cord on the left (cord 6) is then angled back toward the center and the knotting cords from the top right half of the diamond are now hitched onto it—first cord 8, then 9, 10, 11 and 12. The other half of the diamond is done in the same manner.

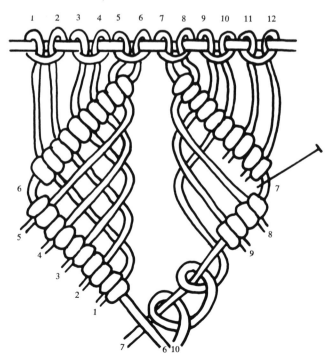

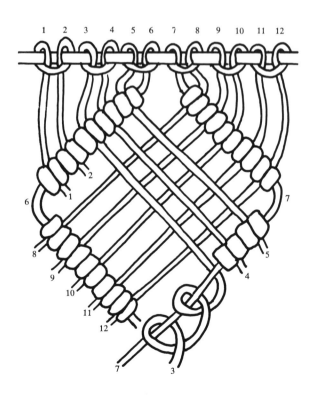

42

VIII C. *Weaving within a Diamond*

Again, the top half of the diamond is formed in the usual manner. The cords within the diamond are then woven in this way. One at a time, the cords on the right are woven over and under the cords on the left. First, cord 8 weaves over and under cords 5, 4, 3, 2, and 1. Cord 8 is pushed up close to the side of the diamond. Next, cord 9 weaves under and over cord 5, 4, 3, 2, and 1, and is then pushed close to the previous one. These steps are repeated with cords 10, 11, and 12.

The bottom half of the diamond is then completed.

VIII D. *Double Diamond with Two over Two Weaving in Center*

You need an even number of cords in the center to weave like this. The method is the same as for VIII C.

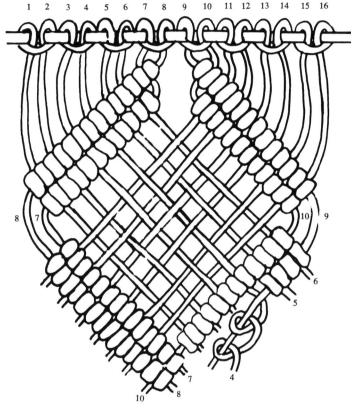

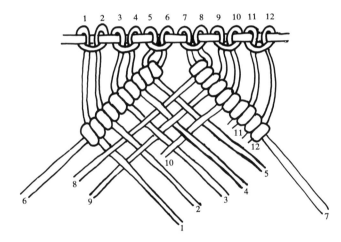

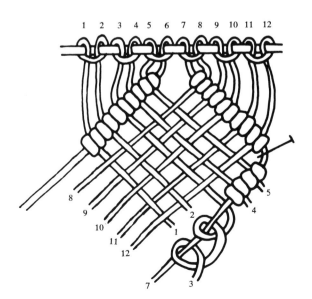

43

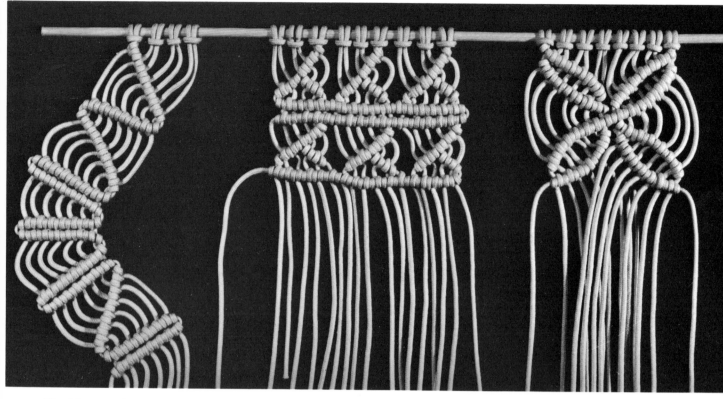

Fig. 20   A   B   C

IX A. *Shaping with Double Half Hitches*
A piece can be shaped with double half hitches by changing the direction of the knot-bearing cord. Follow the lines in the picture to determine how the shape of the sample was made. With this technique, circles and other shapes are possible.

IX B. *Pattern with Diagonal Double Half Hitches*
For the first part, every sixth cord is a knot

bearer. The knot bearer is angled to the left and the cords above it are hitched onto it. Then, the third cord from the top of each motif is used as a knot bearer and angles to the right. The cords above the knot bearer are hitched onto them.

IX C. *Flower Shape with Double Half Hitches*
For a rounded effect, the knot-bearing cords are gently curved as the other cords are hitched onto them.
Cord 1 is curved to the right and the next seven cords (2 through 8) are hitched onto it.
Cord 2 is curved over to the right and the next seven cords are hitched onto it in order (cords 3, 4, 5, 6, 7, 8, and 1).
Cord 16 is curved to the left and cords 15 through 9 are hitched onto it.

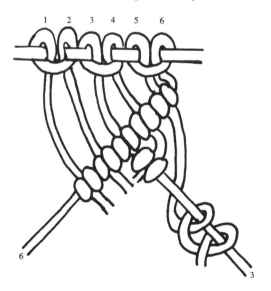

44

Cord 15 is curved over to the left and is used to complete the top half of the flower shape and to begin the bottom part. All the cords are hitched onto cord 15 in the order in which they come from the top.

Cord 1 curves over to the left and the cords above it are hitched onto it.

Cord 2 curves over to the right bottom and the cords above it are hitched onto it.

Cord 16 curves over to the right and the cords above it are hitched onto it.

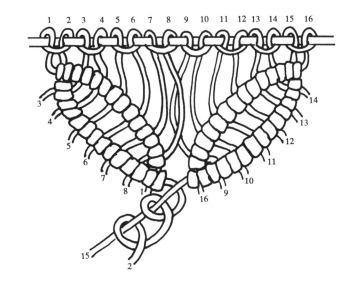

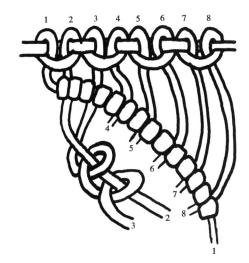

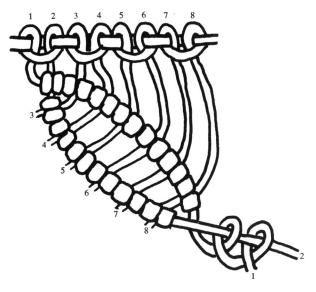

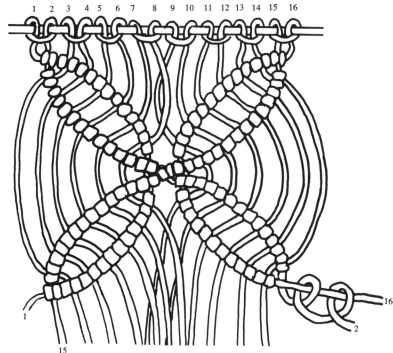

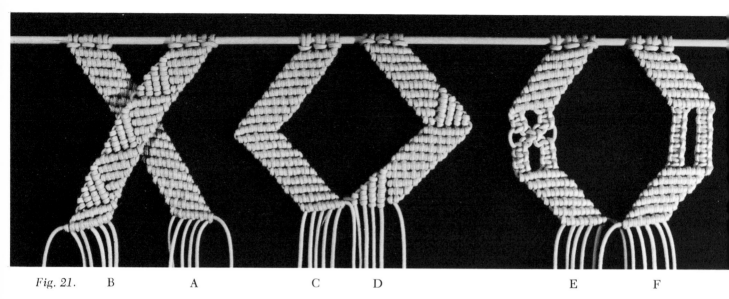

Fig. 21.　　B　　　　A　　　　C　　　　D　　　　　　　　　　E　　　　F

XA. *Angling with Horizontal Double Half Hitches*

A whole section of knotwork can be made to shift position in this way.

　　Row 1—Using cord 1 as a knot bearer, double half hitch from left to right using the rest of the cords.

　　Row 2—Using cord 2 as a knot bearer, double half hitch from left to right using all the cords in the previous row.

　　Row 3 and on—Continue in this same manner.

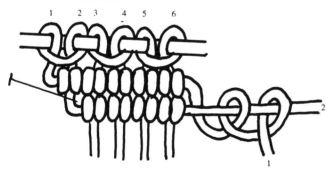

As you progress from one row to the next, shift your pin over to the right a bit.

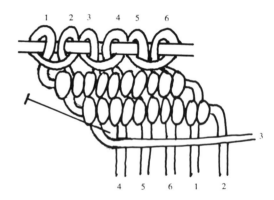

X B. *Angling with Horizontal Double Half Hitches, Using Vertical Double Half Hitches for Textural Contrast*

　　Row 1—Using cord 6 as a knot bearer, double half hitch from right to left, using cords 5, 4, 3, 2, and 1 in order.

　　Row 2—Using cord 5 as a knot bearer, double half hitch from right to left using cords 4, 3, 2, and 1 *only*.

Row 3—Using cord 4 as a knot bearer, double half hitch from right to left using cords 3, 2, and 1 *only*.

Row 4—Using cord 3 as a knot bearer, hitch on cords 2 and 1 *only*.

Row 5—Using cord 2 as a knot bearer, hitch on cord 1 *only*.

Five cords are now just hanging on the left. Go back to row 1 and bring cord 6 straight down, on top of the other cords. Going from top to bottom, vertical half hitch cords 5, 4, 3, and 2 onto it.

Bring cord 5 down, and vertical half hitch cords 4, 3, and 2 onto it.

Bring cord 4 down, and vertical half hitch cords 3 and 2 onto it.

Bring cord 3 down, and vertical half hitch cord 2 onto it.

One section is now completed. Repeat this as many times as desired.

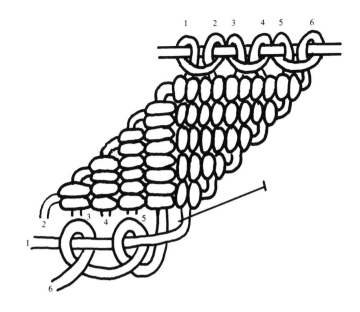

X C. *Angling Back and Forth with Horizontal Double Half Hitches*

Row 1—Using cord 6 as a knot bearer, double half hitch from right to left using cords 5, 4, 3, 2, and 1.

Row 2—Using cord 5 as a knot bearer, double half hitch from right to left using *all* the cords from the previous row.

Row 3—Using cord 4 as a knot bearer, continue as before.

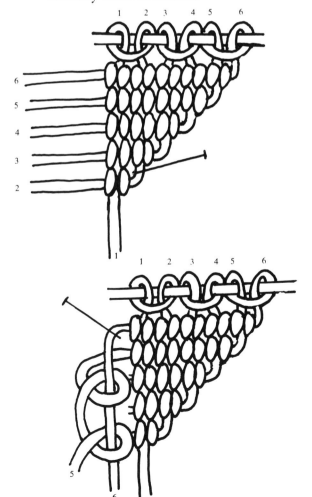

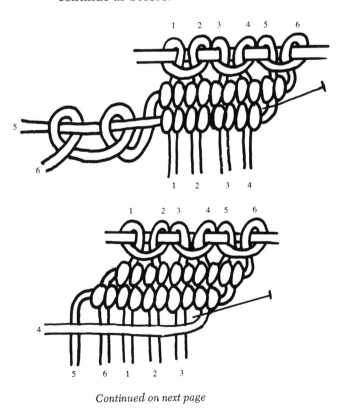

47

Continued on next page

For this sample, continue in this manner until nine rows are completed.

Row 10—In this row, be particularly careful to keep the knots close to the knots in the previous row. Using the first cord on the left as a knot bearer (the same cord as was used as a knot bearer in the previous row), double half hitch from left to right using all the cords in the previous row.

Row 11—Using the first cord that is now on the left, double half hitch from left to right, using all the cords from the previous row.

Row 12 and on—Continue in this same manner.

X D. *Angling with Horizontal Double Half Hitches, using Vertical Double Half Hitches for a Textural Change*
Rows 1 through 5—As in sample X A.
Rows 6 through 9—As in sample X B, with the shaping going in the opposite direction.

The bottom half angles back as in sample X C, and ends as in sample X B.

X E. *Angling and Shaping with Horizontal Double Half Hitches and Alternating Square Knots*
The first six rows angle to the left as in sample X C. A pattern of alternating square knots is inserted. The last six rows then angle to the right.

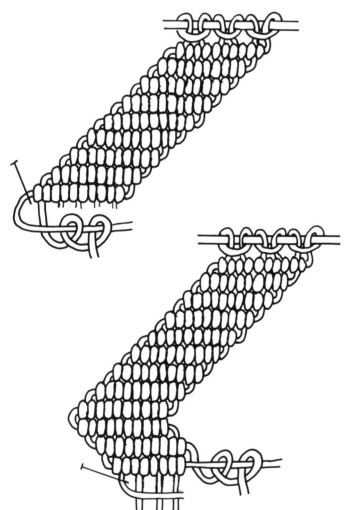

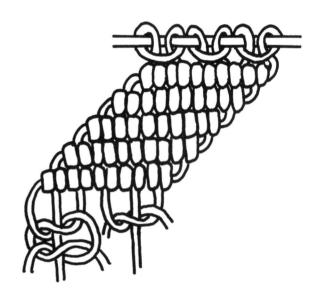

X F. *Angling and Shaping with Horizontal Double Half Hitches and Sennits of Square Knots*
The first six rows angle to the right. The cords are separated and two sennits of square knots are made. The cords are joined again and the pattern angles to the left.

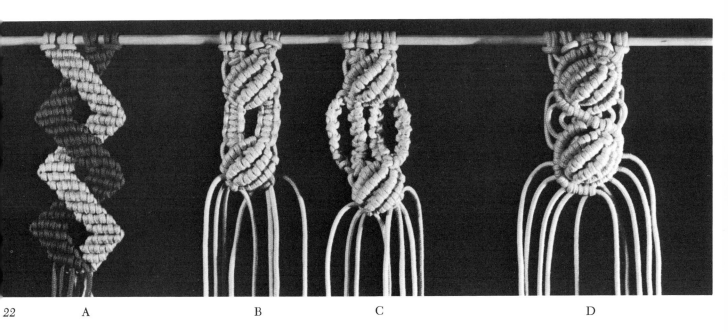

A   B   C   D

XI A.   *Angling with Horizontal Double Half Hitches*

The light-colored section of this band was made by angling with horizontal double half hitches first to the right, then left, then right, then left again. The dark-colored section was angled first to the left, then right, left, and right again. The two sections were then overlapped and intertwined.

XI B.   *Shell Knot Button Using Square Knots and Double Half Hitches. Eight Cord Method*

Row 1—One square knot is made with the first four cords; one square knot with the last four cords.

Row 2—Cord 5 is now used as a knot bearer. Bring it over to the left and hold it at an angle. Double half hitch cords 4, 3, 2, and 1 onto it.

Row 3—Cord 6 is now used as a knot bearer. Bring it over to the left, just below the previous row. Double half hitch cords 4, 3, 2, and 1 onto it.

Rows 4 and 5—Repeat the above with cords 7 and 8 as knot bearers.

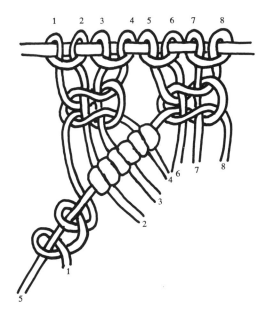

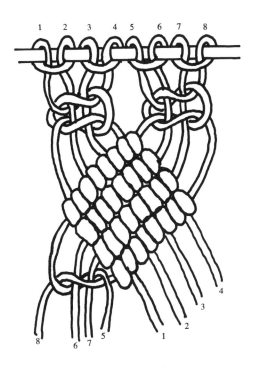

49

Row 6—Make a sennit of square knots with cords 1, 2, 3, and 4. Make a second sennit of square knots with cords 5, 6, 7, and 8.

Rows 7 through 10—Repeat steps 2 through 5 to make another shell knot button.

To Complete the Shell Knot Button:

Row 11—Make a square knot with cords 1, 2, 3, and 4. Make a square knot with cords 5, 6, 7, and 8.

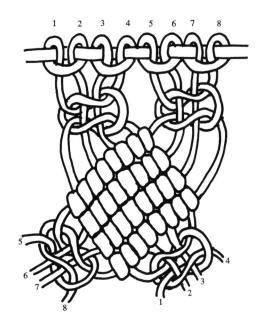

XI C. *Shell Knot Button with Decorative Insert of Chain Knots*

Rows 1 through 5—Repeat the first five steps in XI B above.

Row 6—Make one square knot with the first four cords and another square knot with the second four cords. This completes one shell knot button.

Row 7 and on—Make four single chain sennits below the square knots and end with another shell knot button.

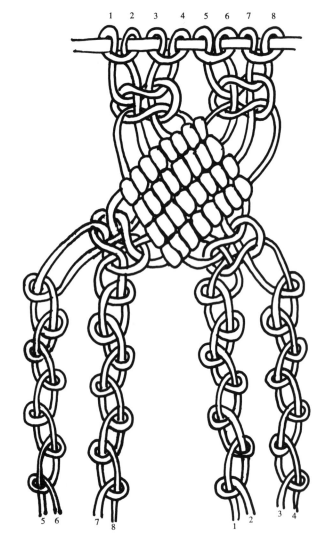

XI D. *Shell Knot Button Made with Ten Cords*
Cords 5 and 6 will be your knot bearers.

1. Curve cord 5 over to the left and down a little. Double half hitch cords 4, 3, 2, and 1 onto it.
2. Curve cord 6 over to the right and down a little. Double half hitch cords 7, 8, 9, and 10 onto it.

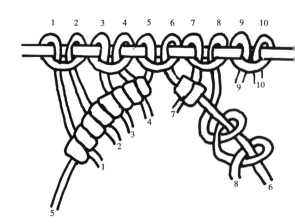

For the time being, put both of these knot bearers aside.

3. Make a square knot with cords 1, 2, 3, and 4.
4. Make a square knot with cords 7, 8, 9, and 10.
5. Using cord 7 as a new knot bearer, double half hitch cords 4, 3, 2, and 1 onto it.

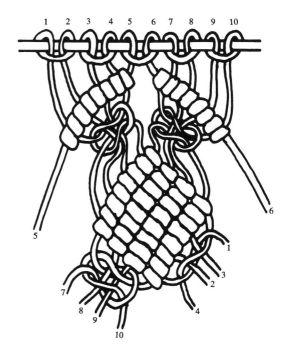

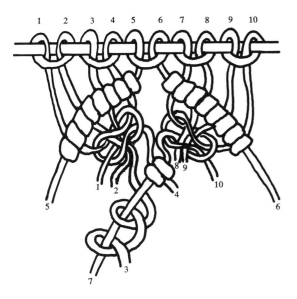

6. Using cord 8 as a new knot bearer, double half hitch cords 4, 3, 2, and 1 onto it.
7. Using cord 9 as a new knot bearer, double half hitch cords 4, 3, 2, and 1 onto it.
8. Using cord 10 as a new knot bearer, double half hitch cords 4, 3, 2, and 1 onto it.
9. Make a *very tight* square knot with cords 1, 2, 3, and 4.
10. Make a *very tight* square knot with cords 7, 8, 9, and 10.

You will now use the knot bearers you put aside before.

11. Curve cord 6 to the left and center. Double half hitch cords 4, 3, 2, and 1 onto it.
12. Curve cord 5 to the right and center. Double half hitch cords 7, 8, 9, and 10 onto it.

The two center cords are crossed as diamonds are crossed.

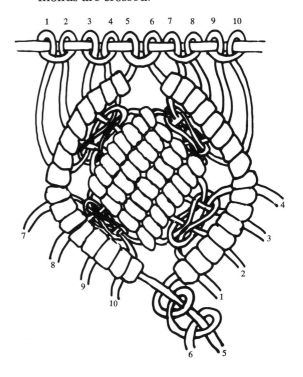

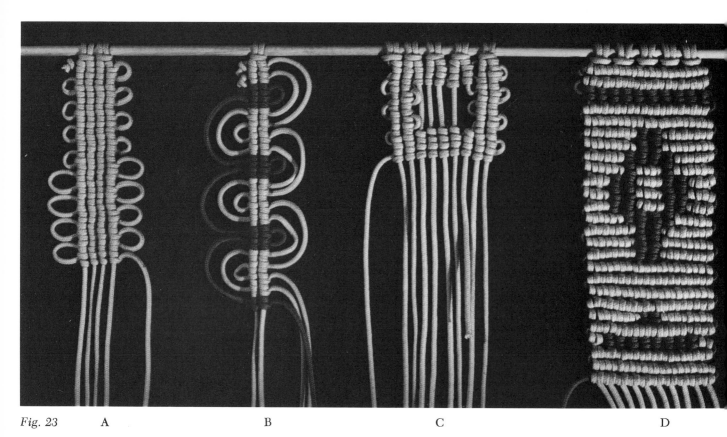

Fig. 23   A   B   C   D

XII A. *Vertical Double Half Hitch with Picots*
The vertical double half hitch is shown on p. 72. To make the picot, place a pin a distance away from the last edge knot. Bring the knotting cord around the pin, and continue knotting back along the next row.

XII B. *Vertical Double Half Hitch with Exaggerated Picots or Swirls*
Three separate knotting cords are used for this.

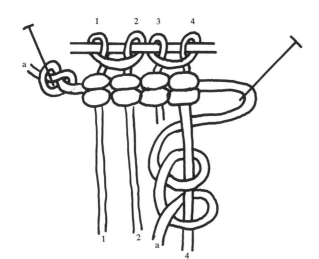

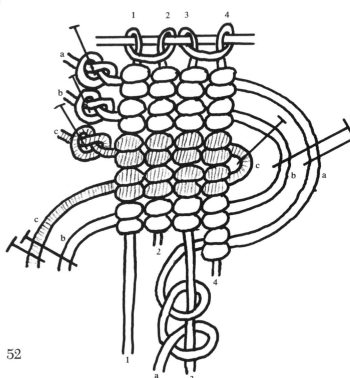

Row 1. Pin a knotting cord (cord A) to the knotting board and make vertical half hitches across the row from left to right (see diagram).

Row 2. Pin a second knotting cord (cord B) to the knotting board and make vertical half hitches across the row from left to right.

Row 3. Pin a third knotting cord of a darker color (cord C) to the knotting board and again make vertical half hitches across the row from left to right.

Row 4. Using the same knotting cord as you used for Row 3 (cord C), make a small picot and vertical half hitch across the row from right to left.

Row 5. Put a pin farther to the right of the knotting to make a larger picot than before. With cord B vertical half hitch across the row from right to left.

Row 6. Put a pin still further to the right than the last one. Wtih cord A, vertical half hitch across the row from right to left.

XII C. *Vertical Double Half Hitches with Some Unknotted Area*

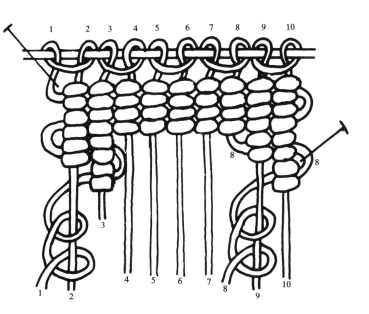

Using cord 1 as a knotting cord, two rows of vertical half hitches were made. The knotting was continued over the first two cords only. Then cord 8 was picked up and used as a knotting cord for vertical half hitches on the last two cords. Cord 8 was brought back to its original position and dropped. Cord 1 was used as a knotting cord again and vertical half hitches were made across the entire row.

XII D. *Cavandoli Stitch*

A combination of vertical and horizontal double half hitches in two colors are used to form a design. The light-colored background is made of horizontal double half hitches; the darker design areas are made of vertical double half hitches.

Ten light-colored cords were hitched onto the dowel. A separate, extra-long, dark-colored cord was cut, pinned to the knotting board and used alternately as a knot bearer and as a knotting cord.

For the horizontal half hitches, the dark cord was used as a knot bearer. Since it was hidden within the knots, the knotting appears light.

For the vertical half hitches, the dark cord was used as a knotting cord. Now it hides the light-colored cords and the knotting appears dark.

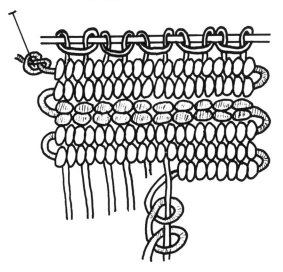

53

Continued on next page

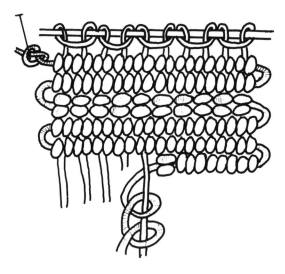

XIII A. *Knotting Pattern Combining Some of the Techniques Shown in Previous Samples*

XIII B. *Another Knotting Pattern Combining Some of the Techniques Shown in Previous Samples*

XIII C. *Alternating Overhand Knots*

XIII D. *Strands of Cords Decorated with Overhand Knots*

XIII E. *Overhand Knots in Two Different Patterns*

In the first row, overhand knots are made with groups of three cords.

In the second row, overhand knots are made with groups of four cords.

The cords are then split and crossed in the pattern as shown, and in the third row, overhand knots are made with the regrouped sets of four cords.

THE HALF HITCH AND SOME VARIATIONS

See page 74.

XIV A. *Half Hitch Sennit That's Been Allowed to Spiral*

A single half hitch was made over and over again around the same core cords. The cord on the right was knotted around the core cords on the left. It spirals of its own accord, but can be coaxed to lie flat.

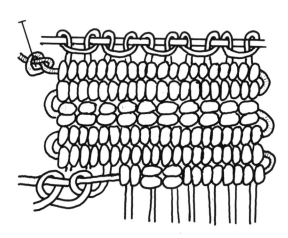

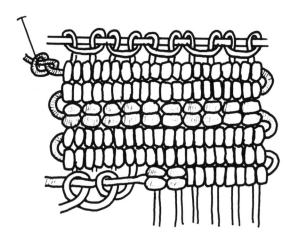

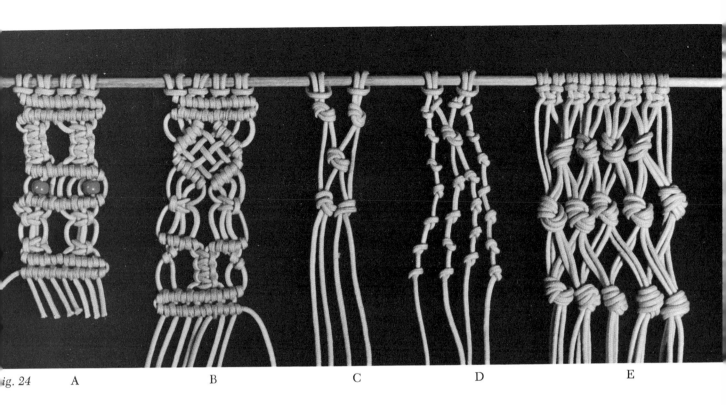

A   B   C   D   E

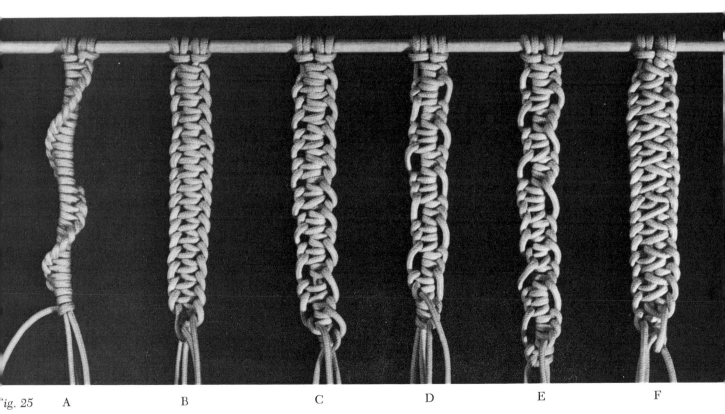

A   B   C   D   E   F

55

XIV B. *Half Hitch Sennit with Knotting Cords Alternating*

Two knotting cords and two central core cords were used. With the knotting cord on the right, a half hitch was made around the core cords. Then, with the knotting cord on the left, a half hitch was made around the core cords. These two steps were repeated throughout.

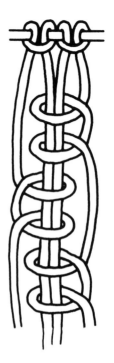

XIV C. *Half Hitch Sennit: Variation Two and Two*

Two knotting cords and two central core cords were used. With the knotting cord on the right, two half hitches were made around the core cords. Then, with the knotting cord on the left, two half hitches were made around the core cords. These two steps were repeated throughout.

XIV D. *Half Hitch Sennit: Variation Three and Three*

Two knotting cords and two central core cords were used. With the knotting cord on the right, three half hitches were made around the core cords. With the knotting cord on the left, three half hitches were made around the core cords. These two steps were repeated throughout.

XIV E. *Half Hitch Sennit—Random Pattern*
Two knotting cords and two central core cords were used. Knotting cords were hitched around the core cords, first from the right, then from the left in a random pattern.

XIV F. *Half Hitch Sennit—with Knotting Cords Alternating and Core Cords Split*
Two knotting cords and two central core cords were used. With the knotting cord on the right, a half hitch was made around the one core cord adjacent to it. With the same knotting cord, a half hitch was then made over the two central core cords.
With the knotting cord on the left, a half hitch was made around the one core cord adjacent to it. With the same knotting cord, a half hitch was then made around the two central core cords. These four steps were repeated throughout.

XV A. *Half Hitch Chain—or Chain Knot Sennit*
Two knotting cords and *no* core cords were used. With the knotting cord on the right, a half hitch was made around the knotting cord on the left. With the knotting cord on the left, a half hitch was made around the knotting cord on the right. These two steps were repeated throughout.
As each knot is made, it is pushed into place, and tends to rest in a diagonal position.

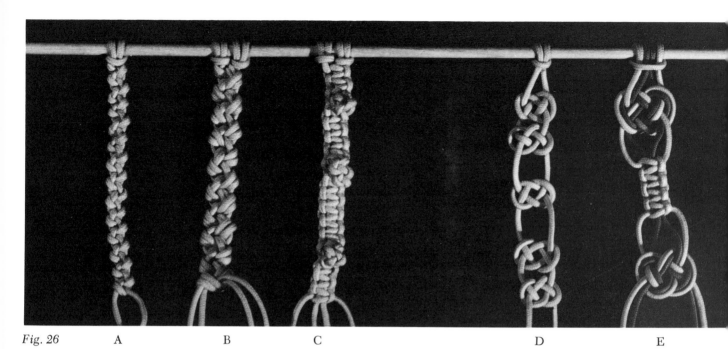

Fig. 26   A   B   C   D   E

XV B. *Half Hitch Chain—or Chain Knot Sennit, Variation*

Four knotting cords and no core cords were used. Two knotting cords were used together as one cord would be used. Then the chain was made as in XV A on the previous page.

XV C. *Square Knot Sennit with Raised Picot Made of Chain Knots*

Four cords were used. A short sennit of square knots was made, using two knotting cords and two core cords. Then, only the two central cords were used, and a short sennit of chain knots was made. The two outside cords were picked up again, and a square knot was made directly below the last square knot. This forced the chain knot sennit to double back on itself and form a raised picot.

XV D. *Spaced Josephine Knots*

See page 74.

To keep a sennit of Josephine knots from spiraling, reverse the direction of knotting after each Josephine knot is completed.

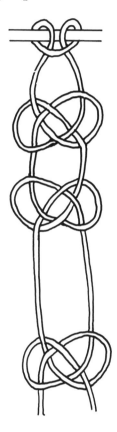

XV E. *Two-Colored Josephine Knot Band with a Short Sennit of Square Knots*
Two light-colored cords and two dark-colored cords were used. The two light-colored cords remained on the outside at all times, while the two dark-colored cords remained on the inside.

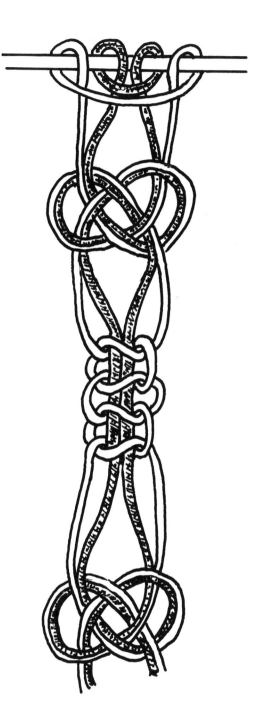

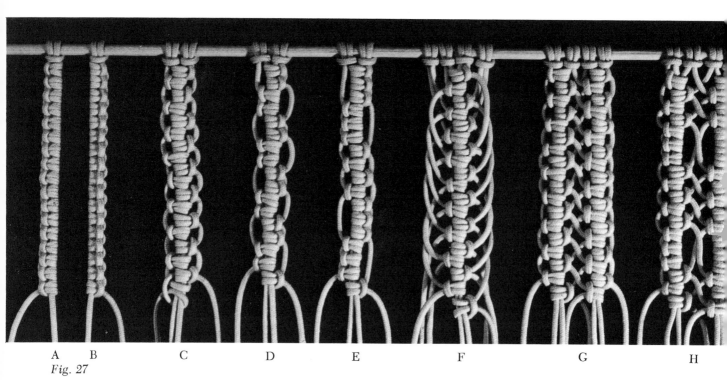

A   B   C   D   E   F   G   H

Fig. 27

REVERSED DOUBLE HALF HITCHES AND THEIR VARIATIONS

A reversed double half hitch is made in two steps:

Step 1—The knotting cord goes OVER, around and UNDER the core cord(s) and through the loop.

Step 2—The knotting cord goes UNDER, around, and OVER the core cord(s) and through the loop.

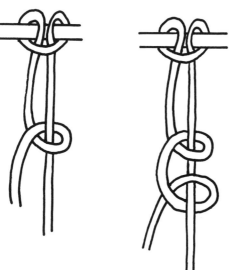

XVI A.   *Reversed Double Half Hitch Sennit with the Knots Forming on the Left Side Only* Two cords were used. Reversed double half hitches were made one below the other, using the cord on the left as the knotting cord and the cord on the right as the core cord.

60

XVI B. *Reversed Double Half Hitch Sennit with the Knots Forming on the Right Side Only*

Two cords were used. Reversed double half hitches were made one below the other, using the cord on the right as the knotting cord and the cord on the left as the core cord.

XVI C. *Reversed Double Half Hitch Sennit with Knots Forming on Both Outside Edges; One and One*

Four cords were used. The two outside cords were used as knotting cords; the two central cords were used as core cords.

Using the cord on the right, one reversed double half hitch was made around the two central core cords.

Then, using the cord on the left, one reversed double half hitch was made around the two central core cords.

This was repeated throughout.

XVI D. *Reversed Double Half Hitch Sennit. Two and Two*

Using the cord on the right, two reversed double half hitches were made around the two central core cords.

Using the cord on the left, two reversed double half hitches were made around the two central core cords.

These two steps were repeated throughout.

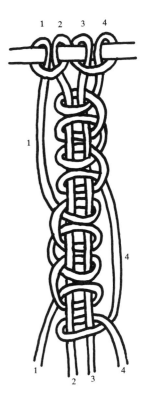

61

XVI E. *Varied Pattern of Reversed Double Half Hitches*

XVI F. *Six-Strand Reversed Double Half Hitch Pattern Using Only Two Core Cords*

The two central cords (4 and 5) were used as the core cords. Using cord 6, one reversed double half hitch was made around the core cords. Then cords 3, 7, 2, 8, and 1 were used in turn to complete one pattern.

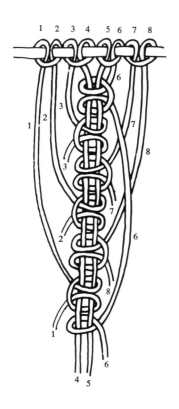

ously. The sennit on the left is started with the knotting cord on the left which knots around the two core cords; the sennit on the right is started with the knotting cord on the right which knots around two core cords. One reversed double half hitch is made on each sennit. For the second reversed double half hitch, the knotting cord from the right-hand sennit (cord 5) is knotted around the core cords of the left-hand sennit; the knotting cord from the left-hand sennit (cord 4) is knotted around the core cords of the right-hand sennit.

These two steps are repeated, with the inside knotting cords interchanging throughout.

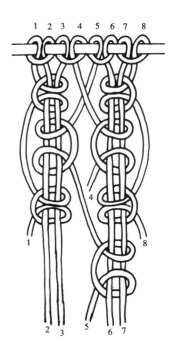

XVI G. *Two Interlaced Sennits of Reversed Double Half Hitches*

Two four-strand sennits of reversed double half hitches are started simultane-

XVI H. *Two Interlaced Sennits of Reversed Double Half Hitches in a Varied Pattern*

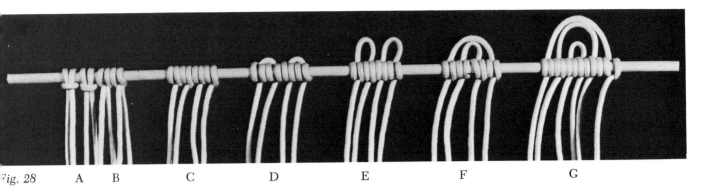

HEADINGS

XVII A. *Reversed Double Half Hitch with Band in Front*

Two different methods of doing this are shown below:

1. The cord to be mounted is folded in half. The center fold is placed on top of, around, and behind the mounting cord or bar. The two free ends are then placed inside the loop and pulled taut.

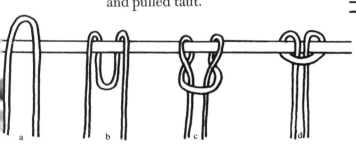

2. The cord to be mounted is folded in half. The center fold is bent forward and down. The two "ears" that are formed are pushed backwards. The loop that is formed from the folded back "ears" can now be slipped onto a mounting cord or bar and be pulled taut.

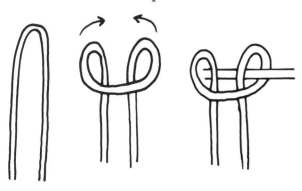

XVII B. *Reversed Double Half Hitch with Band in Back*

Two methods of doing this are shown below:

1. The cord to be mounted is folded in half. The center fold is placed under, around, and in front of the mounting cord or bar. The two free ends are then placed inside the loop and pulled taut.

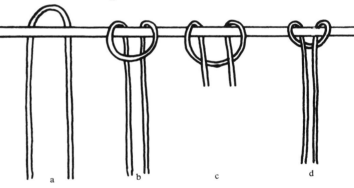

2. The cord to be mounted is folded in half. The center fold is bent backward and down. The two "ears" that are formed are pulled forward. The loop that is formed with the "ears" can now be slipped onto a mounting cord or bar and be pulled taut.

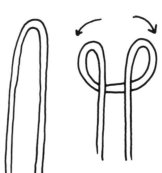
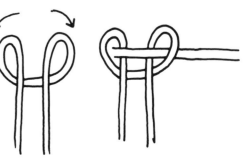

XVII C. *Cords Mounted With Double Half Hitches*

The center of the folded cord is slipped under the mounting piece and is pinned to the knotting board close to the mounting piece. A double half hitch is made onto the mounting piece, first with one cord, then with the other.

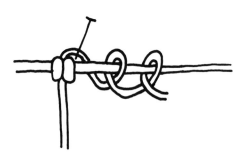

XVII D. *Cords Mounted with Double Half Hitches and a Small Picot*

This is made the same as that in XVII C, except that the folded cord is pinned to the knotting board just a little above the mounting piece.

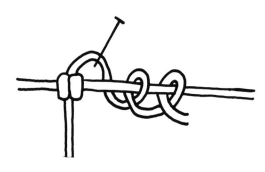

XVII E. *Cords Mounted with Double Half Hitches and a Large Picot*

This is made the same as that in XVII D, except that the folded cord is pinned to the knotting board at a still higher point.

XVII F. *Cords Mounted with Double Half Hitches and a Double Picot*

Two pairs of folded cords are used for this mounting. Both pairs are slipped under the mounting piece and are pinned to the knotting board, one above the other, as in the diagram. First the two cords on the left are double half hitched onto the mounting piece. Next, the inner picot is completed and then the outer picot is completed.

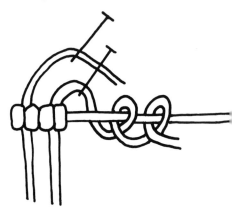

XVII G. *Cords Mounted with Double Half Hitches and a Triple Picot*

Three pairs of cords are used for this mounting. All three pairs of cords are slipped under the mounting piece and are pinned to the knotting board, one above the other, as in the diagram. First, the three cords on the left are double half hitched onto the mounting piece. Next, the innermost picot is completed, followed by the middle picot and the outermost picot.

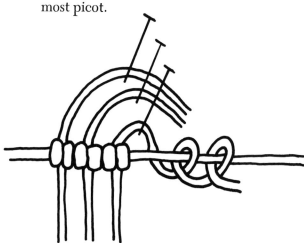

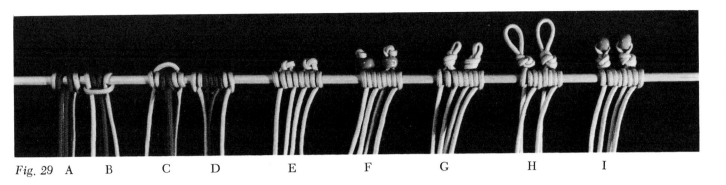

Fig. 29   A   B   C   D   E   F   G   H   I

XVIII A. *Reversed Double Half Hitch Mounting with Inner Cords of One Color and Outer Cords of Another Color. Band in Back.*

Put the outer cord onto the mounting piece as in XVII B 1 or 2, but do not tighten.

Mount the inner cord as in XVII B 1, slipping these inner cords between the outer cords.

Other methods are possible, but this seems easiest.

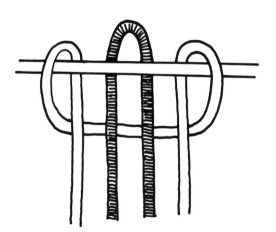

XVIII B. *Reversed Double Half Hitch Mounting with Inner Cords of One Color and Outer Cords of Another Color. Band in Front.*

Put the outer cord onto the mounting piece as in XVII A, 1 or 2, but do not tighten. Mount the inner cord as in XVII A1, slipping these inner cords between the outer cords.

XVIII C. *Two-Color Mounting with Double Half Hitches, a Picot, a Reversed Double Half Hitch*

The outer left cord was hitched onto the mounting piece with a double half hitch as in XVII C. The dark middle cords were hitched on with a reversed double half hitch. The outer right cord was then hitched on with a double half hitch.

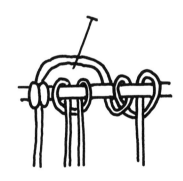

XVIII D. *Two-Color Mounting with Double Half Hitches*

The outer left cord was hitched onto the mounting piece with a double half hitch. Then the two central cords were hitched on in the same manner. The outer right cord was hitched on last.

65

XVIII E. *Mounting with a Single Overhand Knot and Double Half Hitches*
In the center of the mounting cords, an overhand knot is made. The cords are then mounted with double half hitches.

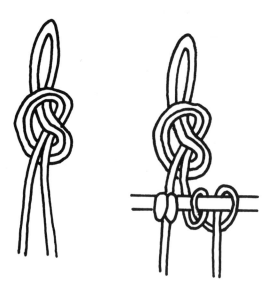

XVIII F. *Mounting with a Single Overhand Knot, Bead, and Double Half Hitches*
An overhand knot is made as in XVIII E. A bead is then slipped onto the two cords and pushed up until it is just below the overhand knot. The cords are then mounted with double half hitches.

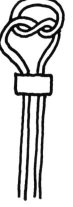

XVIII H. *Mounting with Double Half Hitches, and an Overhand Knot Around the Fold of the Mounting Cords. Large Picot*
This is made the same as that in XVIII G except that the overhand knot is further away from the fold in the mounting cord.

XVIII I. *Mounting with a Bead on Top, an Overhand Knot, and Double Half Hitches*
A bead was slipped onto one strand of the mounting cords and was brought up to the center fold. An overhand knot was made just below the bead. The cords were then mounted with double half hitches.

XVIII G. *Mounting with Double Half Hitches and an Overhand Knot Around the Fold of the Mounting Cords. Small Picot*
The mounting cord is folded in half. Holding the two cords together near the fold, an overhand knot is made around the two cords. The cords are then mounted with double half hitches.

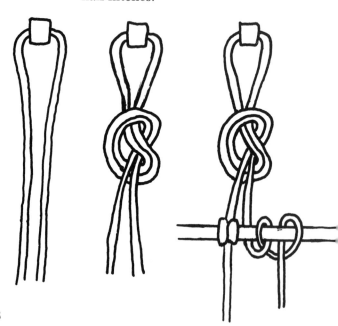

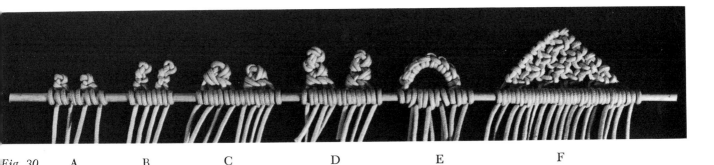

Fig. 30   A   B   C   D   E   F

XIX A. *Small Single Chain Knot Sennit and Double Half Hitches*

A short sennit of two single chain knots was made with two mounting cords. They were then double half hitched onto the mounting piece in the usual manner.

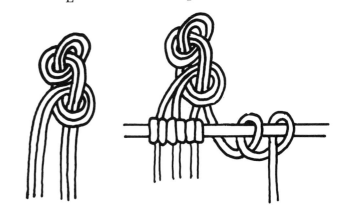

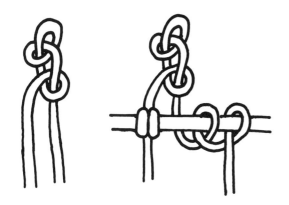

XIX B. *Single Chain Knot Sennit and Double Half Hitches*

A sennit of four single chain knots was made with two mounting cords. They were then double half hitched onto the mounting piece in the usual manner.

XIX C. *Small, Double Chain Knot Sennit and Double Half Hitches*

A short sennit of two double chain knots was made with four mounting cords. They were then double half hitched onto the mounting piece in the usual manner.

XIX D. *Double Chain Knot Sennit and Double Half Hitches*

A sennit of four double chain knots was made with four mounting cords. They were then double half hitched onto the mounting piece in the usual manner.

XIX E. *Reversed Double Half Hitched Scalloped Mounting*

A pair of mounting cords was hitched onto the mounting piece upside down, with a reversed double half hitch. Using one of these cords as a knotting cord, and one as a core cord, a sennit of eight reversed double half hitches was made. The sennit was temporarily put aside. Right next to the first pair of mounting cords,

67

three more pairs of mounting cords were hitched onto the mounting piece with reversed double half hitches. The sennit was then arched around towards the mounting piece and the cords double half hitched onto it.

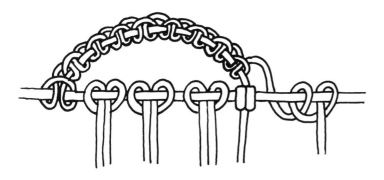

XIX F.   *Pointed Heading of Square Knots Mounted With Double Half Hitches*
One pair of mounting cords was pinned to the knotting board and was opened out to form an upside down "V" formation. Four pairs of cords were hitched onto either side with reversed double half hitches. Starting from the tip, a pattern of alternating square knots was made until a row of four square knots was completed. All of the cords were then double half hitched onto the mounting piece.

XIX G.   (not illustrated in photograph) *Another Method of Making a Pointed Heading*

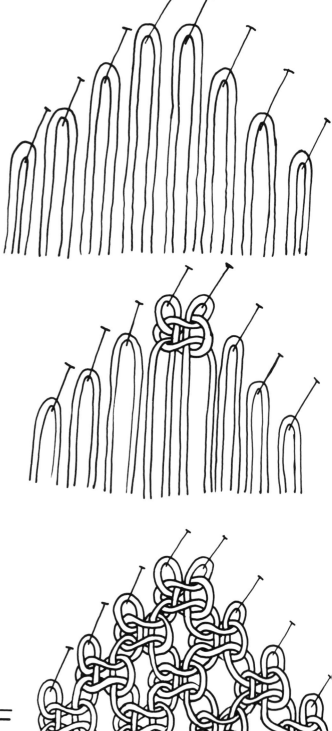

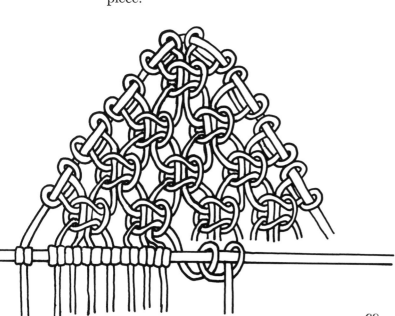

68

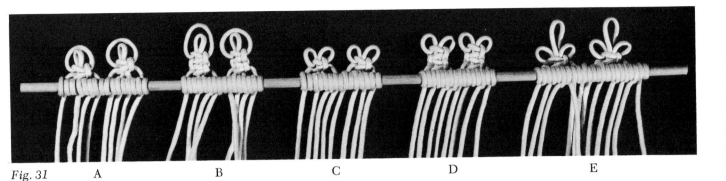

Fig. 31   A   B   C   D   E

XX A. *Single Square Knot Heading with One Picot within Another*

One pair of mounting cords was pinned to the knotting board; these cords are core cords. A second pair is pinned to the board a little above the first; these are the knotting cords. With the knotting cords, one square knot is made around the core cords. The cords are then double half hitched onto the mounting piece in the usual manner.

XX B. *Square Knot Heading with One Picot with Another*

This is made the same as that in XX A, except that two square knots are made around the core cords.

XX C. *Single Square Knot Heading with One Picot Beside the Other*

Two pairs of mounting cords are pinned to the knotting board, one beside the other. The two center cords are the core cords, the two outside cords are the knotting cords. With the knotting cords, one square knot is made around the core cords. The cords are then hitched onto the mounting piece with double half hitches in the usual manner.

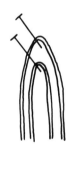

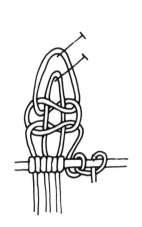
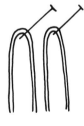
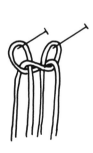
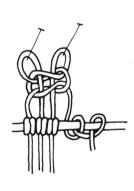

69

XX D. *Square Knot Heading with One Picot Beside the Other*

This is made the same as the sample in XX C, except that two square knots are made around the core cords.

XX E. *Square Knot Heading with Three Picots, One Beside the Other*

Three pairs of mounting cords are pinned to the knotting board, one beside the other. The center pair should be higher than the outside pairs. The two outside cords are the knotting cords; the four inner cords are the core cords. With the two outside knotting cords, one square knot is made around the four core cords. The cords are then double half hitched onto the mounting piece in the usual manner.

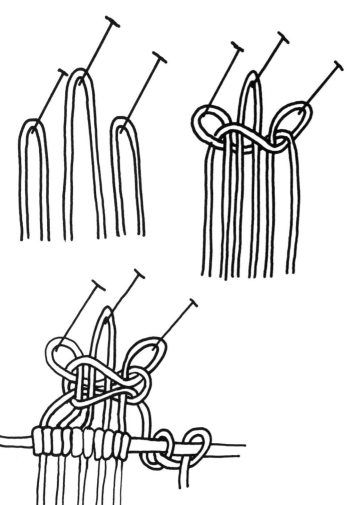

CIRCULAR PIECES

It is best to work a circular piece on a knotting board that can be rotated easily. Knotting cords can be mounted on anything that is round—either a solid ring, or a ring made of cord. Cords can be hitched onto the ring with reversed double half hitches, double half hitches, and sometimes even in a more fanciful manner.

Circles are usually worked from the center out, since it's more convenient to add cords than to drop them. Any combination of knots can be used, but as the circle grows, more cords are generally needed. There are many different ways in which cords can be added.

The samples illustrate some ways of adding cords.

XXI A. For the mounting ring, a cord was cut, and shaped into a ring with the ends overlapping. Ten pairs of knotting cords were mounted onto this ring with reversed double half hitches. Sennits of alternating square knots with an open net-like effect were made as in IV A. New cords were added onto the "floats" between the alternating square knots. Pairs of cords were hitched onto each "float" with a reversed double half hitch. They were then knotted into sennits of square knots.

XXI B. For the mounting ring, a small curtain ring was used. Cords were mounted onto the ring with reversed double half hitches. A small pattern of alternating square knots was made.

A new knot-bearing cord was pinned to the knotting board. The cords from one group of square knots were double half hitched onto the new knot bearer. Then two pairs of new knotting cords were hitched onto the knot bearer with reversed double half hitches. The last two steps were repeated all around the circle. A second row of double half hitches was made and the knotting pattern continued.

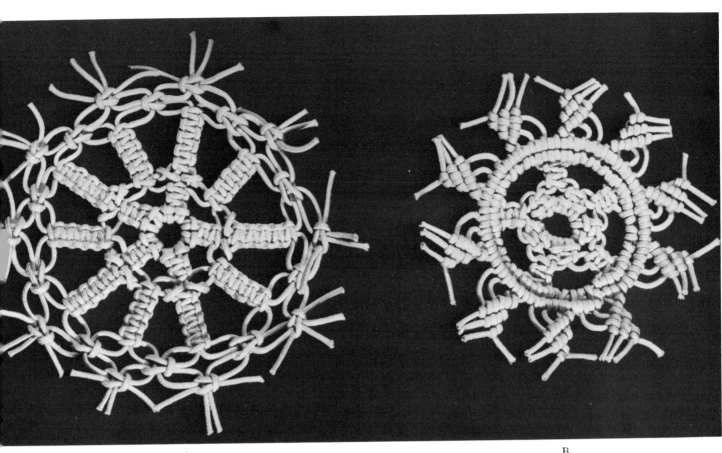

32   A   B

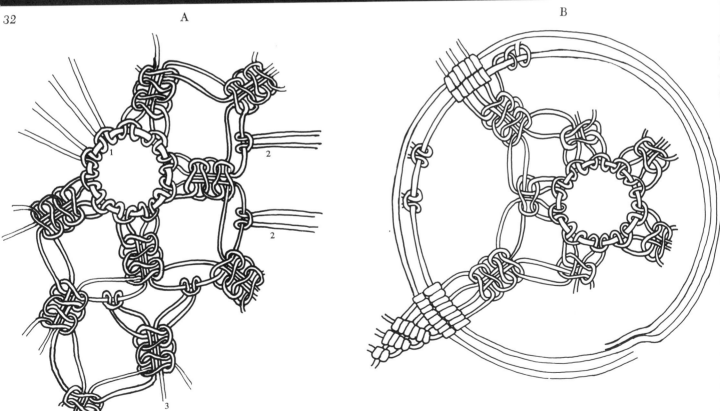

71

NAME OF KNOT	HOW IT'S MADE
HALF KNOT	
SQUARE KNOT	Half Knot as Above
ALTERNATING SQUARE KNOT	
HORIZONTAL DOUBLE HALF HITCH	
VERTICAL DOUBLE HALF HITCH	
OVERHAND KNOT	

	COMPLETED KNOT

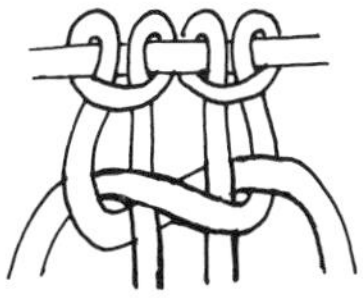

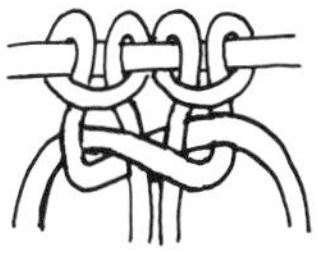

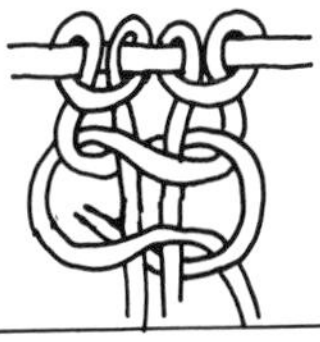

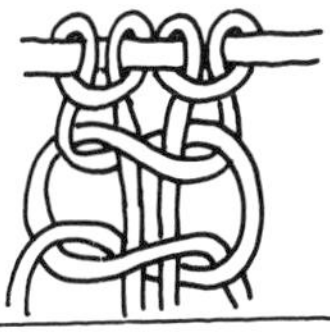

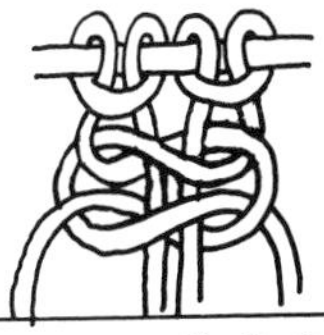

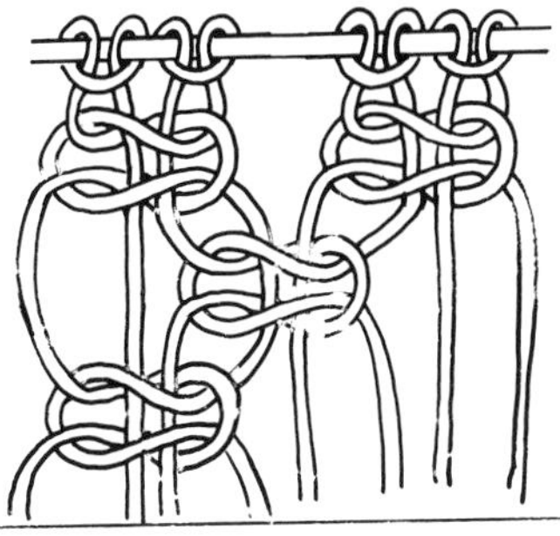

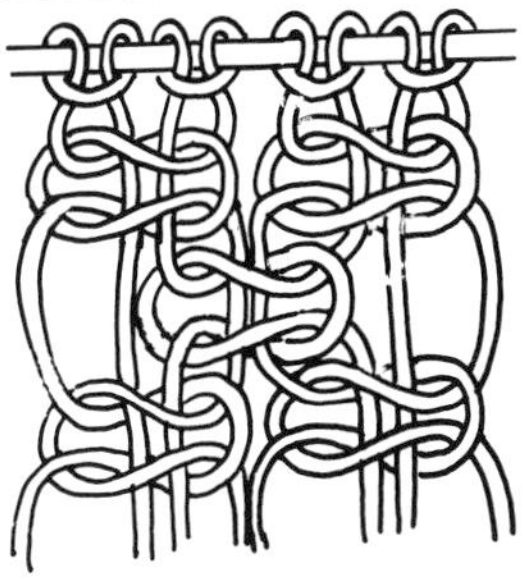

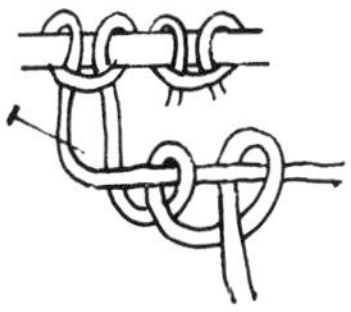

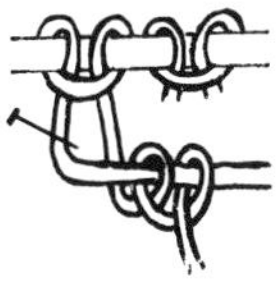

Reverse Direction

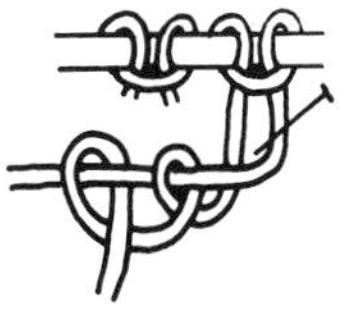

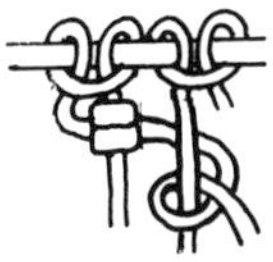

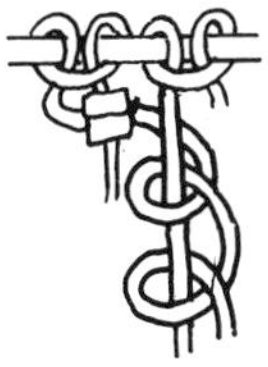

Reverse Direction

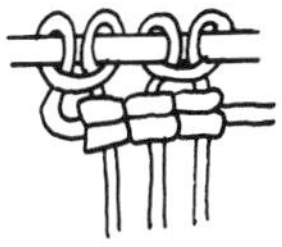

Vertical Double Half Hitch

The vertical double half hitch is merely a horizontal double half hitch turned on its side. However, in the vertical double half hitch the knotting cord remains the same throughout, and therefore gets used up quickly.

The knotting cord is placed *under* the knot bearing cord and a vertical double half hitch is made as in the diagram. It is pushed close to the previous row of knots. The *same* knotting cord is then placed *under* the next knot bearing cord and "snapped" into place close to the previous row of knots. A vertical double half hitch is made around this next knot bearing cord.

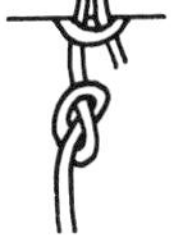

NAME OF KNOT	HOW IT'S MADE
HALF HITCH	
CHAIN KNOT	
REVERSED DOUBLE HALF HITCH	
JOSEPHINE KNOT	
REVERSED JOSEPHINE KNOT	
WRAPPING	Pull here ⟶

	COMPLETED KNOT

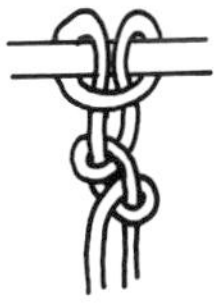

Wrapping

ugh wrapping is not technically a knot, it has many uses with macramé.

cord many times longer than the length of the wrapping. Fold the cord un-
y as in the diagram. Place the folded cord next to the cords to be wrapped. Take
nger cord and bring it around the other cords. Keep on wrapping around and
d, always placing the wrapping cord above the previous turn. When the
ped portion is as long as desired, slip the end of the wrapping cord through the
Pull on the "tail" cord at the bottom of the wrapped section. When the top end
urely within the wrapped section, both ends can be trimmed.

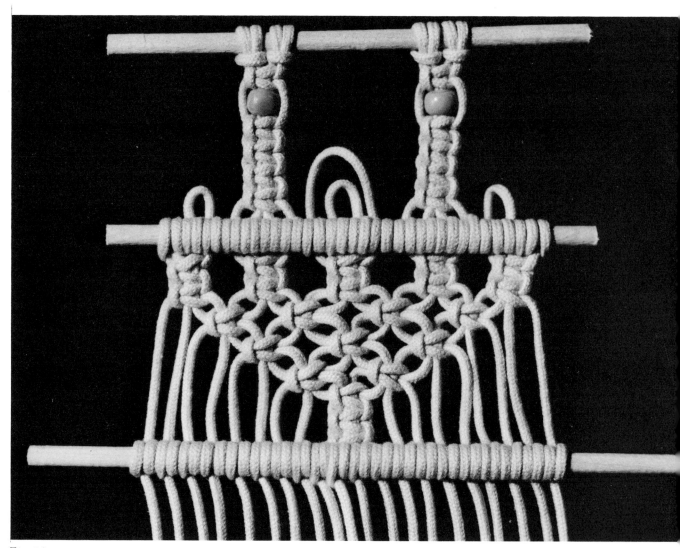

Fig. 33

XXII. *Adding or Increasing the Number of Cords*

In this sample, one way of adding cords is shown. The sample was started with four pairs of cords hitched onto a dowel with reversed double half hitches. Two sennits of square knots were made and the cords were then double half hitched onto a second dowel. At this point, more cords were desired. Between the two sennits, two additional pairs of cords were mounted with double half hitches and a double picot XVII F). The pair of cords on either side of the sennits were double half hitched on

with a single picot (XVII E). The two outermost cords were hitched on with a reversed double half hitch with the band in the back (XVII B).

There are many other ways of adding on cords. Two of these waysare shown on the circular samples, XXI A and B. Other variations are shown in sample XXIII. Actually, any place that will hold a new cord securely is fair game. Cords don't necessarily need to be mounted straight down. They can be mounted on a slant, or sideways, and the knotting can continue in a new direction.

76

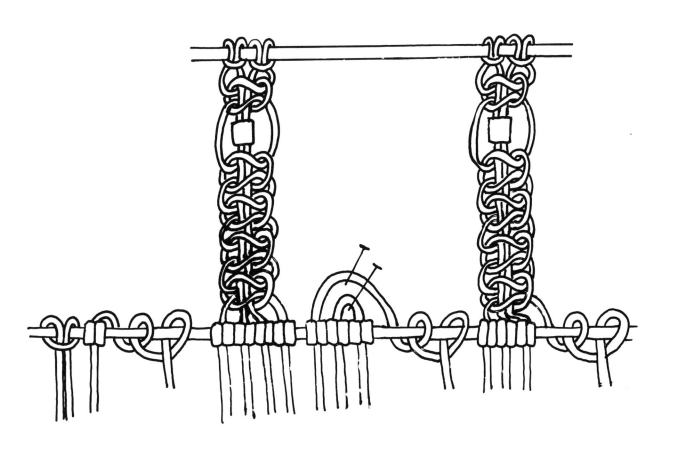

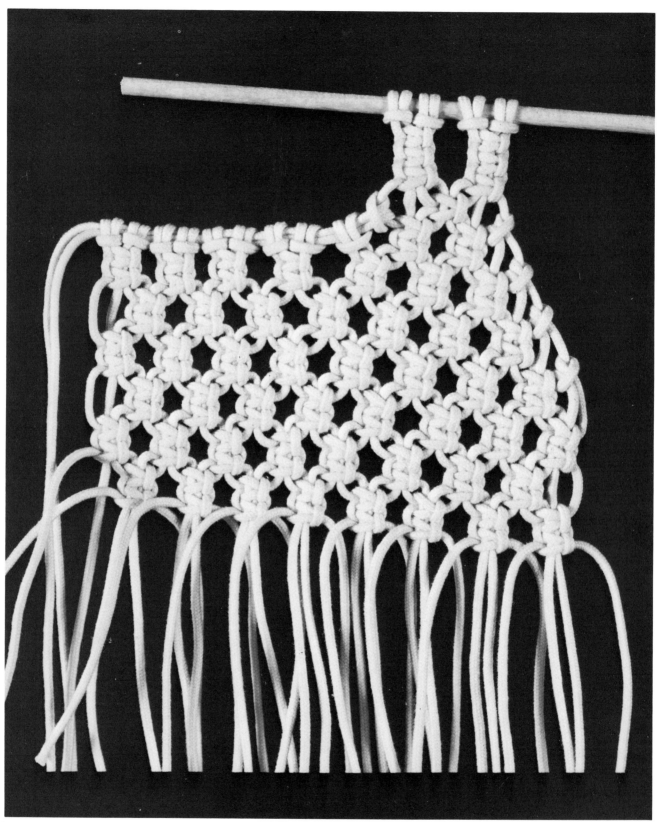

Fig. 34

XXIII. *Shaping Pieces*

This sample illustrates two different methods of shaping a piece of macramé.

The right side of the sample has a gradual outward curve. In a pattern of alternating square knots, such as in this sample, vertical floats form along the edges. To achieve the gradual curve, one pair of new cords was hitched onto each vertical float. The new cords were immediately incorporated into the knotting pattern. The left side of the sample has a rather abrupt outward curve. A new pair of cords was hitched onto a float at the edge of the sample. The new cords curved over to the left—and became new mounting cords. Additional cords were mounted onto them, and the alternating square knot pattern was continued.

These methods of shaping are particularly well suited to shaping articles of clothing. As a guide for your knotting, you can draw your pattern onto a piece of paper and pin the paper to your knotting board, or you can buy a commercial pattern and pin it to your knotting board.

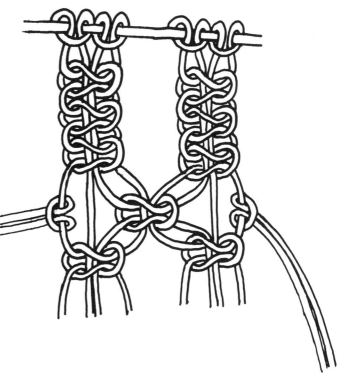

And these are just a few of the variations possible with just a few knots—and a little imagination.

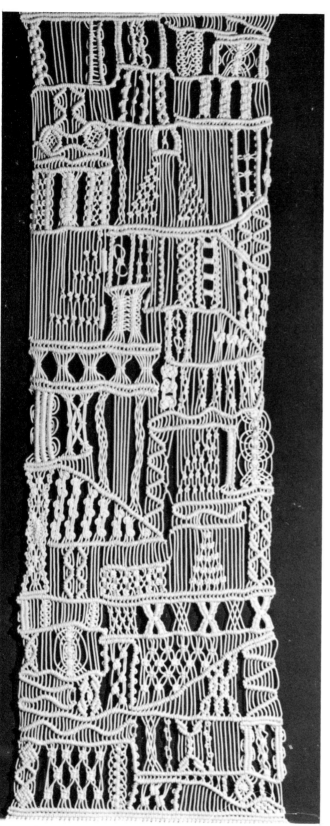

Fig. 35 Window Panel (Macramé Montage). Braided nylon fiber. 22″ x 56″. *Joan Michaels Paque.* Photo, *Hank Paque.*

Fig. 36 Belt. *Melissa Diamanti.*

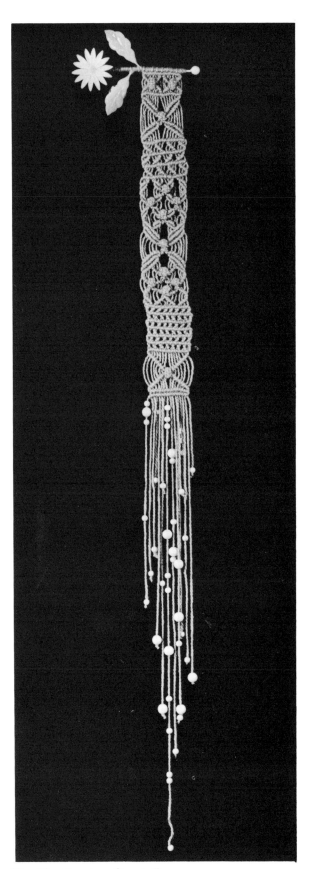

37 Belt. *Melissa Diamanti.*

Fig. 38 Hanging. *Connie Brown.*

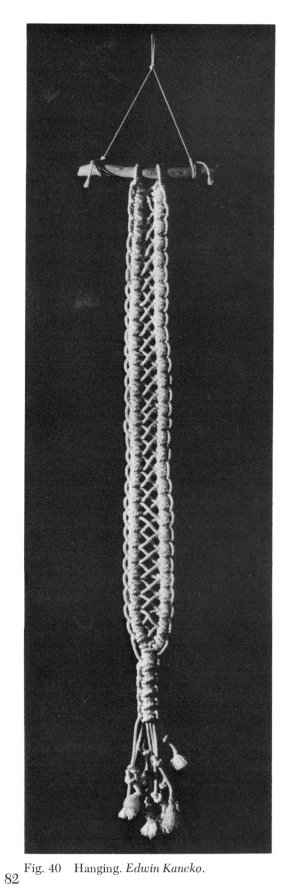

Fig. 39 Sampler. *Ella Bolster*.

Fig. 40 Hanging. *Edwin Kaneko*.

82

Fig. 41 Close-up of a section of a sculptural piece.
Edwina Drobny.

83

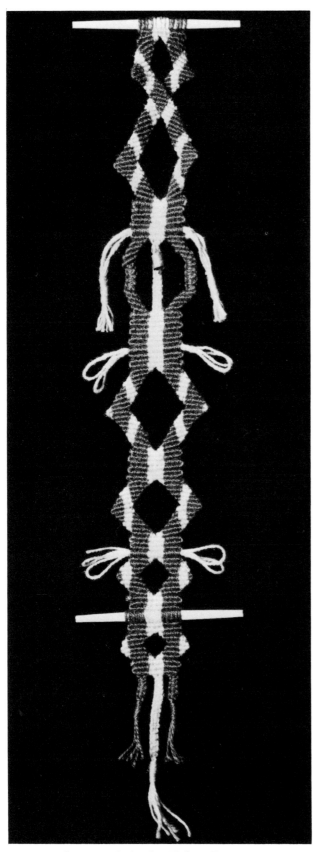

Fig. 42 Playing with Angles. *Helene Bress.*

Fig. 43 Macramé Wall Hanging. Natural polished cotton. 9″ x 41″. *Joan Michaels Paque.* Photo, *Hank Paque.*

3

HOW LONG IS LONG ENOUGH?

How long is long enough? What if you run out of a cord? What are some ways of shortening cords temporarily? And what other materials and equipment work well with macramé? These are some very practical problems that need some very practical solutions.

EQUIPMENT

The equipment needed to get started in macramé is delightfully simple. The only essentials are a knotting board, scissors, pins, and the yarns you will use. A few very helpful accessories are rubber bands, a crochet hook, a large-holed tapestry needle, a measuring device, and graph paper or paper with a grid of squares and angles.

KNOTTING BOARDS

Most projects in macramé will be worked on a flat work surface, or knotting board. To make knot-

ting easier, strong pins will be pushed into the knotting board. You will pull against these pins while making and tightening the knots. Therefore, a sturdy surface and one that will accept pins is needed.

The two materials mentioned earlier and most satisfactory for this purpose are:

1. A polyurethane or plastic foam kneeling pad or pillow form. *Plastic foam*—not foam rubber. A convenient size is 12″ x 16″. The kneeling pad can be purchased in hardware and dime stores; the pillow form in fabric or upholstery stores.

2. Insulating board about 12″ x 16″. Insulating board is generally available in lumberyards where, occasionally, scraps can be found. Often a whole sheet (48″ x 96″) or a half sheet (48″ x 48″) must be purchased. However, a whole sheet is relatively inexpensive. The cost would be reduced, of course, if you could share the sheet with some other people. Some craft suppliers carry this type of board, too. Some brands of insulating board are more satisfactory than others. If the pin penetrates the material without your having to apply too much pressure and if you can

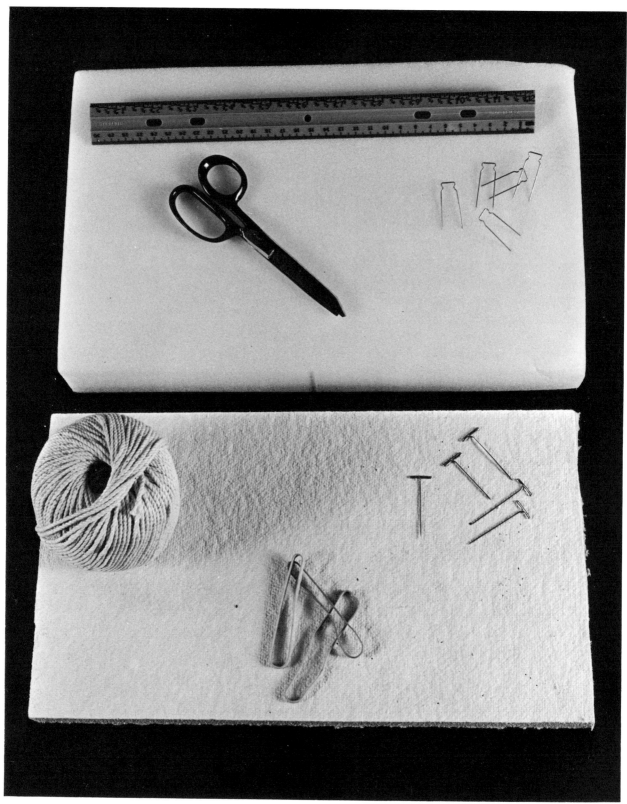

Fig. 44 Basic Materials and Tools for Macramé.

pull against the pin without displacing it, the board should work well for macramé.

If you cannot obtain a foam kneeling pad or a small piece of insulating board, you can make a knotting board for yourself out of the following materials. They will be somewhat less satisfactory than a polyurethane pad or an insulating board, but they will work adequately.

3. Several thicknesses of corrugated cardboard taped or glued together at the edges. The sides of empty boxes you find at the supermarket are ideal for this purpose. A convenient size is 12″ x 16″, but it doesn't matter if it is a little larger or smaller. Put enough thicknesses of cardboard together to make the board about one inch thick.

4. *A very firmly* stuffed pillow. It must be stuffed firmly enough so that the stuffing will not move as you are working on the pillow.

5. A few thicknesses of cork glued at the edges or taped together. A board made with cork should be at least ¾ of an inch thick. To reduce the cost, a few layers of cork may be glued to corrugated cardboard to get it up to the necessary thickness. Use glue around the edges only.

Or, make your own as of old:

"Make the cushion as an oblong flat-shaped pillow, 12″ long by 8″ wide, and stuff it with sand to render it heavy, cover it with good Ticking [sic] and arrange the lines woven in the Ticking evenly along the length of the cushion, as they can then be used as guides for the horizontal lines of the work. An ornamental cover of scarlet ingrain twill, or blue silk can be arranged over the ticking cover, if the latter is not considered ornamental enough, but it is not necessary. Prepare a piece of fine linen or silk, similar in shape to the Covers used in other Pillow Lace making to pin over the lace while in progress to keep it clean."*

* S.F.A. Caulfield and Blanch C. Saward, *Dictionary of Needlework*, 1885.

KNOTTING OR MOUNTING SURFACES FOR VARIOUS SPECIAL USES

While working on a belt or other small piece, a clipboard lined with a piece of polyurethane foam is convenient. The top of the knotting can be fastened under the clip and the knotter can pull against this. It is a good traveling companion.

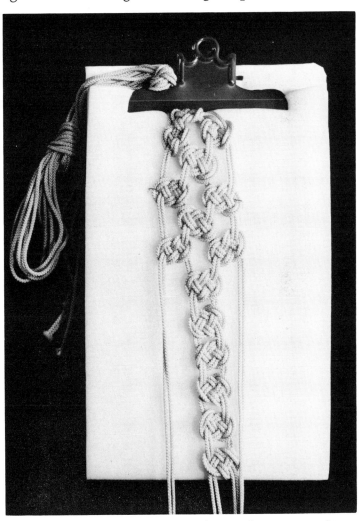

Fig. 45 Clipboard lined with plastic foam. Belt in progress. *Steven Bress.* Photo, *Seymour Bress.*

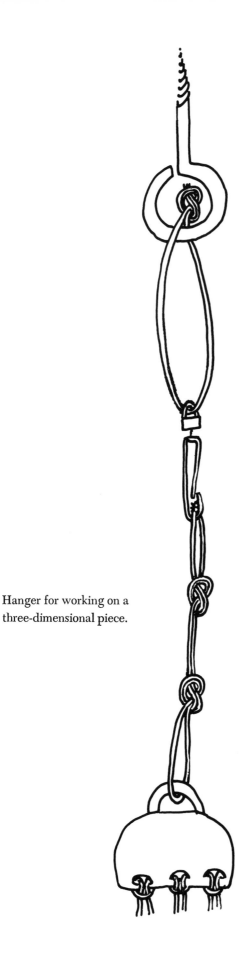

Hanger for working on a
three-dimensional piece.

For large pieces, or when macramé comes to fill your heart and home, you might find the following helpful.

I think that a draftsman's drawing table is ideally suited for macramé. You can raise, lower, and tilt it to any angle which is most comfortable for you for any given project. Cover the top of the table with insulating board.

My upright tapestry loom now has a piece of insulating board clamped to its front surface. (A sturdy easel would be its equivalent.) This provides a permanent work area and a comfortable one. You can sit or stand before this and work. When you stop working, the knotting can stay pinned to this surface. Tangling of cords is minimized in this way.

Three-dimensional hanging pieces present their own problems. Suspending the piece from a hook in a doorway works well—except that lighting and traffic are often problems.

Here is another solution that's more convenient in several ways. It allows you to work wherever you please, sitting or standing. The piece you are working on may be raised or lowered to meet your needs. All that is involved is a screw eye mounted in the ceiling near where you work, and two specially prepared cords.

TO MAKE A HANGER FOR WORKING ON THREE-DIMENSIONAL PIECES

Screw a large screw eye into the ceiling.

Cut a strong cord two yards long. You may need a longer cord if your ceiling is higher than eight feet.

Slip a swivel hook onto the cord. (A swivel hook is the type used for dog leashes.)

Slip one end of the cord through the screw eye in the ceiling.

Join the two ends of the cord with an overhand knot.

88

Cut another cord two yards long.

Put it through the top of your macramé piece and tie the two ends together.

Make overhand knots along this cord about every two inches.

Hook your hanging onto the swivel hook of the ceiling cord at whatever height is comfortable for you. You may sit or stand as you work. When your hanging needs to be raised, unhook it, and move it up a notch or two. For a wide hanging, two sets of hangers will work well.

SHAPED PIECES

Since cords can be added to or eliminated from a piece of macramé, macramé pieces can be made in almost any shape you please. Clothing, for example, can be made by knotting directly over a paper pattern. Using forms as a base, on the other hand, allows you to construct three-dimensional pieces, Martha Hoering worked the bell in Figure 48 around a cone of yarn. Pins penetrate the yarn easily. Styrofoam forms, dress forms, and wig stands are just a few of the things you can use as a base on which to construct three-dimensional pieces. When a slick surface must be used, the knots can be urged to stay in place temporarily with double-stick cellophane tape or masking tape.

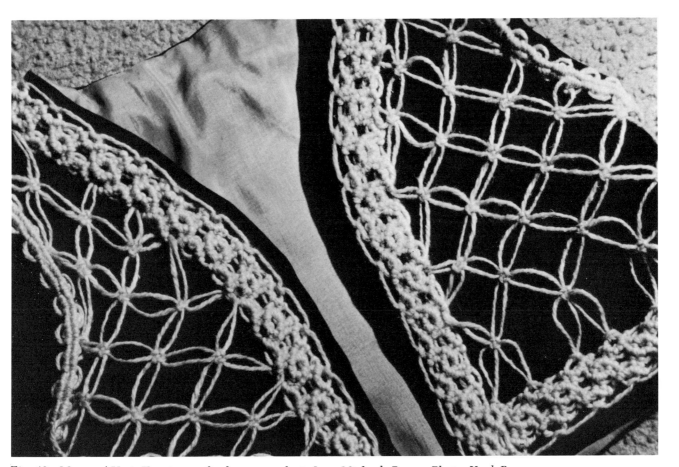

Fig. 46 Macramé Vest. Two tones of ochre over velvet. *Joan Michaels Paque.* Photo, *Hank Paque.*

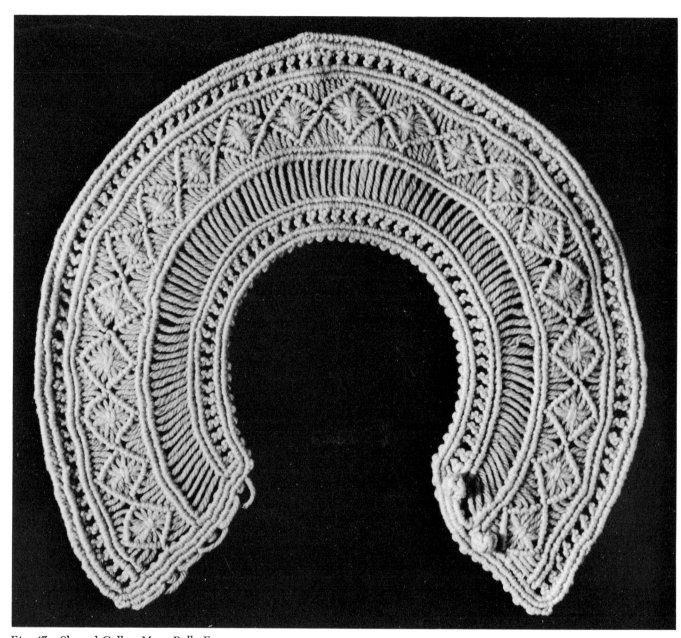

Fig. 47 Shaped Collar. *Mary Belle Frey.*

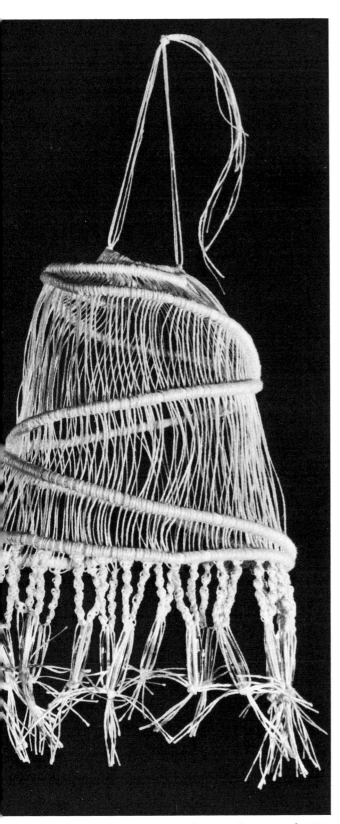

OTHER MISCELLANEOUS EQUIPMENT

Scissors: Any pair sturdy enough to cut the cords you choose.

Pins: Sturdy pins are important. "T" pins, sometimes called "Wig" pins are most satisfactory for use with insulating board. They can be found in craft shops, sewing supply stores, or where hair accessories, such as bobby pins, are sold. It's well to have about two dozen on hand. "U" pins, sometimes called "Tidy" pins work beautifully with the plastic foam. They are usually sold where sewing or upholstery supplies are sold.

Rubber Bands: One method of shortening the working cords you use is to "bundle" up each long cord and hold each "bundle" with a rubber band. If you choose this method, you'll need as many rubber bands as there are cords in your project. (Ways to shorten cords will be described later. See pages 97-98.)

Knitting Bobbins: Sometimes large knitting bobbins can be used to shorten cords. They are available in knitting stores and come with directions for use.

Or, pull skeins can be made without any equipment. (See pages 98-99.)

Crochet hook and large tapestry needle: These are used primarily to end cords off when finishing a project.

Measuring tools: For small projects, a yardstick is very satisfactory for measuring the length of cords you need. When you begin to work on larger pieces, other means are more satisfactory. Two chairs set at an appropriate distance apart will serve well. I think, however, that a weaver's warping board is the most satisfactory for measuring long cords. One may be purchased at a weaver's supply house or reproduced simply at home. Methods for using these devices will be described later.

48 Bell. How did she do it? For a knotting base, Martha Hoering [used] a cone of yarn. She pinned the center of a heavy cord to this [cone]. Onto the heavy cord, she hitched some fine cotton yarn. The [heav]y cords meander around and the fine cotton cord is double half-[hitc]hed onto it. *Martha Hoering.*

MAKING A MEASURING BOARD

You will need the following materials which are readily available in any lumber yard:

One pine board—ask for size 1″ x 12″ x 42″. The actual measurements of the board they will give you will be ¾″ x 11½″ x 42″.

Eight 3″ finishing nails. Get a few extra ones in case they bend as you hammer them in.

Put in nails as indicated on the diagram.

With this measuring board, you can measure cords as short as 18 inches and as long as 12 yards. The board is small enough to be put away in a closet when not in use.

ACCESSORIES FOR USE WITH MACRAMÉ

To add to the fun and excitement of macramé, start the happy search for beads, buckles, bells, seeds, feathers, shells, and anything you feel might add interest to a piece of knotting.

Beads: All kind of beads are available, but knotters have a special problem. Often macramé is worked with heavy yarns, and often more than one strand of yarn must pass through the hole of a bead. Therefore, beads with large holes are generally needed. With care, the holes in some beads can be enlarged. For example, the holes in wood or cork beads can be enlarged either by drilling them out or by poking a heated rod through their centers.

ENLARGING HOLES IN WOODEN OR CORK BEADS

Drilling: Hold the bead firmly in a vise or with a pair of pliers, then drill with a hand or electric drill.

Burning out the center: Have ready some asbestos or some other fireproof and heat-resistant material such as a ceramic tile or brick, and an ice pick or a steel rod about 12 inches long and about ⅛ inch in diameter. The rod can be purchased in hobby stores where they are generally sold for use as the landing gears of model airplanes.)

Place the bead in a vise or hold it with a pair of pliers. Heat the rod in the flame of your stove. When the tip of the rod is red hot, pick the rod up at the opposite end. Push the rod through the center of the bead.

While the rod is still hot, try burning lines and dots on the bead itself and turn an otherwise ordinary bead into a rather unique one.

Fig. 49 Beads, Buckles, Bells, Seeds, Feathers, Shells. Accessories for use with macramé.

Filing: The holes in some beads might be enlarged by filing them with jeweler's files. Many hardware stores, as well as some of the better stocked craft and hobby stores, carry jeweler's files.

NOW FOR THE HUNT

Somewhere within your home, you probably have the beginning of a bead collection—a broken necklace or a worn-out beaded purse. The dime store can hold some treasures: try the jewelry counter and the toy sections. Import houses often have strings of glass beads as well as beads made from seeds or wood. For a very special piece, you might select beads from a jeweler, a lapidary shop, or a museum shop. Some specialty shops in the larger cities deal only in beads and these, of course, are good places to investigate.

Handmade beads and macramé combine particularly well. Some potters make and sell them themselves or sell them through craft or bead shops. You can make beads yourself. Clay, *papier-mâché,* instant *papier-mâché,* large seed pods, scraps of wood, sea shells, and square and round tubing available from hobby stores, are just some of the raw materials you can start with.

The search for buckles and rings of various sizes may lead you to fabric shops, notions counters, hardware stores, and marine supply houses; for decorative buckles, to leather supply shops, museum shops, shops that sell American Indian handicrafts, as well as to antique shops.

For bells you might try import houses, dime stores, and gift shops.

For seeds (not to be confused with "seed beads" which are tiny beads that are impractical for use with macramé) look in import houses or dime stores. They often have strings of beads made from seeds.

Try craft shops for feathers. If you're adventurous and not too squeamish, you can sometimes find freshly killed birds on country roads. One bird has a lot of feathers.

It's fun to use shells you've collected yourself, but not always possible. Craft shops, tropical fish stores, and shell specialty stores are good sources for these.

A macramé piece may be mounted on holding cords or it may be started on almost anything that strikes your fancy. Here are some mounting pieces to consider:

Dowels	Purse handles
Sticks	Buckles
Plastic rods	Ceramic pieces
Bamboo	Curtain rods
Parts of old chairs	Knitting needles

More ideas will be discussed in the chapter on design.

MEASUREMENTS

How long is long enough? Usually, it's longer than you think! For several good reasons, teachers and writers wish you wouldn't ask that embarrassing question. Unless a project has been knotted before, and is going to be repeated *exactly*, there is no one, direct, specific answer.

This leaves the teacher or writer in a rather uncomfortable spot. He may guess just right—and then all is well. If he overestimates, you will have yarn left over—and he will be blamed for wasting your material. If he underestimates—well, that really is a nuisance!

Here is the basic problem.

In order to determine *exactly* how much yarn you need for a particular project, you need to know the amount of take-up (amount of yarn consumed in making a knot) plus how many knots and which kinds you will be placing on each cord. Only rarely will you have all this information and so I offer the following suggestions.

If you don't have a plan in mind, just want to create a piece as you go along, and don't know how open or close the knotting will be, you can take a chance and estimate with this rule of thumb:

The length of each cord should be about four times the length of the finished piece.

HOWEVER, IF THE CORDS ARE TO BE FOLDED IN HALF, the length of each cord should be 8 TIMES THE LENGTH OF THE FINISHED PIECE, and only half as many cords will be needed.

This rule of thumb usually works well for those pieces that have some open and some closed areas.

For example, let us say that you are planning a narrow hanging about one yard long. You plan to use 24 cords mounted on a dowel. You would measure, then, only *12* cords, each eight yards long. When folded on a dowel, they will give you the 24 cords you need, and each cord will be four yards long.

The chart on pages 102-106 lists a large variety of cords and tells how many cords you will need per inch using any of these cords. That information should be of help in determining the number of cords you'll need for a specific project.

To determine the TOTAL AMOUNT OF YARDAGE needed for a given piece, multiply:

the length of each cord $\times$ the number of cords
   = the total amount of yardage required for the piece

94

g. 50 Test Samples. May Shields finds this visual record very helpful. *May Shields.* Photo, *Seymour Bress.*

There are many good reasons for making a sample before you start on a particular project. A sample gives you the opportunity to experiment with different knotting patterns and gives you time to get the "feel" of the yarn. After experimenting with the type of pattern you plan to use, you can then measure your finished sample, and be able to approximate the amount of yarn you'll need for your actual piece.

Here's a suggestion on how to make a sample:

Cut four cords, each cord six feet (or two yards) long. Fold each cord in half and mount each cord on a cord or on a small dowel. Experiment with the cords, try different knots and several different patterns. When most of the yarn is used up, measure your finished sample.

The formula for determining the length of cords you will need for your project, based on a sample is:

$$\text{length of starting cords of your sample} \div \text{length of finished sample} = \text{your base number}$$

The base number multiplied by the length of your planned piece will give you the length of each cord you will need for your project. REMEMBER, though, IF THE CORDS WILL BE FOLDED IN HALF, double the length and cut only half as many cords.

your base number × length of your planned piece
= length of each cord. (Double this if the cords are to be folded in half.)

95

Whether or not your cords are to be folded in half, ADD A FEW INCHES FOR A FRINGE AND FOR WORKING SPACE. Very short ends are hard to work with.

With experience, you'll learn that some knots consume more yarn than others. Then, you'll either compensate for this in figuring the amount of yarn you'll need, or you'll learn to splice very well.

It goes without saying that a dense knotting pattern. The knotting cord in vertical half hitches gets used up at a phenomenal rate. Core cords of sennits, on the other hand, have practically no take-up at all.

HOW TO MEASURE

When measuring yarns with a yardstick, wrap the yarn around and around the yardstick the long way until the proper length is reached. Cut and use this first cord as a measuring guide for the others. Cut the remaining cords using the first cord as a guide and place each cord in a separate pile. This keeps the cords from tangling.

TWO-CHAIR METHOD OF MEASURING

The two-chair method works like this. Place the chairs half as far apart as the total length of the cords needed. Tie one end of the cord to chair 1. Bring the cord around chair 2 and back to chair 1. One cord has now been measured.

Continue in this way. When the total number of cords has been measured off, cut the cords at Chair 1 *only*. The halfway mark is around Chair 2.

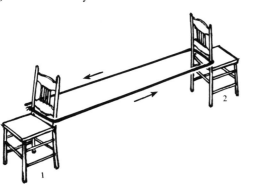

MEASURING BOARD

I feel that the measuring board described on page 92 is the most satisfactory device of all for measuring macramé cords. Place the board on a table. Make a loop near the end of your string and secure it with an overhand knot. Place the loop around the nail (A). To measure off an eight-yard cord, take the cord and bring it around nail (B); bring the cord back around nail (C); bring the cord over to the right again and around nail (D) and then back again, but this time around nail (E). You have now measured off four yards.

To measure off the other half of this cord, follow the same path you just took—but in reverse. The first cord will serve as a guide. When you get back to nail (A) you have measured off one eight-yard cord. Repeat these steps for all the cords of this length you need.

To remove the cords from the board, cut the cords at the *starting nail (nail A) only*. Nail (E) is your halfway mark. Cords can be removed one at a time. If you remove them at nail (E), they are already folded in half and can be mounted onto your mounting piece directly.

CHART I   CHART OF AVERAGE SIZES

Belts and Sashes
Belts—Waist measure plus a few inches for overlap.
Sashes—Waist measure plus about 20″ fringe on either side.
　　(To estimate the yardage needed for each strand of a sash: take waist measure, multiply it by 4, and add about 40″ for the fringe.)

Leash—5 feet.

Pillows
　　square—12″ x 12″ or 14″ x 14″
　　round—same
　　floor—24″ square

Place Mats—12″ x 18″
　　　　　　　14″ x 21″

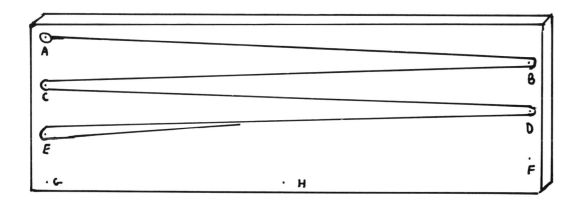

Purses
    Evening—4½″ x 7½″
    Handbag—8″ x 10″
    Small Tote—10″ x 10″ plus fringe
    Large Tote—14″ x 14″ plus fringe

Runners—14″ x 28″

Stoles—17″ x 60″ plus a fringe on each end
      22″ x 90″ plus a fringe on each end

MOUNTING CORDS

After measuring off your cords, the next logical step is to mount them. This may be done in several ways. The two simplest methods were shown on page 4 and page 63. More elaborate ways are shown in Chapter 2 of this book.

SHORTENING CORDS

Most often your cords will be very long and knotting would become tedious if the cords were not shortened. There are several satisfactory ways of shortening cords.

1. Starting from a point about 18 inches below your mounting piece, wind the cord around your palm. Keep wrapping the yarn round and round your palm, always placing the cord *alongside* the previous cord and working out toward your fingertips. When you have completely wound the cord,

slip it off your hand and place a rubber band around the center. If the winding was done carefully, the cord will release easily as the knotting progresses. If done sloppily you'll have to undo it occasionally, and rewrap.

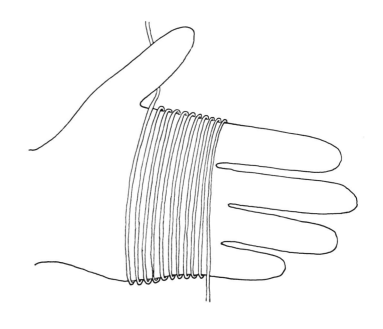

2. A variation of this is known to weavers and other craftsmen as a "butterfly." Again, start from a point about 18 inches below the mounting piece.

Begin by putting the cord between your thumb and index finger of your right hand.

Bring the cord across your palm and bring it around your little finger.

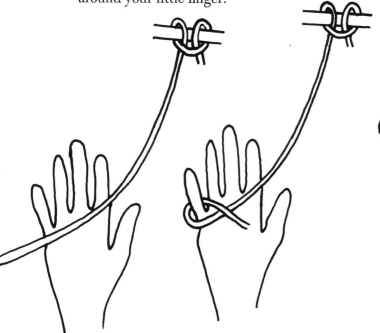

Next, bring the cord around the outside of your thumb and then between your thumb and index finger.

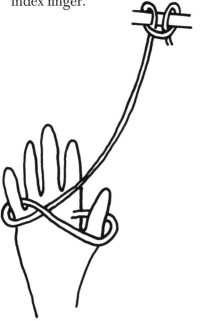

Continue in this way back and forth.

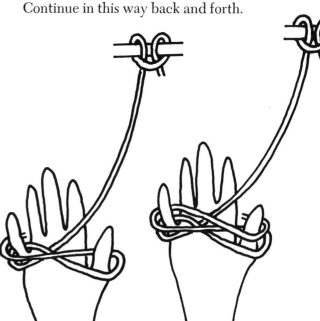

Try not to overlap the cord as you bring it around your fingers. Keep the cord moving up toward the tips of your fingers.

Stop winding when you have a few inches of cord left.

With your left hand, firmly hold the center of the "bobbin" you've formed.

Remove the bobbin from your fingers.

Wrap the free end of the cord tightly around the middle of the bobbin several times.

Tie the loose end of the cord with one or two hitches.

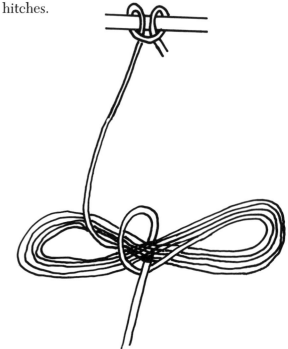

g. 51   Fish. At one point in time, when fine threads were used for macramé work, fish bobbins of this sort were used.
Steven Bress.

What you've actually made is a small pull skein. The cord should release easily and continually. The description is wordy, but the butterfly is easy to make and pleasant to use.

3. If neither of these two shortening methods appeal to you, you might like to try using knitting bobbins. Sometimes extra large ones are available in yarn shops. Directions for use should come with them. You'll need one bobbin for each cord you have.

APPROPRIATE MATERIALS

And now for the yarns or cords. Generally, knotters look for a strong, smooth, hard-twisted, non-elastic cord. This combination of qualities works well for macramé. With experience—and care—other combinations can be used to good advantage.

99

The following chart is designed to give you an
idea of some of the available yarns and their
characteristics.

Fig. 52

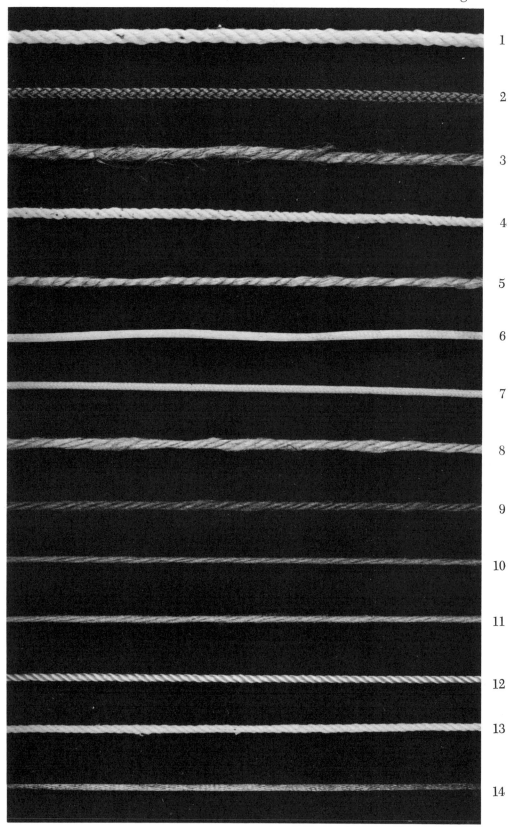

1

2

3

4

5

6

7

8

9

10

11

12

13

14

Fig. 53

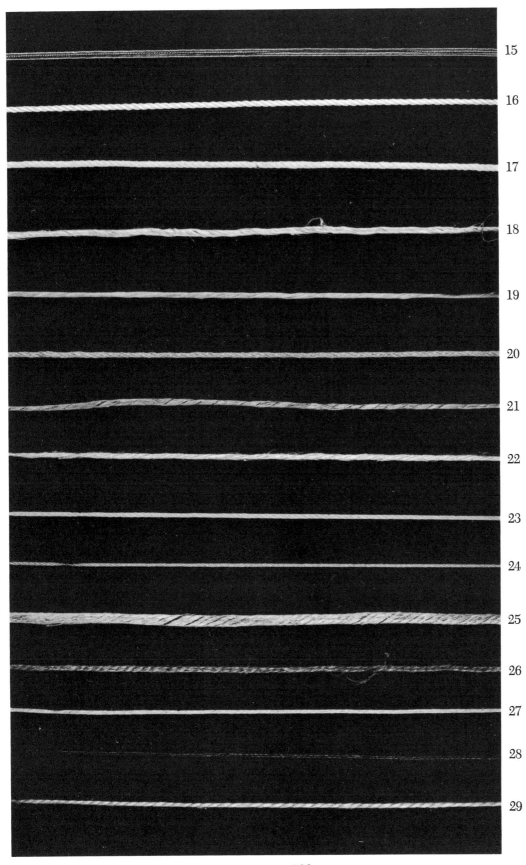

15
16
17
18
19
20
21
22
23
24
25
26
27
28
29

These cords are shown actual size.

CHART II   CORDS SUITABLE FOR MACRAMÉ

Type of Cord	Composition	Qualities	Tension Required	Cords per Inch	Color Range	Availability	Possible Uses
1. Seine Twine #72 also called Mason Cord & Chalk Line	Cotton	Easy to work with. Pattern will be well defined. This weight cord will work up quickly.	Firm	5	White	Hardware stores, though not as available as the smaller sizes	Very bulky belts, wall hangings.
2. Polypropylene Cord	Polypropylene	Firm, but yielding. Easy to knot. Works up quickly.	Firm	6	Wide	Specialty shops, arts & crafts shops, mail order	Belts, wall hangings.
3. Jute, 3 Ply	Jute	Easy to work with. Some people are made uncomfortable by the lint it sheds.	Firm	5½–6	In this size usually in natural only	Hardware stores	Belts, wall hangings, purses.
4. Seine Twine #36 also called Mason Cord & Chalk Line	Cotton, also available in Nylon	Easy to work with. Pattern will be well defined.	Firm	6	White	Hardware stores. Not as available as smaller sizes.	Bulky belts, wall hangings.
5. Jute, 2 ply	Jute	Easy to work with. Sheds lint. In time, will fade in strong light.	Medium-Firm	6	Wide	Craft suppliers, weaving yarn stores, mail order	Belts, purses, wall hangings, decorative items.
6. Rayon Satin or Rattail #2	Rayon	Easy, pleasant to use. Very smooth, but knots stay in place. Lustrous.	Firm	7	Wide	Craft suppliers, mail order	Belts, decorative items, wall hangings, neck pieces, evening purses.
7. Tubular Cotton	Cotton	Easy and pleasant to work with. Knots well. Slightly springy. The samples in Chapter 2 were made with this cord.	Firm	7½	Several colors available	Craft suppliers, mail order	Belts, purses, decorative items.

Type of Cord	Composition	Qualities	Tension Required	Cords per Inch	Color Range	Availability	Possible Uses
8. Rug Yarn	Rayon & Cotton	Easy to work with, easy on the hands. "Pills" or forms fuzz balls when handled a great deal.	Medium-Firm. If pulled too hard becomes crabbed-looking, and may break	6½–7	Wide	Readily available at dime stores, knitting departments	Belts, purses, wall hanging, clothing, necklaces, table mats, pillows.
9. Rug Yarn	Wool	With a little care works easily and well.	Medium	7	Wide	Yarn suppliers, but not usually among knitting yarns. Weaver's supply shops.	Clothing accessories, wall hangings, very good for accents, such as twining, wrapping and rya knots within a macramé project.
10. Knitting Worsted	Wool	Very soft, very stretchy. Knots often become obscured. Not recommended unless handled very delicately.	*Very* Light	8	Wide	Knitting shops, dime stores	Clothing accessories that won't get hard wear, e.g. neck pieces. Also for accents as rya knots.
11. Knitting Worsted	Orlon	As the above. It is very soft and stretchy, and the knots often become obscured. You can **make** it work for you, but other yarns are much more cooperative.	*Very* Light	8	Wide	Knitting shops, dime stores	As above.
12. Seine Twine #21	Nylon	Slippery, but knots easily and well. Not recommended for very beginners.	Firm	9	White, sometimes gold & green	Hardware stores	Belts, purses, necklaces, wall hangings, mats, runners.
13. Seine Twine #21	Cotton	Easy to work with. Pattern will be well defined. Good for beginners.	Firm	8	White, sometimes yellow or gold	Hardware stores—Most carry sizes #21 or #18	Belts, purses, wall hangings, mats, runners.

103

Type of Cord	Composition	Qualities	Tension Required	Cords per Inch	Color Range	Availability	Possible Uses
14. Rayon Satin Cord or Rattail #1	Rayon	Easy and pleasant to use. Very smooth, but knots stay in place. Lustrous.	Firm	8	Wide	Specialty yarn stores, craft shops	Belts, decorative items, wall hangings, neck pieces, evening purses.
15. Soutache	Rayon	Knots well, but Soutache is a flat cord. If you want it to be knotted perfectly, you must adjust the cords as you work.	Firm	9	Wide	Craft suppliers	Belts, decorative items.
16. Seine Twine #18	Nylon	Slippery, but knots easily and well. Not recommended for very beginners.	Firm	11	White, sometimes gold & green	Hardware stores. This and #21 are among the most common sizes	Belts, purses, necklaces, wall hangings, mats, runners.
17. Seine Twine #18	Cotton	Easy to work with. Pattern will be well defined. Good for beginners.	Firm	11	White, sometimes yellow or gold	Hardware stores. Most carry either #18 or #21	Belts, purses, wall hangings, mats, runners.
18. Sisal	Sisal	Comes in a wide variety of sizes. Very stiff and wiry. Difficult to use. Can be tamed by dampening it a little as you work. If too wet it tends to unply and come apart. Hard on hands. Gloves are recommended, or band-aids in strategic places.	Firm and Insistent	7	Natural, sometimes in a few colors	Hardware stores	Tote bags, wall hangings. In heavier weights, door mats.

Type of Cord	Composition	Qualities	Tension Required	Cords per Inch	Color Range	Availability	Possible Uses
19. Waxed Linen	Linen with a waxed coating	Waxed Linen is particularly well suited for macramé. It works easily, though it is not recommended for very beginners. Knots stay where you place them. Shaped pieces retain their shape without any stiffening.	Medium Firm	10	Natural, brown, black	Weaving yarn shops, some craft shops	Jewelry, decorative 3-dimensional shaped pieces, wall hangings.
20. Macramé Cord	Cotton	Easy to use. Knots easily and well.	Medium	8	Wide	Craft suppliers	Jewelry, belts, small-scale wall hangings.
21. Polished India Twine	Jute	Stiff and wiry, but once knotted, stays in place well. Hard on hands—gloves or band aids recommended. Slower to work with than softer yarns. Knots are somewhat irregular, because of the unyieldingness of the yarn. Interesting effect.	Firm	10	Natural	Hardware stores, five and dime stores	Decorative items, e.g. wall hangings or screens.
22. 10/5 Linen	Linen	Often used by weavers for rug warps. A pleasure to work with. Knots show up well. Works easily.	Medium	11	Wide	Weaver's yarn supply stores	Necklaces, purses, belts, runners, mats, pillows, wall hangings.
23. Navy Cord	Polished cotton	Stiff, wiry, knots well and gives a clean, crisp appearance. Will loosen or come undone at end if not finished in a secure way. Has good body. Not good for beginners.	Very Firm and Insistent	12	Wide	Craft supply houses	Belts, necklaces, wall hangings.

Type of Cord	Composition	Qualities	Tension Required	Cords per Inch	Color Range	Availability	Possible Uses
24. Heavy Crochet Thread	Cotton	Easy and pleasant to use. Good body. Doesn't squash down or crush. Knots well defined.	Medium	17	Wide	Dime stores, craft suppliers	Good for articles with a delicate look–necklaces; intricate, complex belts, small hangings.

GOOD MACRAMÉ CORDS—NOT SO READILY AVAILABLE

Type of Cord	Composition	Qualities	Tension Required	Cords per Inch	Color Range	Availability	Possible Uses
25. Spring Twine—Heavy Weight		Very rigid. Makes crisp, neat piece.	Very Firm	5	Natural	Upholsterer's supply stores	Wall hangings, large tote bags.
26. Tarred Marline	Linen	Stiffer than stiff, but with determination, it is workable. Strong smell that disappears in time. Odor is pleasant to some, offensive to others. Very sturdy.	Very Firm	8	Medium brown	Marine supply shops	Outdoor hangings; as an accent color and texture to pieces in lighter natural tones.
27. Mattress Twine	Linen	Pleasant and easy to work with. Crisp looking.	Very Firm	12	Natural	Upholsterer's supply stores	Jewelry, belts, purses.
28. Upholstery or Mattress Twine	Linen	Although this is very stiff, it knots well and makes a crisp fabric which will hold its shape. You need to "place" the knots a bit.	Very Firm	12	Black and perhaps natural	Upholsterer's supply stores	Wall hangings, flat and 3-dimensional.
29. Perle Cotton 3/2	Mercerized Cotton	It's rather fine, but works easily and well.	Medium	15	Wide	Weaver's supply shops	Jewelry. Several strands together to make a belt.

106

Certainly there are more yarns than those listed. I've tried to list the most relevant yarns and cords and those which are potentially available to the average knotter. If you do search out or stumble upon other yarns that appeal to you, make a sample swatch using them. This will quickly show you the potentials of the yarns. Note down the characteristics as listed on the chart and you'll have a good record for future reference. Keeping notes is really helpful.

Some of the comments in the chart necessarily reflect my own prejudices. The yarns are listed to give you a starting point. Before embarking on a project, you might like to make a sample to see if you agree with the listings.

The chart gives you an overview of the most readily available yarns. Only a few sizes of seine twine and jute are listed. Larger, smaller, and in-between sizes are available, but you may have to hunt for them.

SPLICING

Sometimes it happens! You run out of cord, or a cord breaks. All is not lost. There are several relatively easy ways of remedying this situation.

Usually you are aware that a cord is shortening and that you'll soon need to replace it. In such a case, you can often arrange to replace it at your convenience and in a convenient spot. Here are the most convenient spots:

1. When making sennits of square knots, or half square knots, the core cords are easily replaceable. Any core cord can be replaced this way.

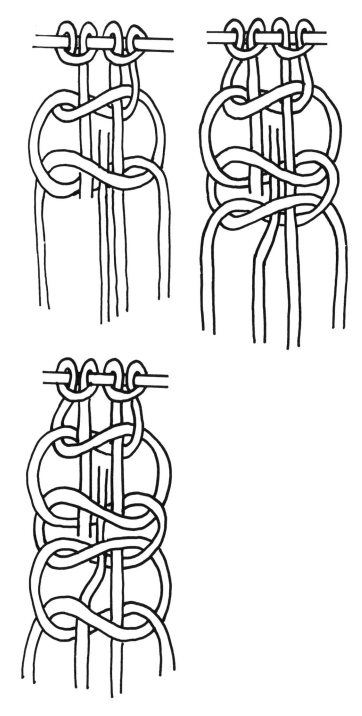

2. When you are making a sennit as above and a knotting cord begins to shorten too quickly, you can interchange the knotting cord with one of the core cords and continue knotting. If you are a perfec-

tionist, you may not like this method, because upon close scrutiny the change is slightly noticeable.

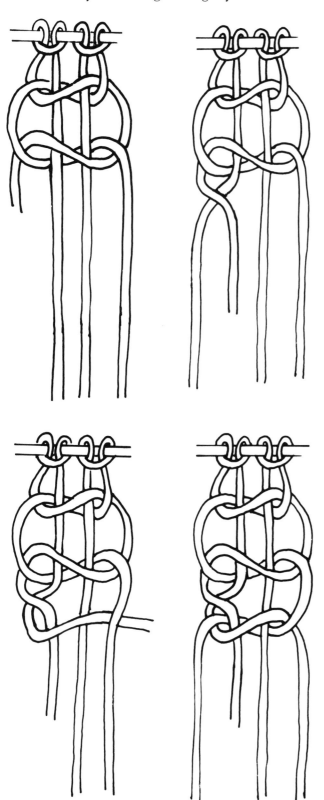

3. When making double half hitches, the knot-bearing cord is simple to replace. Overlap the old knot-bearing cord with the new one, and do several double half hitches over both ends together. Clip off the old cord, and continue with the new one. If the knot-bearing cord is very thick, you might like to cut out a ply or two of both the old and the new cords, and then overlap them.

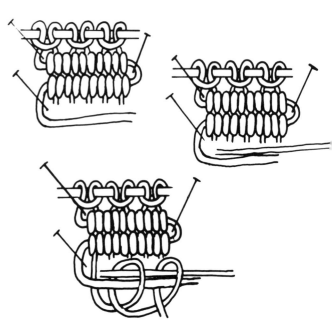

Although the splicing techniques described above are the easiest to manage, other situations can be remedied, too.

4. Sometimes an old and a new cord can be knotted together, on the wrong side of the piece, and the macramé portion can go right on. This method of splicing will only work when the knotting is dense enough to hide the joining knot. The knot-bearing cord in vertical half hitches can usually be replaced in this way.

5. Another method is to drop the short cord before it gets shorter than four inches. Pin a new cord to your board, leaving a tail of about four or five inches. Continue knotting, using the replacement cord. When the piece is completed, return to the spot where you added the new cord and either weave the old and new ends back into some knots to keep the cords from coming loose, or knot the two ends together, or stitch the ends

down inconspicuously, or, if necessary, glue the ends down. If the piece will not be washed, any white glue will do. If it will be washed, it's best to use a waterproof fabric glue.

And now for the traditional way of splicing two cords together.

6. In this method of splicing, the old cord is joined directly to a new cord. Most yarns used for macramé are composed of several strands—or plies —twisted together.

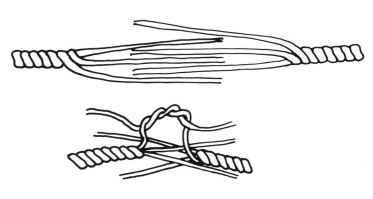

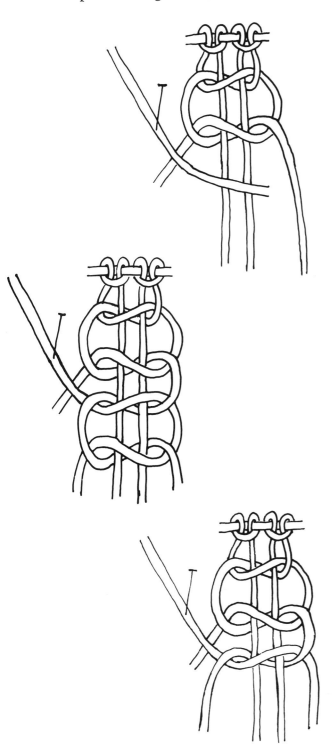

Untwist the new and the old cord for a distance of about two inches. Overlap the plies from both cords (see diagram). Twist a ply from one cord together with a ply from the other. (If possible, twist them in the direction opposite to the way they were originally twisted. They seem to hold together better this way.) Twist the rest of the plies together in the same way. When all the plies are twisted together, the knotting can be continued. If the splice is not too secure, a thin solution of glue can be used to hold it in place. Also, if the splice is too thick, one or more sets of plies can be cut out.

Fig. 54 Soft Neckpiece. Made of soft yarns, square knots, and finger weaving at the shoulder part. It's ended with a few rows of overhand knots. *Marjorie Newell.*

4

BEGINNINGS AND ENDINGS

& some in-betweens

ENDINGS

Incongruous as it may seem, let's start with some endings. Different types of projects have problems unique unto themselves, but they all come to an end. Often, the same type of ending can be used for diverse projects.

Care should be taken in choosing an appropriate ending. The lines or contours of the endings should follow or be in keeping with the feel of the rest of the piece. A delicate, prim wall hanging, for example, could be spoiled by ending it with fat clumps of overhand knots and an untrimmed fringe.

Fringes and macramé are a natural. A fringe may be secured with overhand knots, wrapping, or double half hitches. A fringe may be trimmed evenly all across or deliberately unevenly, but with thought, please. Sloppiness may make something unique, but doesn't often produce good design.

The strip sampler on page 236 illustrates several different ways of ending a piece. Other examples can be found throughout the book.

The overhand knot method is one of the most common ways of ending a piece. The neckpiece in Figure 54 and the sash in Figure 55 are two examples of this.

111

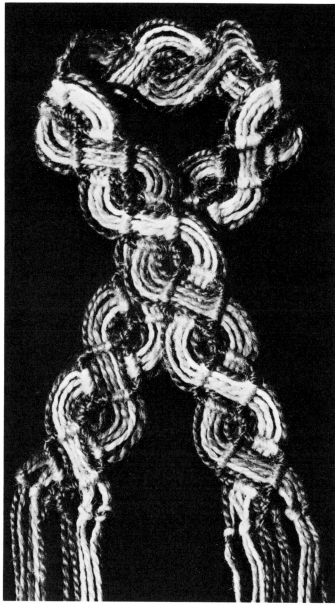

Fig. 55   Sash. This tri-colored jùte sash is ended with a row of overhand knots. *Ella Bolster.*

Fig. 56   Meticulously constructed purse. It is ended with a few rows of double half hitches and a fringe. *Marie Grassi.*

Wrapping produces a less bulky, neat fringe. The ending cords may be wrapped with a color the same as the fringe, or with colors to match other parts of the hanging. The strip sampler and the gold hanging on page176 are two good examples of this.

If the cord isn't too wiry or springy, a row of double half hitches can end the piece and a fringe left below it. The row of double half hitches can be straight or shaped.

The bottom rear of the hanging on page 217 is shaped with double half hitches and trimmed. If the cord is springy, a row of overhand knots below the double half hitches will usually keep the cords in place.

Tassels can be an effective "ending" on window shades or at corners of pillows. One way to make a tassel is like this:

For the core of your tassel
  —Measure off a batch of cords twice the length of your tassel-to-be. (You can do this easily around a piece of stiff cardboard cut to the length of your tassel.)

For the decorative portion of your tassel
  —Measure off some more cords about six times the length of your tassel. These cords may be the same color or a contrasting color. It's impossible to give exact numbers, but more cords can be added or some can be removed, if necessary. Have the number of cords be a multiple of four, e.g., 16, 20, 24.
  —Place the longer cords on top of the core cords.

—Cut two more cords for the "hanger" part of your tassel.
—Put the "hanger" cords around the center of all the tassel cords. Draw the cords together tightly and make a knot.

—Pin the "hanger" cords to your knotting board and do some decorative knotting with your long tassel cords.
—Knot the "hanger" cords into a decorative sennit.
—Trim all ends.
—Stand back and admire!

There are many instances when fringes and tassels are not desirable. Here are a few ways you can end a piece without either.

1. Turn the piece on to the wrong side. With a large-eyed tapestry needle or crochet hook, bring the ends up and through a few knots in the previous rows. If the piece will not get any abuse, and the cord is not springy, the cord can then be trimmed. If the piece will be handled a bit, after the cord is tucked back into a few knots, make an overhand knot in the cord, leave a little tail, and trim.

2. Another method of getting the cords to the wrong side of the piece is to make a final row of reversed double half hitches. The cords are now on the back of your piece, and may be tucked back into a few knots as above, or treated as those which follow.

3. Ends can be brought to the back and stitched down by hand.

Fig. 57 Tassels. Linen tassels for shade pulls. *Mary Belle Frey*. (See text for how-to description.)

4. Ends can be brought to the back and glued down with white glue or special fabric glue. If the piece is washable, be sure the glue is also washable. Fabric glues are usually washable; white glues are usually *not*.

5. Clothing, pillows, and purses will often be faced or lined. Ends should be treated as above and then the piece should be faced or lined in the usual manner.

ENDING OF ENDINGS

A little ingenuity will go a long way. When all else fails, improvise. You're bound to come up with a good solution.

The choices for mounting or starting pieces are infinite. They run the gamut from a piece of string to precious gems. As you browse through this book, you'll see many interesting mounting pieces, and in Chapter 5 there are some ideas which may intrigue you.

Plain headings and more fanciful ones are described on pp. **63-70.** While you may start your project on almost anything that suits your fancy, you may have to improvise some way to mount your cords. A piece of driftwood will serve as a good example.

Here's some driftwood.

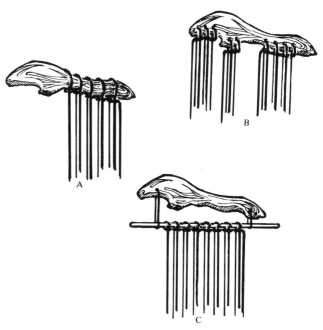

You may want to:
1. Mount the cords directly around the piece as in "A"
2. Drill some holes in it and mount the cords as in "B"
3. Drill a few holes in the driftwood and suspend a bar from it as in "C"

Each way will give you a different effect—but all three ways will work.

ig. 58   Tassels. These blue and white tassels hang at the end
a long sash. Perle cotton. *Mary Belle Frey.*

Sometimes, you want to get started *right now*, but you're not quite sure *what* you want to start on. Within limits, you can transfer your work from one bar to another after the work has begun. Transferring your work from bars of equal size (e.g., from a ½ inch dowel to a ½ inch plastic rod) is relatively easy. Just butt the two ends together, and gently slip the piece off one bar directly onto the other.

The same method holds for transferring your work from a larger rod to a smaller one. In that case, there will be a small area of strings showing before the knotting part begins.

You can even transfer your work to a considerably larger starting piece. To make such a transfer, remove your macramé piece from its original mounting bar. The original mounting hitches will open to about twice their original size. The rest of the knottng will *not* become undone. You can then slip your piece back onto any suitable mounting piece.

BELTS AND SASHES

Belts have their own set of requirements.

"D" rings and "O" rings are versatile and well suited for macramé belts. Wooden, metal, and strong plastic rings are sometimes available in sewing supply shops; metal rings can be found in hardware stores, marine supply stores, and in craft shops which sell leather-working supplies and equipment. Two "O" or "D" rings mounted together form a good buckle. One of the first projects in the book is made this way. (See page 00.)

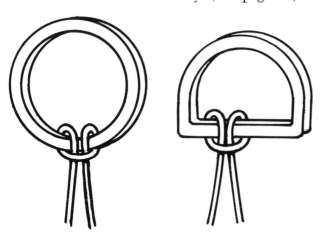

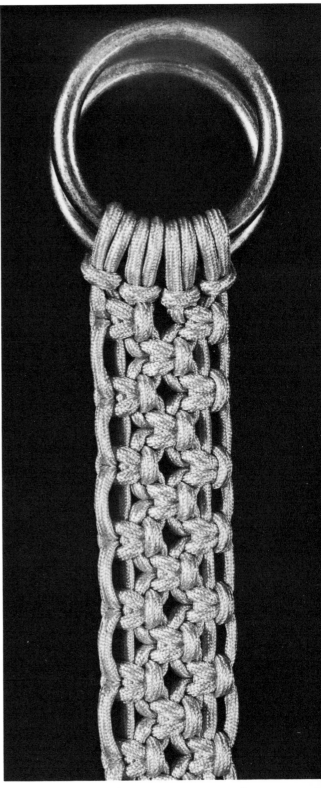

Fig. 59 Belt. Eight heavy orange rayon cords were mounted onto two large rings. A simple pattern of alternating square knots was used to make this handsome belt. *Melissa Diamant*

116

Another way to use these rings is to mount the starting cords on one ring with double half hitches, make the belt a few inches shorter than your waist measurement, and mount the other ring at the end. Double half hitch the cords onto the second ring, bring the ends to the back and finish in one of the ways described under endings.

To hold the belt together, make a tie cord about 18 inches long. Slip this through both rings and tie it in the middle. Small curtain rings or finger rings from the dime store can also be used for these belts.

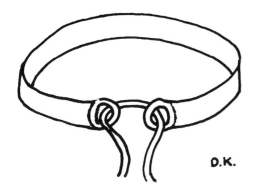

D.K.

Any buckle may be used for a belt. You can mount the cords directly onto the buckle or start the belt at the tip.

1. Mount the cords directly onto the buckle. Knot your belt long enough to completely circle your waist, plus an additional few inches for overlap. In the pattern on the overlap, provide secure places into which the "tongue" of the buckle can fit securely, such as alternating square knots.

2. Start the belt at the tip, perhaps with a point as described in the knot variations section. Continue knotting until the belt completely circles your waist plus a few additional inches for an overlap. Divide your cords, and make a few sennits of square knots about 1½ inches long. Fold the sennits around the buckle and secure them by sewing them down on the back of the belt. End off the cords. (See diagram on next page.)

A belt may also be started with a loop and held together with a large knot, button, bead, or bar at the other end. See p. 121 for more details.

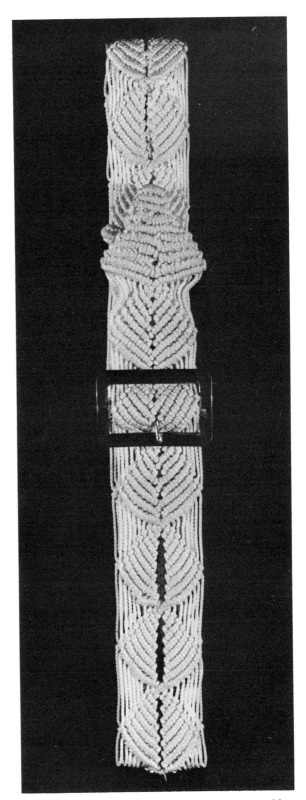

Fig. 60 Belt. Belt of white nylon seine twine. Note the ingenious way in which spaces were created so that the belt could be secured. *Margaret Overholt.*

117

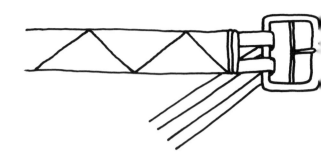

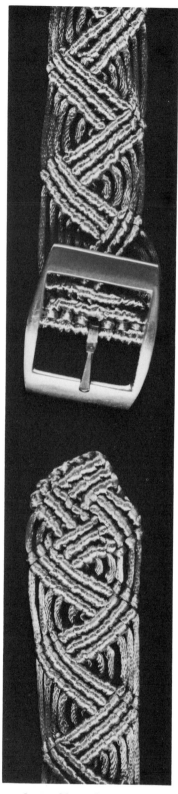

Fig. 61 Belt with Buckle. This interesting
pattern of double half hitches was done in a
smooth shiny rayon cord (rattail). *Doramay
Keasbey.*

A leather belt may be trimmed with macramé as in "A" on next page.

This can be done by making several sets of holes about six inches apart down the length of the belt. To come out properly, there must be an even number of sets of holes, i.e., 4, 6, 8. Mount your cords through the first set of holes at one end of the belt, and start knotting. When the knotting reaches the second set of holes, push the ends through those holes, bring the cords up through the next set of holes and begin knotting again. At the last set of holes, push your cords through to the back of the belt and make some square knots to secure the macramé, or glue the cords to the leather.

Perhaps you have a leather belt which is no longer being used. You can cut off a few inches from the beginning of the belt and a few inches of the tip of the belt. Push or punch a few holes in each piece, as in "B". Mount your macramé cords through these holes and knot until the belt you are knotting and the tip which was cut off the leather belt go around your waist properly. Push the ends through the tip end of the leather belt and end them as in one of the "endings."

If you did the above belt, you now have a strip of leather left over—the center of the belt you just cut up. How about pushing or punching some holes on either end of this piece of leather, as in "C"? Mount cords in the holes and do some fancy knotting. Tie it around your waist as a sash. Note: Be sure that the leather portion is smaller than your waist so that the sash will tie around the knotting and drape well.

A sash may be knotted in the same general pattern from end to end, or knotted rather solidly around the waist portion, and ended with long fringes—plain or elaborate. The overlap for a sash is usually about 20 inches for each side, 40 inches total.

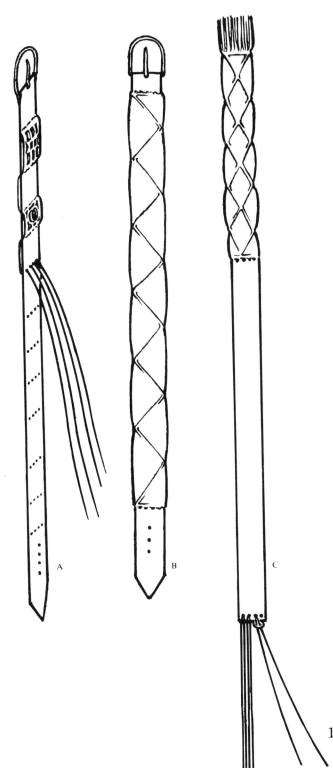

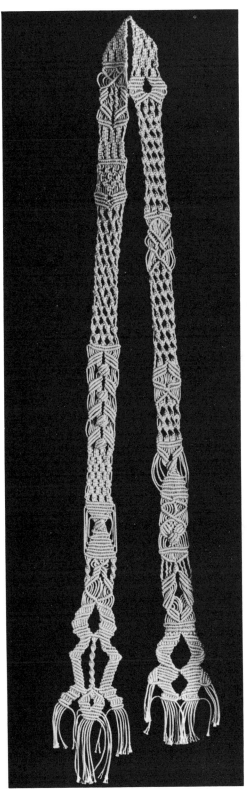

Fig. 62 Sash. Trudy Nicholson freely improvised the knotting on this elaborate sash. Gold, heavyweight, crochet cotton. *Trudy Nicholson.*

119

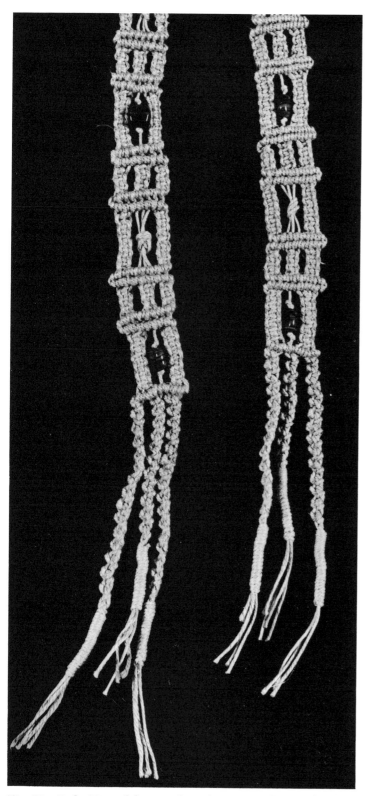

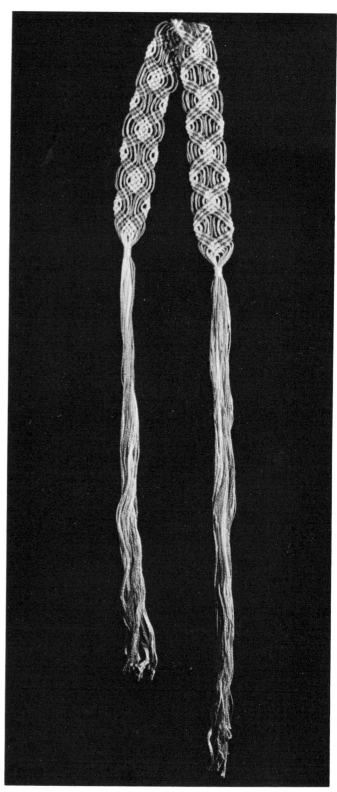

Fig. 63 Sash. Natural linen sash with variegated green beads. The fringes are made of chain knot sennits which are wrapped at the ends to hold them securely. *Helene Bress.*

Fig. 64 Sash. Marie Grassi ended her colorful sash by wrapping the cords at the waist and then letting the cords cascade down. *Marie Grassi.*

NECKLACES

Fig. 65 Sash with Handmade Ceramic Beads. Here's a different type of sash. It's narrow at the sides and back, wide at the front, and ties in the back! *Hannelies Penner.*

Where to start? How to end?

Possibilities are numerous. Probably the simplest of all is to start with a string, mount cords directly onto it, and tie the mounting string with a bow in the back.

You can start a necklace with a loop at one end and end it with a bead, button, or bar which will fit through the loop and close the necklace. A bead works well if the loop and bead are matched well, but I think the button or bar is a bit more secure.

To start a necklace in this way:
1. Take two of your cords, and fold them in half.
2. Tie an overhand knot just below the fold.
3. Leave enough of a loop to accommodate your bead, button, or bar.

To end with a bead:
1. Take one or more cords and pull them through the bead from the right.

Fig. 66 Three Belts. Here are some ideas for the "in-between" portion of your belt or sash.
Trudy Nicholson, Ella Bolster, Helene Bress.

2. Then take an equal number of cords and pull them through the bead again, but this time from the left.
3. Now take these cords, and make a square knot below the bead.
4. Work the ends back into the piece.

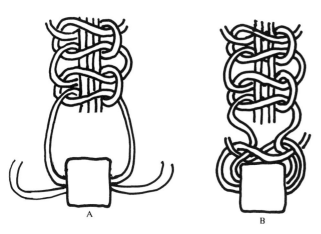

It's often easier to find a button that fits the starting loop than to try to match up a loop and a bead. If you're going to use a button to close your necklace, finish the knotting portion by stitching or gluing the ends down, or by bringing the ends back in—as described previously in "Endings," pages 113-114.

Find a button that fits the loop securely and sew it onto the end.

To end with a hook and eye:
A sturdy hook and eye arrangement will work well, too. These can be sewn directly onto the finished piece.

Other starting points:
Start at both ends and work toward the center. You can control the symmetry well this way. (*See diagram on next page*)

Start at the center back and work around toward the front. Leave an opening big enough for your head to go through. Pin the center of your cords to your knotting board and work first one side, then the other.

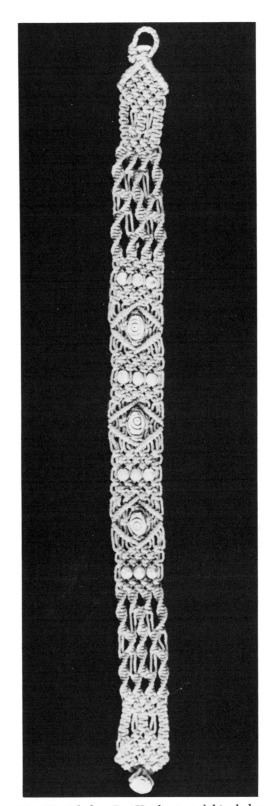

Fig. 67 Choker. Peg Hardy *started* this choker with a bead and *ended* with a loop. *Peg Hardy.*

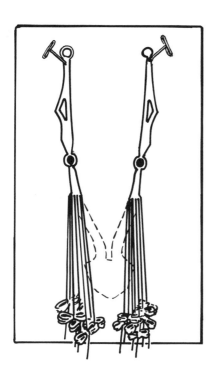

start here

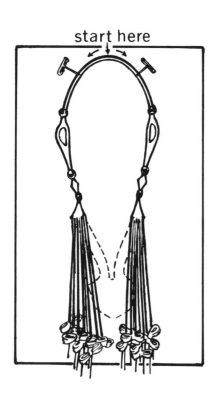

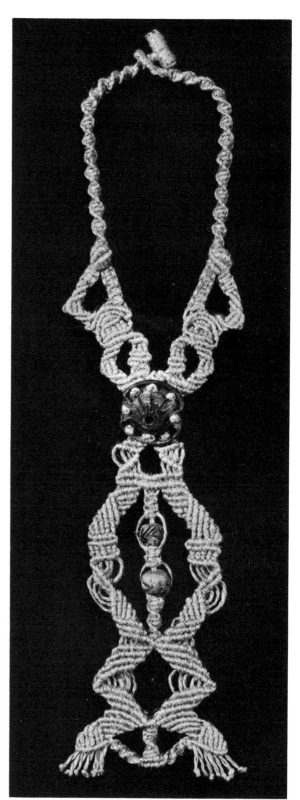

Fig. 68 Neckpiece. Trudy Nicholson started this piece on the ceramic disc in the center—and worked her way down. She then decided it would make a nice neckpiece, turned the piece upside down—and completed the neck part. *Trudy Nicholson.*

124

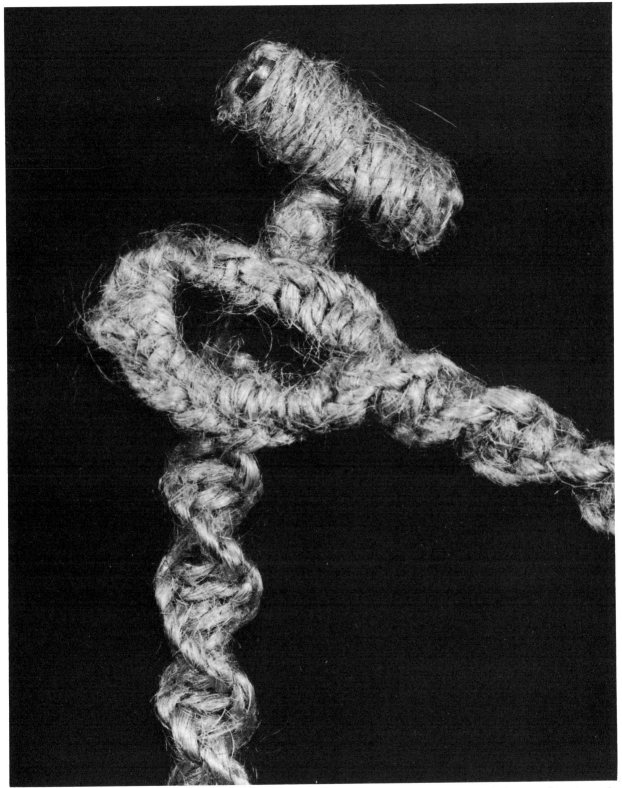

Fig. 69 Close-up of Neckpiece. This neckpiece closes with a loop and a bar. Trudy Nicholson used a piece of hollow tubing for the bar, ran her cords through it, wrapped the bar, and secured the ends with glue. *Trudy Nicholson.*

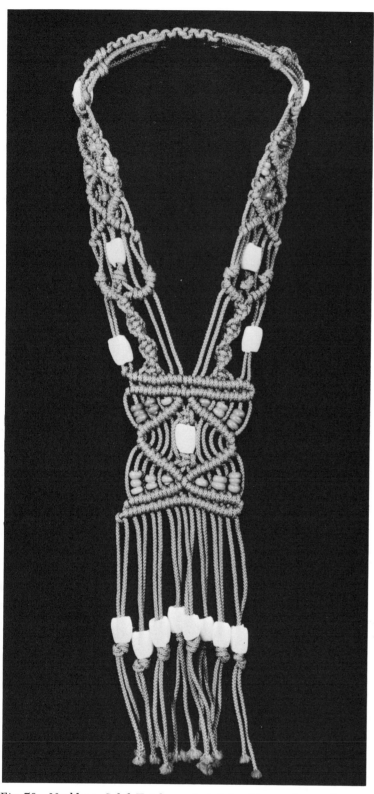

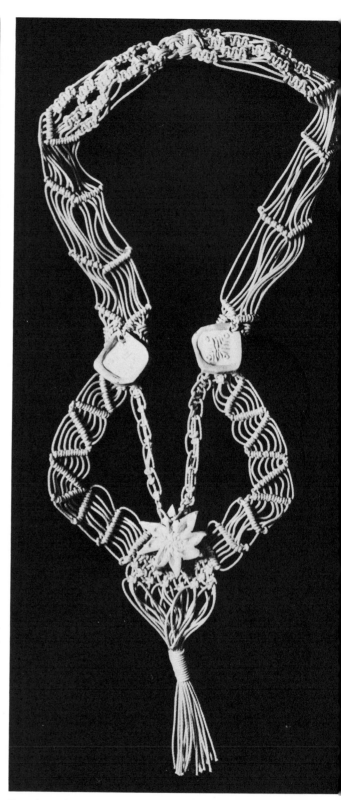

Fig. 70 Necklace. Sybil Fainberg started her blue, polypropylene necklace in the center back and joined the two sides for a pendant effect in the front. *Sybil Fainberg.* Photo, *Seymour Bress.*

Fig. 71 Shaped Necklace. Here's another necklace started in back and worked around toward the front. The ceramic pieces interest to this crisp, prettily shaped piece. Navy cord. Cer pieces, *Debbie Hopkins. Marjorie Mills.*

Start on necklace rings. Rings of this shape can often be found where costume jewelry is sold. Your cords can be mounted directly on those rings. The cords can be mounted all around or just in the center.

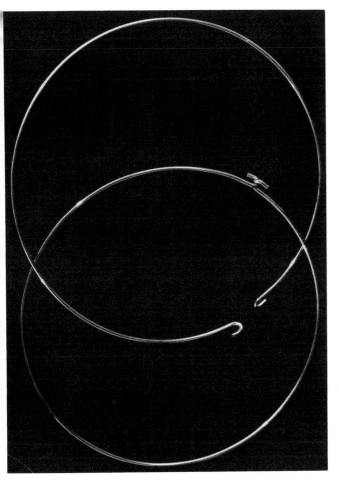

Fig. 72 Necklace rings—shown open and closed. Necklaces can be started on rings of this sort.

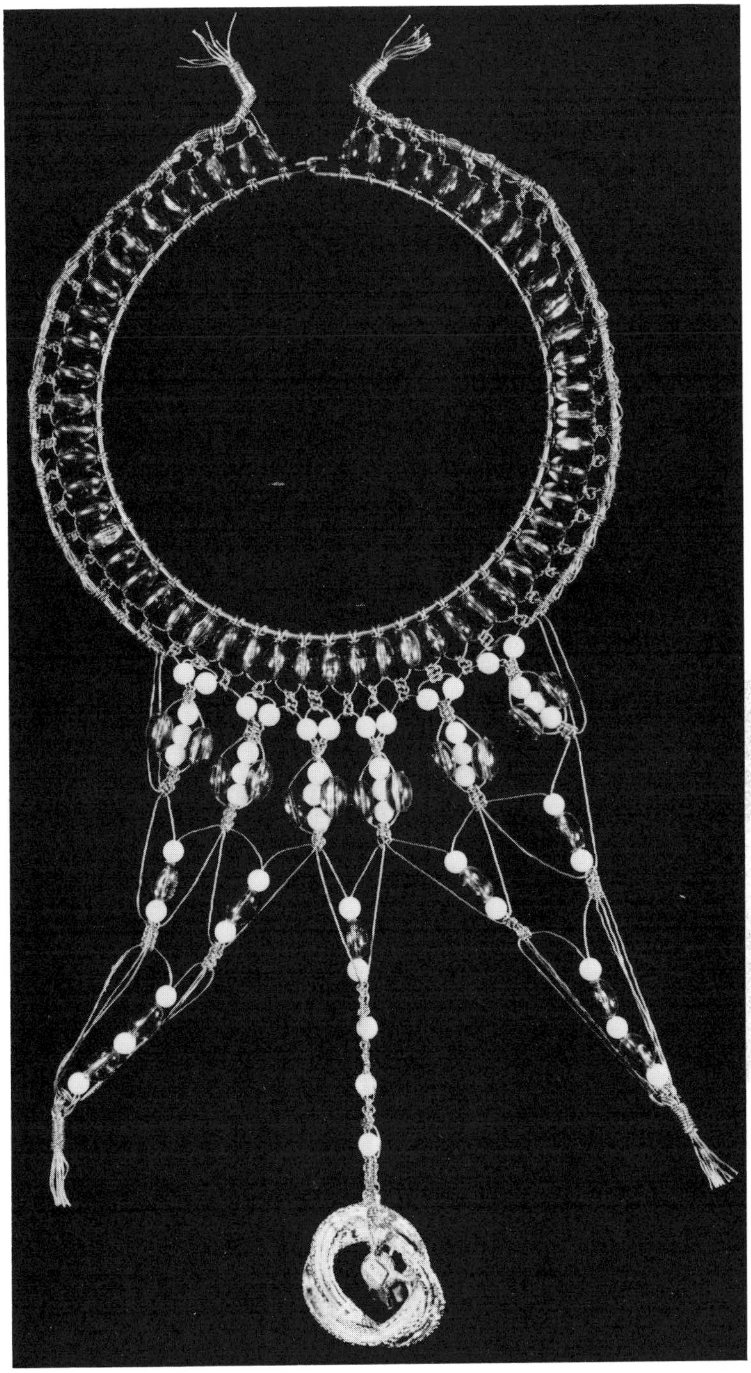

Fig. 73 Necklace. Gold lamé, green beads, and a discarded brooch were the materials used to obtain this glamorous effect. It was started on a metal ring. *Peg Hardy.*

The necklace by Peg Hardy (see Figure 73) was started on a ring of this sort. If carefully planned, several sets of pendants can be made to slip on and off the ring, to suit your mood or outfit.

Start at the bottom of the pendant part and work toward the back. To end a pendant started this way, you may use any of the three endings first mentioned: bead, button, or bar. If the pendant is large enough to fit over your head, you can end it by overlapping the ends and use the wrapping method to bind the ends together. (See Wrapping, p. 74)

A good way to join two sennits coming from opposite sides, as on a necklace, is to clip the filler cords short from both sennits.

Using the outside cords from side A as new core cords, knot around these filler cords with the outside cords of side B. When the knotting is completed, bring the ends of the knotting cords into the center of the sennit. Jeanne Vernon's pendant is done this way.

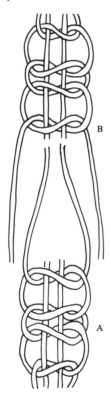

Some necklaces have no beginning or end, or at least so they appear. Joan Michaels Paque's necklace on p. 214 is one of this type.

You'll probably get some additional ideas just by looking at the photographs in this book. As you work, still more ideas will surely occur to you.

Fig. 74 Neckpiece. This neckpiece started on the round ceram disc. It radiated out from here, went down, up, and rambled a around. Jute. Ceramic pieces, *Ebby Malmgren. Trudy Nicholson.*

Fig. 75 Brilliant red, hot pink, and orange pendant. In a deliberate attempt to avoid a fringe at the front center, Jeanne Vernon chose to start in the front and work her way around to the center back. She ended the necklace so skillfully that it's impossible to see where she overlapped sennits. *Jeanne Vernon.* (Description and diagram of this type of ending in text.)

EARRINGS

Earrings can be made by mounting your cords on earring rings. (See p. 200.) If you use very fine cords, you may even try knotting *within* the loops.

PURSES

The variety of purses is endless. There are casual, dressy, tote, and evening purses. Some standard sizes are suggested in Chart I. Here are some beginning, ending, and construction ideas. It's a good idea to make a full-size paper pattern before starting, to see if the size and shape are really what you want.

In terms of construction, one of the simplest purses is made out flat like this:

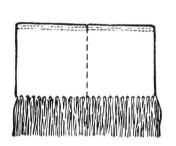

It is mounted on a very heavy cord or group of finer cords and knotted on a flat board. When the knotting is completed, the purse is folded in half and sewn together on the open side. The fringe from the front and back halves are then knotted together. Wrapping makes a neat ending for this kind of purse and also closes the bottom. A handle may be made of the same cords used to make the purse and stitched onto the purse.

Envelope purses may be made flat, too.

Upon completion of the knotting, fold the purse on the lines indicated in the diagram, and sew the front and back seams together. Purses may be started at the bottom or the top and have fringes, or have the ends tucked away. If gussets are desired, they may be made separately and stitched to the sides of the purse.

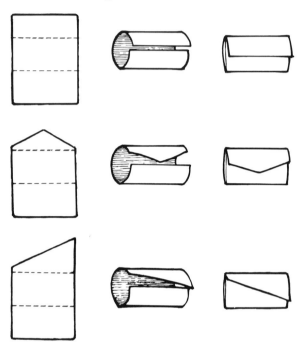

The body of a purse may be made in one piece by knotting it around a base. A good base, for example, is a polyurethane pad or pillow form.

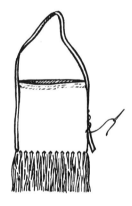

Encircle the base with your mounting cord. Pin the cord directly onto the pad. Work from the top down. Rows of double half hitches make a firm and sturdy bottom or base for the purse. The ends may be brought inside and knotted together so that they won't pull out—or they may be fringed, or ended as the bottom of bottles. (See p. 141.)

A purse may also be made in three pieces. The long strap will be used as the bottom of the purse, gussets, and straps.

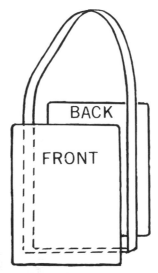

Fig. 76 Tote Bag. Lola Liebner fashioned this handsome jute tote bag in four pieces—front panel, back panel, gusset for three sides, and handle. Courtesy *Mrs. E. Lakin Phillips. Lola Liebner.*

Fig. 77 Ecuadorean Purse. The cords of this purse are mounted directly onto a simple, wooden handle. The back and front are knotted separately for about 1½″ and then joined at the sides. The cords are brought to the inside at the bottom and the purse is lined. Gift from *Allen Bress*.

Of course, purses can be started on purse handles. Dowels, bamboo rods, half-round moldings, rings, metal frames or wooden frames with a bar on which cords can be mounted all serve as good starting points for purses.

Conversely, a purse may be started from the bottom up, and may be mounted on a leather or wooden base.

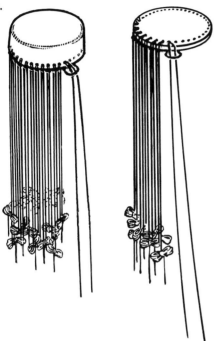

One thing to watch for in making a purse is to be sure the opening is large enough for you to reach into it easily. When using bag handles, knot the back and the front separately for a few inches before starting to knot them together. You may also work the back and front separately, and then sew them together to within a few inches of the top.

If you make short sennits near the top of your purse, you can weave a cord over and under the sennits and make a drawstring purse.

Unless the knotting is very close, you'll probably want to line your purse. You might want to sew the lining directly to your purse or try this idea:

Make a set of interchangeable, different-colored linings for your purse and secure them in place with sturdy snaps or hooks and eyes. The character of your purse will change slightly with each different color, and the purse will blend with more of your clothes.

Fig. 78 Purse. Jute purse with a shell knot flap. *Helen Levin* with an assist from *Madge Schneider*. Photo, *Seymour Bress*.

Fig. 79 Purse. Handsome, sturdy purse of cotton seine twine and wooden beads. Shown open. *Richard Mathews.*

Fig. 80 Purse. Three triangular tabs form the beginning of this purse. They're designed to nest on top of the diamonds when the purse is closed. Seine twine. *Helen Levin.* Photo, *Seymour Bress.*

Fig. 81 Handwoven Purse with Macramé Overlay. The knotted handles on this purse are particularly versatile. They can be shortened or lengthened at the wearer's discretion or pleasure. *Richard Malmgren, M.D.* Photo, *Seymour Bress.*

Fig. 82 Knapsack. Have you ever thought about making your own knapsack? Richard Mathews has, and has done so very successfully. *Richard Mathews.*

PILLOWS

Pillows and purses are made in a similar fashion. As for pillows, here are some ideas.

You might do well to make a full-scale paper pattern of pillows too, to make sure they will suit your needs. Standard sizes are listed in Chart I, but it is fun to vary these.

The easiest way to make a pillow is to do your knotting directly around the form on which the finished pillow will be mounted. You will be sure to knot it to the proper size this way. Square, rectangular, and round polyurethane pillow forms are available, and these make good bases. Sometimes you can have forms cut to your specifications.

You can make a pillow on a flat board and fold it to shape when you're finished. Or, if a gusset is desired, make the back, front, and gusset separately and then stitch them together.

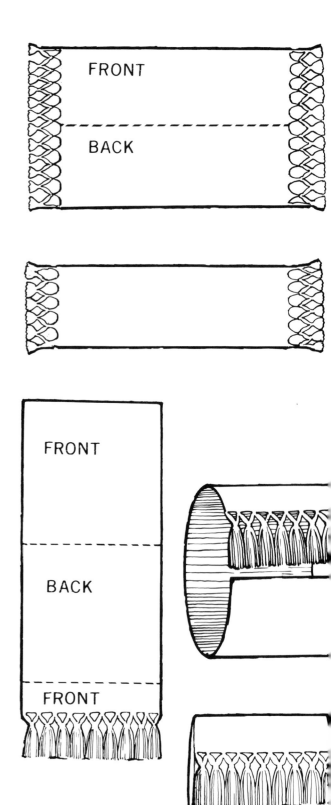

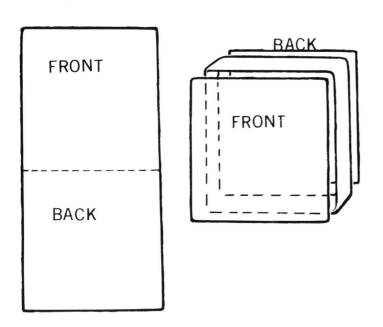

The end cords may be hidden in the lining by using any of the methods mentioned previously— or they may be used decoratively, as part of the design.

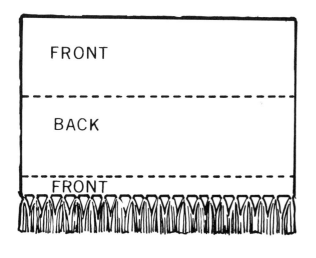

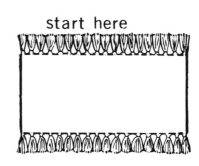

MATS

Now for some pretty place mats. Again, note the standard sizes as listed in Chart I. Make a paper pattern of a shape that pleases you, and start knotting. Here are some designs that work well with macramé.

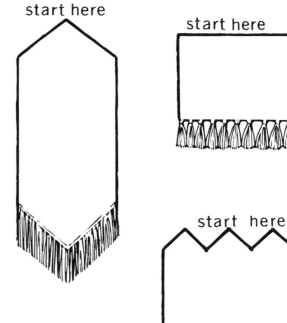

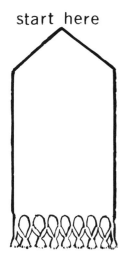

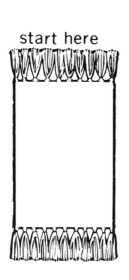

Fig. 83 Covered Bottle. *Virginia Harvey* knotted this particularly handsome cover with white nylon upholsterer's twine. Courtesy *Russell W. Harvey. Virginia I. Harvey.* Photo, *William Eng.*

There's something intriguing about covering a bottle. First, let's start at the top and work down. For your first attempt, choose a bottle that has a good resting place for the starting cords near the top of the bottle.

Cut your cords in multiples of four.

To Mount: Take one of your cords and use it as a mounting cord. Pin it to your knotting board and hitch the rest of your cords onto it.

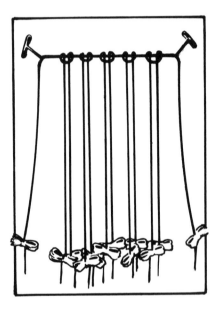

Now, remove all these cords from your knotting board and transfer them to your bottle.

Wrap the mounting cord around the "nesting place" in your bottle. To close the circle on your mounting cords, bring the right cord over the left cord and, holding the cords firmly, make a double half hitch onto the right cord with the left cord. Pull tight. Then, drop the two mounting cords and use them in your knotting pattern. (*See diagrams on next page*)

Knot in the pattern of your choice. If the bottle widens, you may want to add extra cords as you progress. See p. 76 for some methods of adding on cords.

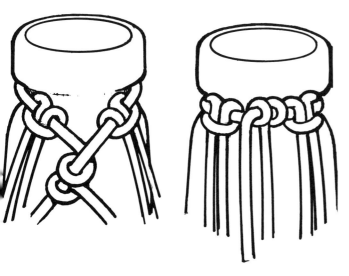

The simplest way to end your cover is to make a fringe near the base of the bottle.

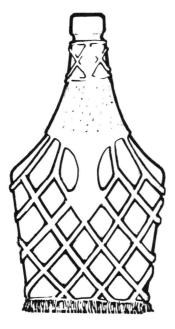

A particularly neat and satisfactory way of finishing the base (or bottom) of the bottle is to do row after row after row of double half hitches in spiral fashion, gradually decreasing the number of cords, until they are all used up.

Start with any *two* cords and use them as your knot bearers. Do about four complete double half hitches over these two knot bearers. Drop one knot bearer and cut it off short. Pick up another cord to replace the one you cut off, and do about four

Fig. 84 Covered Bottle. The pattern intertwines in an interesting way. The knotting was done with yellow nylon seine twine in the manner described in the text. *Jeanne Vernon.*

141

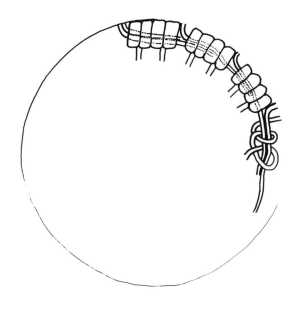

more double half hitches. Drop the oldest knot bearer, cut short, pick up another cord to replace it, and continue in this manner until all the cords are cut off. Work the last cord back under the other cords.

There is no hard and fast rule about how many double half hitches you do with each pair of knot bearers. Start with four. If you have many cords, you may have to reduce the number of double half hitches you do with each pair of knot bearers. On the other hand, if you seem to be eliminating cords so fast that there may not be enough left to cover the bottom, do more than four double half hitches around each pair of cords.

Another way of ending the knotting is to have the knotting go right to the base of the bottle, and even a bit onto the bottom of the bottle. The cords can be trimmed and glued down. If this causes the bottle to become wobbly, a heavy piece of fabric, cardboard, or a thin piece of wood may be glued to the bottom.

TO HANG A BOTTLE

Perhaps you'd like to hang a bottle, or a vase, a jar, or even a bowl. Then you could start at the bottom and work up. When knotting from the bottom up, it may be easier to work with your bottle, jar or vase—upside down. This is easy for wide-necked pieces, but what about a narrow-necked bottle? Well, try this—or devise your own ingenious method. Fill a tall, wide-necked jar or flower pot with sand or lightly crumpled newspaper or tissue paper. Insert the neck of your bottle into the jar, and adjust the sand or paper so that the bottle doesn't wobble. (See diagram on next page.)

The next thing you'll find is that you can't stick pins into a piece of glass. Tape can help you out of a temporary jam.

Here's one method of working:

Draw an outline of the bottom of your bottle and pin it to your knotting board. Pin a ring to the

Fig. 85 Bottom View of Bottle. The cords were gradually decreased, as described in the text. The bottom is flat and the bottle doesn't wobble when standing. *Jeanne Vernon.*

center of the outline. The ring must be smaller than the base of your bottle and large enough to accommodate the number of cords you're working with. Often 12 or 20 cords and an open knotting pattern are used in hanging pieces. Knot in sennits or in any pattern of your choice. When the knotting is wide enough to cover the bottom of your bottle, transfer the knotting from your board to your upside down bottle and continue knotting.

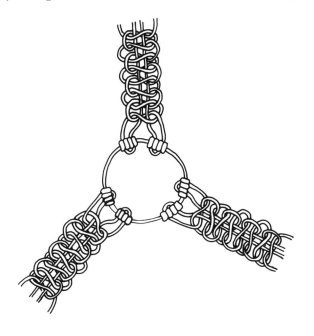

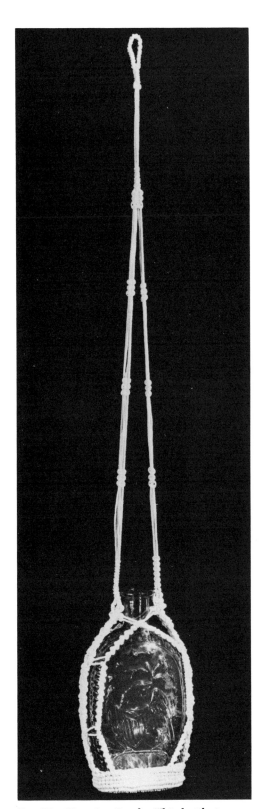

Fig. 86 Hanging Bottle. This bottle is cradled in knotting that starts at the bottom and ends at the top. *Jeanne Vernon.*

143

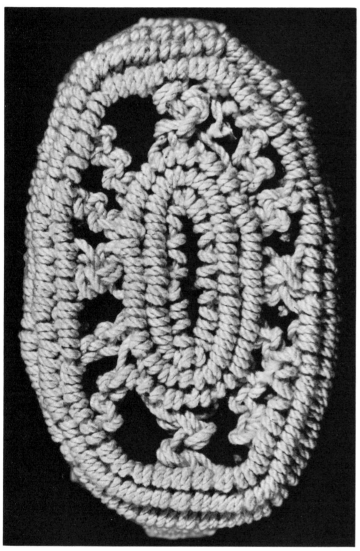

Fig. 87 Bottom of Hanging Bottle. The knotting for this bottle was started in the center with an oval-shaped holding cord. Cords were added as needed to widen the knotting and cover the whole bottom. *Jeanne Vernon.* (More description in text.)

The following is a particularly good method if your knotting will be dense:

Draw an outline of the bottom of your bottle and pin it to your knotting board. Start in the center with a mounting cord in the same general shape as the bottom of your bottle. Work out from the center, increasing the number of cords as you go along. (For more specific instructions on how to do this, refer to the method for working circular pieces on p. 71.) When the knotting is large enough to cover the bottom of your bottle, transfer your work to your upside-down bottle. Knot around the bottle, decreasing near the neck, if desired.

When all of your knotting is completed, you'll want to join the ends so that the piece can be hung. The easiest, but not always prettiest, way to do this is to gather all your cords together and make one large overhand knot at the point where you'll be hanging your piece. Trim the ends.

Another way is to again gather all the ends. For this method, you'll probably have too many ends and if you used them all, your hanger would be too bulky. See if any can be cut off. The core cords of sennits can be cut close and won't weaken the piece appreciably if they are cut off. Overlap the remaining cords and bind them together by the wrapping method or by square knotting the ends together. Jeanne Vernon's pendant on p. 129 uses the latter technique.

To make a Loop:
Gather all the ending cords together. Make a sennit of square knots starting at about the height you'd like to hang your container. Fold the sennit over. Clip the core cords short. Make another square knot just beneath the first square knot in the sennit. Make a few more square knots. Work the ends back in or clip and glue the ends.

If you'd rather have two or more hanging loops, the cords can be split and wrapped in smaller groups.

88 Close-up of the loop formed for her hanging
e. *Jeanne Vernon.*

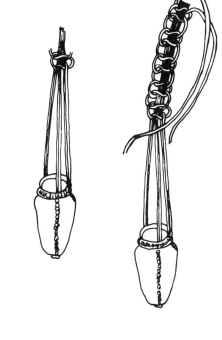

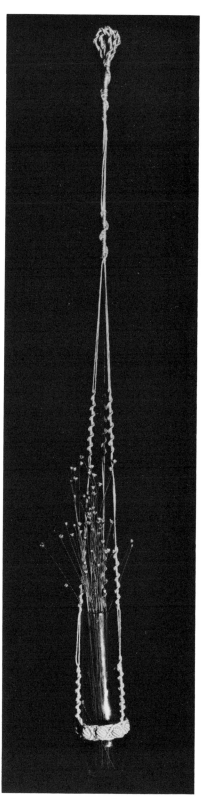

Fig. 89 Hanging Bottle. Here's another hanging container that was worked from the bottom up. The technique is the same as the other bottle, but the knotting pattern is quite different. *Jeanne Vernon.* *Fig. 90* Flower Container. This glass flower holder has a built-in depression which comfortably houses a strip of shell knots. *Jeanne Vernon.*

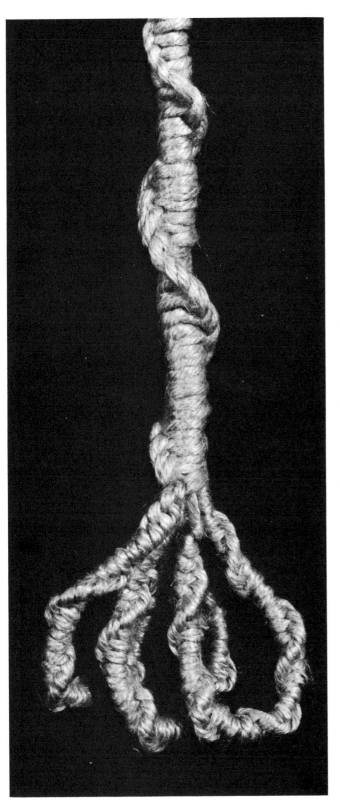

Fig. 92 Close-up of the flower container in Figure 90. *Jeanne Vernon.*

Fig. 91 Close-up of hanger for the container in Figure 90. *Jeanne Vernon.*

146

A clever, complex Hanger. See if you can figure it out!
nne Vernon.

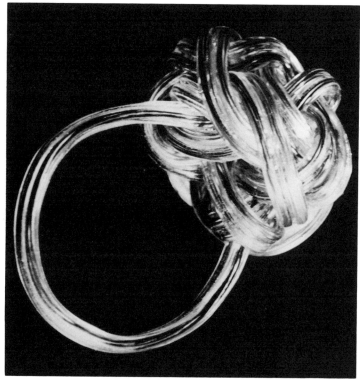

Fig. 94 Ring. And some things have no beginnings or endings—
or so it seems. Connie Kazen started this ring with electrical wire.
She left a loop the size of her finger, made one Josephine knot
above the loop, and then just wove the free ends, in and out, in
and out, until she ran out of wire, or the ring was fat enough. She
then tucked the ends in, and they became part of the ring. You
can't see where it began—or ended. *Connie Kazen.*

Fig. 95 Mexican Stole. Handspun wool yarn is knotted in an open pattern so that the fabric will drape well when worn. Courtesy *Barbara T. Hodge.*

Plate 1 Connie Kazen's Fish. If there were a beauty contest for fish, this one would certainly take the prize. Mrs. Kazen has created a very graceful, flowing, three-dimensional fish. She drilled holes into the plexiglass background in the general shape of the fish, hitched on some cords, and knotted down with the top cords and over toward the tail with the bottom cords. She used white navy cord which she painted after the fish was completed. *Connie Kazen.*

Plate 2 Twined and Knotted Purse. Doramay Keasbey has blended macramé and twining superbly in this handsome purse. *Doramay Keasbey.*

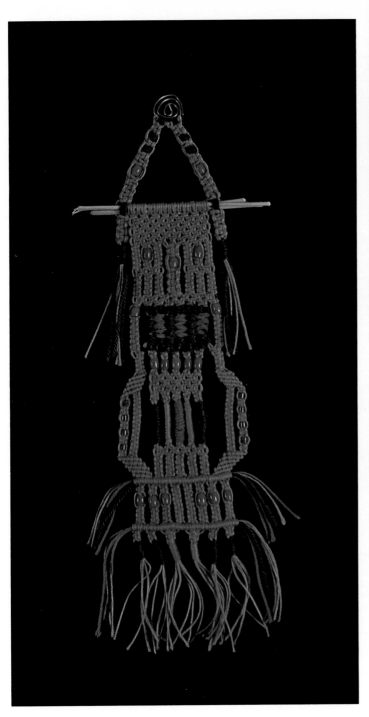

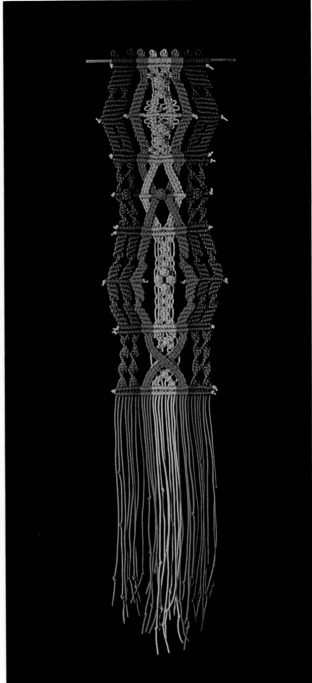

Plate 4　Wall Hanging. *Ella Bolster.*

Plate 3　Hanging. Solid color areas have been added to this little gold linen hanging by twining and wrapping. Beads and additional knot-bearing cords add still more color. *Helene Bress.*

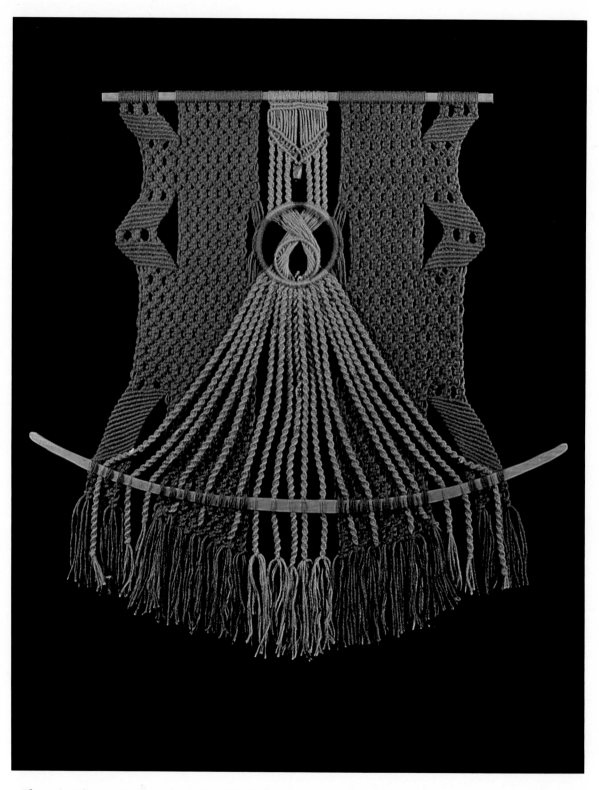

Plate 5 Blue and green hanging. Made by request to go with a blue and green handwoven pile rug. Rug wools. Courtesy *Dan Bress. Helene Bress.*

Plate 6 Close-up of blue and green hanging. The "evil eye" bead in the center wards off evil spirits! *Helene Bress.*

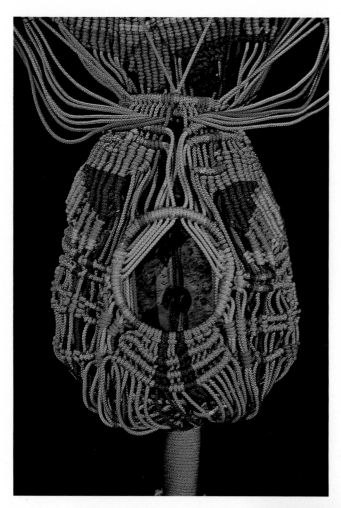

Plate 7 "To Harry," close-up of one section. Complete hanging shown in Chapter 8. *Madge Schneider.*

Plate 8 Top view of Pandora's Box. Vertical and horizontal double half hitches. *Susan Gable Williamson.*

Plate 9 Strip Sampler. *Helene Bress.*

Plate 10 (top left) This spiral wreath is just a dressed-up embroidery hoop. Based on an idea by *Paul Johnson*. *Plate 11 (bottom left)* Bell Pull. The wreath effect that Ella Bolster achieved on this bell pull is quite effective. The square knot is the only knot used! The background is green rayon satin cord done in alternating square knots, and the wreaths are red rayon satin cords. *Ella Bolster.*   *Plate 12 (middle)* Small dowels of graduated sizes, a few bells, and a minimum of yarn are all that's needed for this simple tree. Green jute is used here. Variegated yarns work well for this too. Size of this tree, 22″. Any size can be made.   *Plate 13 (top right)* A three-dimensional tree this time. A clay top painted red (a ring could be substituted), embroidery hoops in graduated sizes, a few bells, and yarn are the materials needed. Green nylon seine twine was used for the basic knotting and bright red chenille and gold lamé for accents. Chenille doesn't knot well and so the chenille was twined below the first embroidery hoop and gently hitched onto the other hoops.   *Plate 14 (bottom right)* Bell Pull. This handsome bell pull was designed and knotted by Ella Bolster. She used a ring for a starter, red and green polypropylene cords, a few bells, some double half hitches, and some imaginative handling. *Ella Bolster.*

5

DIVINE INSPIRATION: DESIGN

Designing your own piece of work can be fun, agonizing, exciting, painful, exhilarating, or any combination of these. When the design works, and you've created something that's pleasing to you, the feeling is one of great pleasure.

There are many different approaches to the problem of design. The particular piece, combined with your own personality, will determine which approach you'll use.

If you've never designed anything on your own before, you may be timid about starting now. You may feel that the only thing you can do is to copy something you've seen. Artists and designers frown upon this, but sometimes it's helpful just to get you started. When you copy though, it is expected that you will give the original artist credit by saying, "Knotted by [*your name*], after an original by [*artist's name.*]"

The hope is that you'll only *start* by copying, and that you'll soon begin to change things—the color, order of knots, placement of beads, proportion, etc.—thus gradually designing your own work.

Sometimes you may just have a very vague idea of what you want to do. You must decide upon the kind of cords, color, approximate finished length, and how you want to start, but you don't have to have the design of the work well formed in your mind. You can just hitch on your cords, start working, and design the work as you go along. One idea usually leads to another. This is not to imply that as you knot one section, the next automatically forms under your fingers.

For some, it *almost* will; for others, it will require much thought. My feelings are that if you just do anything at all that pops into your head, your finished work will look as if you've just done anything at all that popped into your head, and you'll have an erratic, poorly designed work. If you stop occasionally, however, to consider the part you have completed and look back to see if a pleasing composition is forming, you are more likely to form a well composed, integrated work.

Of course, you can plan your work in advance, on paper or in your head, and proceed in this way. Even when you do have a specific idea, it is still wise to stand back every once in a while and evaluate what you have done to be sure that the next part will fit in as you planned.

In designing, there are many points to consider. For example, the materials and knotwork should be appropriate to the particular project. If you're making a stole, the materials should be relatively

149

soft and the knotting open so that the stole will drape well. That combination would be disastrous for a knapsack, however.

Color needs to be handled with discretion in macramé. If different-colored cords are used in adjacent areas, the effect can become very cluttered or muddy looking. Color can be used effectively by keeping the color areas distinct and clear.

Colors can be added to a work with beads, twining, Ghiordes, or rya, knots, and weaving. Also, colors can be hidden within sennits—and be made to emerge when desired. Colors can be made to appear and disappear in Cavandoli work, i.e., close work consisting of horizontal and vertical half hitches. (See page 53.)

Fig. 96 Dress (detail). This dress is made with a tightly knotted yoke, cuffs, and hem, and free-flowing yarn in between. For the sake of modesty, it's been lined. *Mary Belle Frey.*

Generally, a smooth, hard, twisted cord is used in macramé, and texture and surface interest is achieved with knots. A change of knotting pattern and areas of open spaces will change the texture. For special effects, feathers, beads, unusual yarns, and Ghiordes knots can be used.

Most often we think of macramé in terms of knotted areas and pay little attention to the open areas. Open areas with just a few, discreet knots can be very effective.

Smaller open areas are important, too.

Can you visualize this? A large, irregularly shaped piece of driftwood, a sennit of square knots made with heavy natural jute, and a pink satin ribbon, these last two items held together with a big rhinestone pin.

Surely that's unique, but is it pleasing? Is it good design? Sometimes it becomes very important to us to create something different. To be successful, I think it should be pleasing as well. "Pleasing," however, is in the eye of the beholder. My hypothetical driftwood-jute-satin-rhinestone is a horror to me, but may be someone else's delight. The important thing is, though, that it be pleasing to you and not just different.

Execution is not directly a design concern. I insert it here, however, because I believe that poor workmanship can spoil an otherwise good design. Extemporaneous sloppiness is sometimes encouraged as an art form, but it seldom comes off successfully. For example, if some cords become too short to be used, you can let them hang where they will and incorporate them into your design. I think that you should take a good look at your work and/or your conscience however, and decide whether the cords are hanging there for beauty—or laziness.

When you become interested in an art or craft, you see ideas for designs almost everywhere. At first, though, you may wonder how you'll ever think of things to make and where you'll get good design ideas for them. After a while, you'll wonder how you're ever going to complete all your prospective projects and ideas in just one lifetime. You

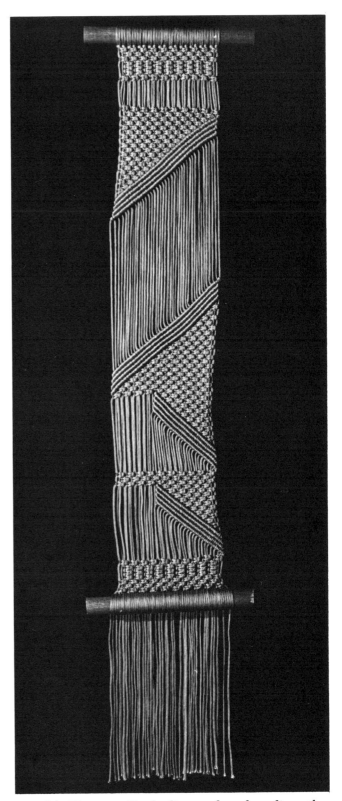

Fig. 97 Hanging. Simple lines—and a few discreetly placed knots. *Richard Mathews.*

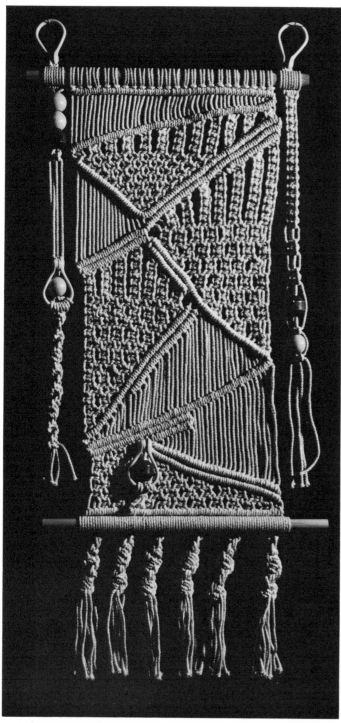

Fig. 98 Wall Hanging. The open areas play as important a part as the knotted ones. A few wooden beads and shower curtain rings are added for color and design interest. Made of heavy cotton seine twine. *Marion Roscheck.*

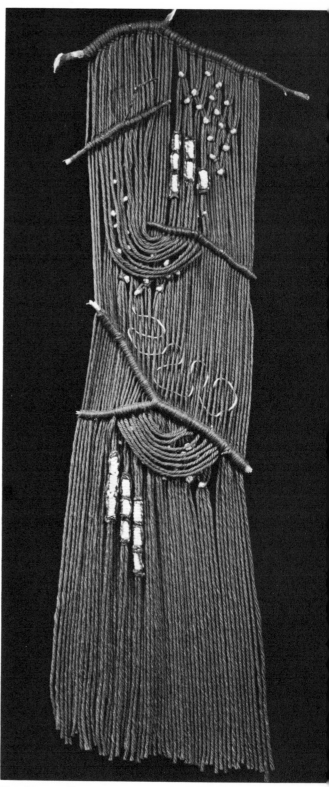

Fig. 99 Wall Hanging. Open, flowing, and rhythmical. *Lola Liebner.*

152

also begin to collect strange assortments of things and justify your bizarre behavior by saying, "It will be just perfect for the next piece I do," or, "It's my only vice."

While leafing through a magazine in the dentist's office, I came upon a picture of a lovely church. The more I looked at it, the more ways I saw of interpreting it in macramé. I can't reproduce that one for you to see, but do offer this one for your contemplation—a magnificent Norwegian Stave church.

Fig. 101 Norwegian Stave Church. Just pause a moment and reflect on some of the ways you might interpret the forms in this lovely church in a piece of macramé. Photo, courtesy *Horace M. Johnson.*

g. 100 Wall Hanging. The densely knotted areas are relieved th several smaller completely open areas in direct contrast to the evious pieces. Two tones of sisal with found objects as decorative cents. *Marion Roscheck.*

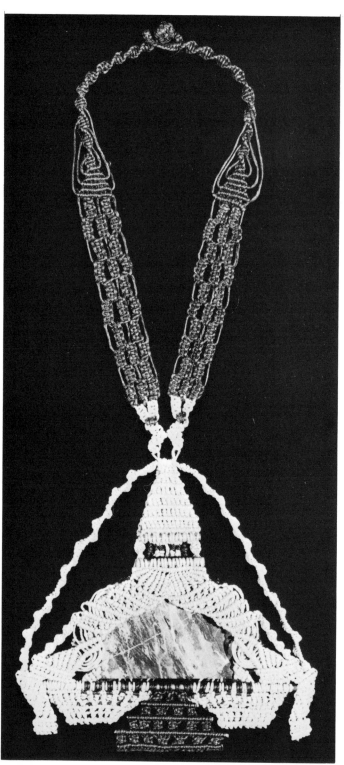

Fig. 102 Pendant. Trudy Nicholson captures the lines and spirit of the lovely Nepalese outdoor church in her pendant. *Trudy Nicholson.*

Architectural shapes are often adaptable to macramé. Modern buildings, old buildings, castles, and churches from different countries are all worth observing.

Fig. 103 Nepalese Church. When in Nepal, Trudy Nicholson was quite impressed with this Buddhist Temple, or Stupa. It sits on top of a hill, all by itself, and is quite a contrast to its surroundings. Courtesy *Trudy Nicholson.*

Fig. 104 Back view of pendant to show the technical details of how the stone was enclosed. *Trudy Nicholson.*

Fig. 105 A Child's Castle. 1971. Close-up of one section. Natural jute, wood beads, and stained Tinker Toy parts. This castle was made as a gift to the Huntington Cooperative Nursery School, which Paul Johnson's daughter, Lisa, attended. Owners: *Beverly and Tom Howe. Paul Johnson.*

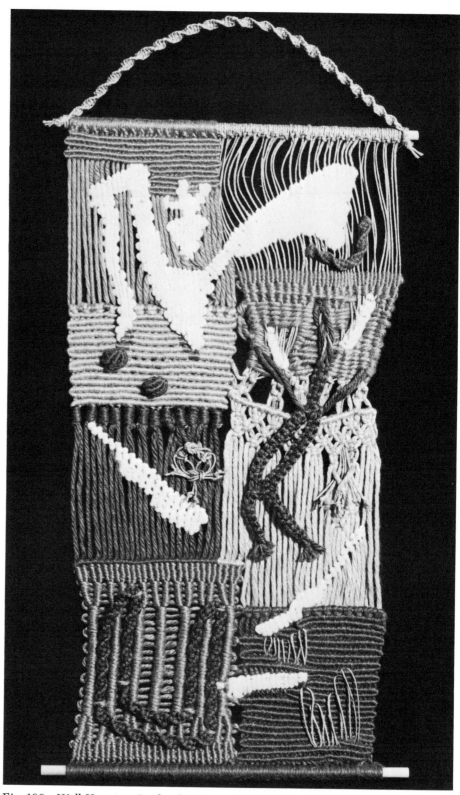

Fig. 106 Wall Hanging. In this free interpretation of a poster by Matisse, Peg Hardy used many different techniques, including wrapping and twining. *Peg Hardy*.

Sometimes paintings, or a part of a painting, may spark an idea in you. A poster by Matisse was the inspiration for this piece by Peg Hardy. (Fig. 106)

Here's a line drawing by Paul Klee. Any part of this could be interpreted in macramé. I'm fond of the dome-shaped part, and may interpret it three dimensionally, on a rather small scale. I think that waxed linen or a thin wire would work well.

Fig. 108 This line drawing by Paul Klee offers many possibilities for interpretation in macramé.
Courtesy, Paul Klee Foundation, Kunstmuseum, Berne.

Forms and materials from nature can be good sources of inspiration. The shape of a plant or an animal may be used directly as in some of the illustrations, or abstractly. Natural materials, such as shells, driftwood, and feathers can be incorporated directly into a piece.

ig. 107   Sketch for Wall Hanging. Here's the simplified orking sketch that Peg Hardy made for her wall hanging. *Peg ardy*.

Fig. 109 Spider Web. This clever spider has just composed her web of double half hitches and a few sennits of square knots. *Sylvia Pocock*.

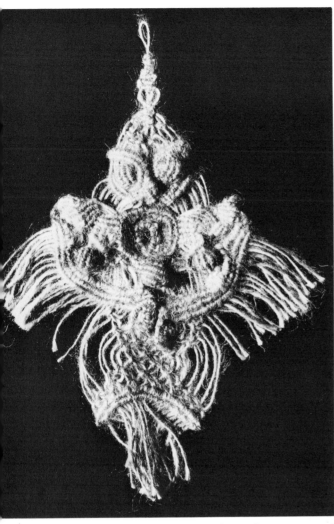

g. 110 Turkey Red Owl. 1971. Paul Johnson has interpreted
s very special breed of owl in his own fanciful way. Hand-dyed
e. 9″ x 14″. *Paul Johnson.*

Fig. 111 Lobster. Hannelies Penner saw a piece of silver
jewelry that was made in a shape similar to this. It intrigued her and she began studying pictures in children's
books and in art magazines. She then put the pictures aside
and made a sketch of her own. This lovely pendant is the
result of her efforts. *Hannelies Penner.*

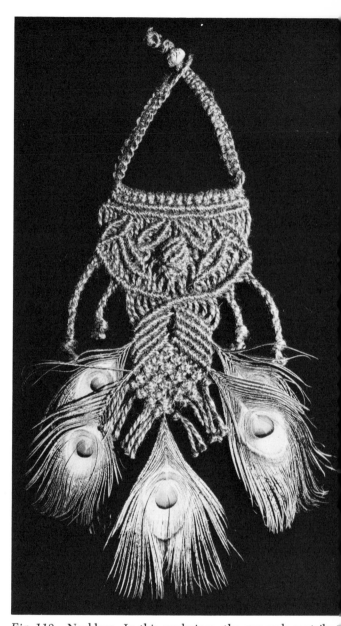

Fig. 113 Necklace. In this neckpiece, the peacock contribut[es?]
in a very personal way. Courtesy *Thurid Clark. Karen Wise.*

Fig. 112 Peacock Pendant. In Eastern folk art the peacock is interpreted in unique ways. Using peacock colors
and memories of the folk art she had studied, Hannelies
Penner created this pendant. *Hannelies Penner.*

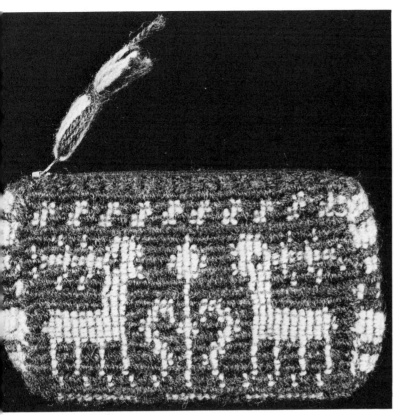

Fig. 114 Little Purse. Among the heirlooms in the Penner family is a blue-and-white huck fingertip towel from Germany. It is embroidered with reindeer and plant forms. Hannelies Penner modified the folk art motifs and interpreted them in macramé, using vertical and horizontal double half-hitches, or the Cavandoli method of knotting. *Hannelies Penner*.

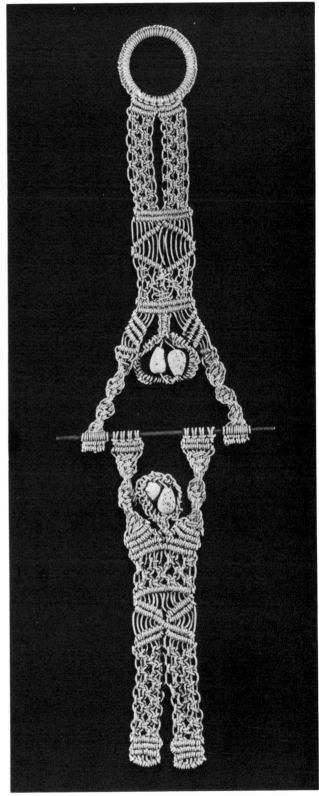

Fig. 115 Acrobats. Here the human form is portrayed playfully and successfully. *Linda Hendricks*.

161

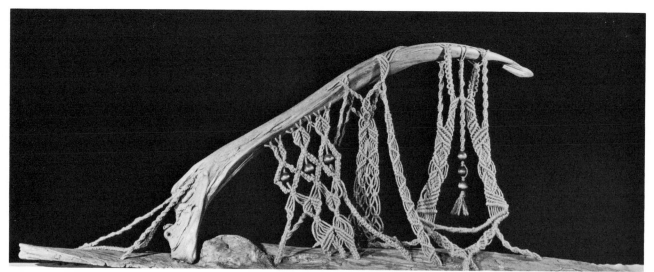

Fig. 116 Driftwood. Driftwood was the starting point for this dramatic piece. *Jeanne Vernon.*

Fig. 117 Close-up of one section of the driftwood piece. *Jeanne Vernon.*

Seashells can be used in many ways. Holes can be poked into some kinds with a sharp pointed object or they can be knotted into pieces as described in the section on enclosing objects, or used as in this pair of neckpieces:

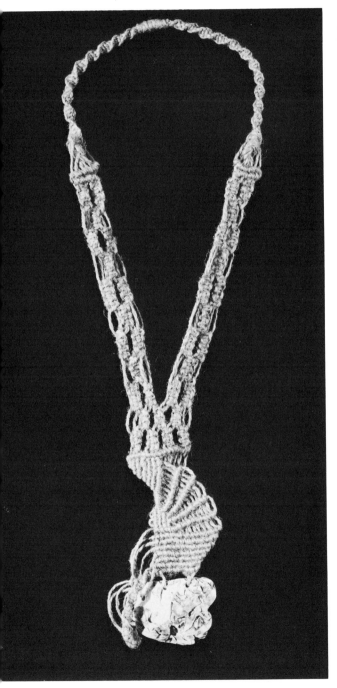

Figs. 118 and 119 Neckpieces. Trudy Nicholson made this pair of jute neckpieces for good friends. The oyster shells were carefully selected from a great heap of shells. These necklaces were among her first projects! *Trudy Nicholson.*

The neckpiece incorporating shells that Paul Johnson knotted has quite a different feel to it. (See page 206.)

And the form of the shell itself can inspire a whole piece of macramé.

"Found Objects" may inspire a project—those miscellaneous nothings that you collect because you can't pass them up. They're pretty, or useful, or unusual, or have sentimental value, and will surely come in handy someday.

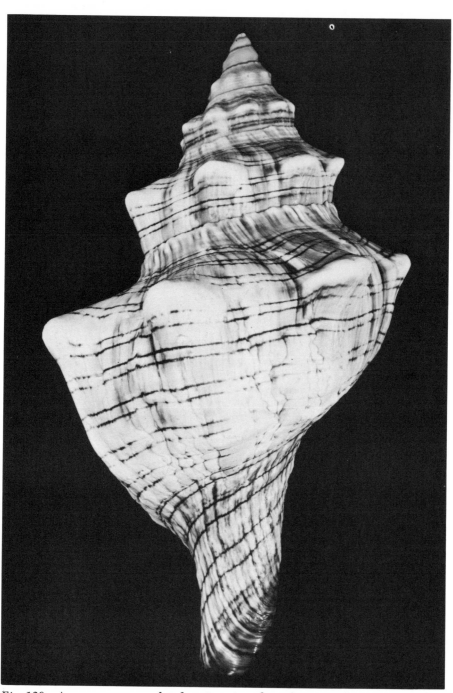

Fig. 120 Among my uncompleted projects is a three-dimensional piece in which I'm trying to capture the graceful swirls of this shell. It will be a rather literal interpretation.

Fig. 121 Pendants. Here's a collection of pendants that Dr. Elizabeth Harris made using some of her "found objects." If you will look closely, you'll see a lump of lead from leftover type, a washer, odds and ends of string, and grommets. *Elizabeth Harris.*

I found some wooden hoops in an antique shop, and immediately began to think in circles. Friends were intrigued with the same idea, and working completely independently of one another we came up with these creations.

The technical approach, the materials used, and the designs for each of these are quite different, but each tried to keep the motion of the circle, each in her own way.

Fig. 122 Circular Hanging. Doramay Keasbey completely covered her hoop and worked from the top, around and down. She used natural cotton seine twine and two cork floats—seagoing materials. *Doramay Keasbey.*

166

Fig. 123 Knots in Orbit. During one of the moon flights, Ella Bolster created these Knots in Orbit. She started with the innermost hoop and worked her way out, adding hoops and yarns along the way. Her moon-age materials are all synthetic—plastic hoops, plastic beads, and white nylon yarn. *Ella Bolster.*

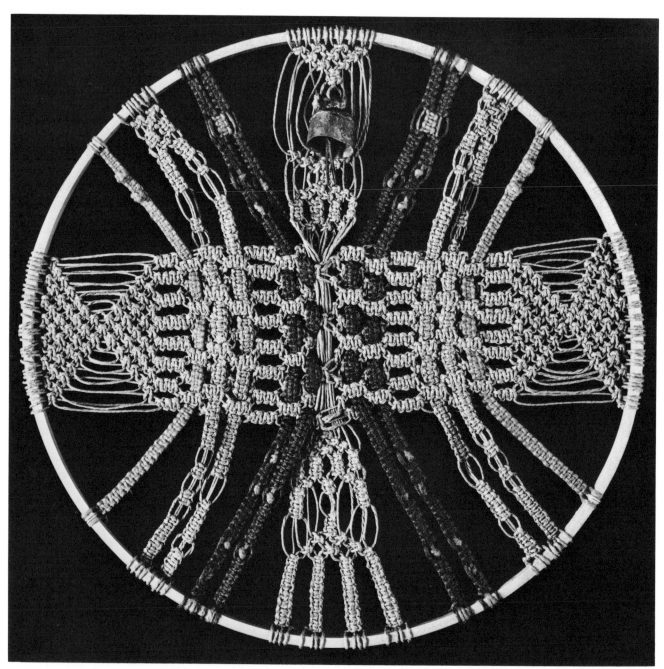

Fig. 124 Circular Hanging. Only my circular piece is earthbound. I started in the general vicinity of the North Pole, went on down South, and crossed over Equator-wise. I used a rough wooden hoop, natural India jute, brown and orange linen, and an antiqued brass bell. *Helene Bress.*

While still on this hoop-circle binge, I spotted a basket-ball hoop in a department store. I looked at my husband. He did some fast mind-reading, and said, "No." So we took it home. . . .

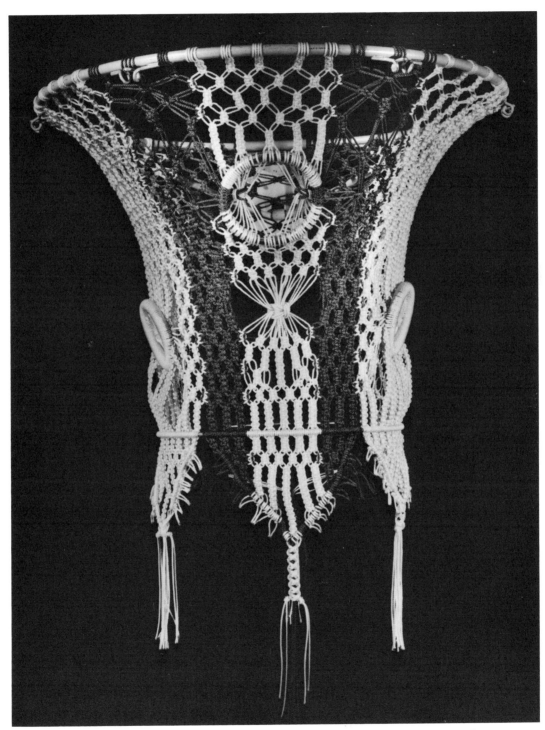

Fig. 125   Basketball Net. Yes, my sons *will* use it! It's made of gold and green nylon seine twine so that it will withstand hard wear and weather. *Helene Bress.*

Fig. 126   Reproduction of an antique Oriental coin.

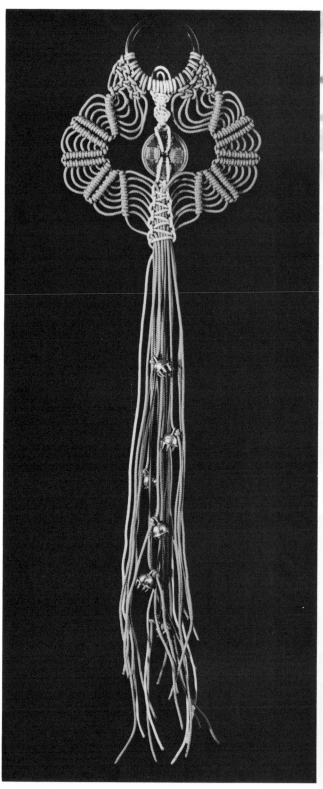

Fig. 127   Hanging. The reproduction of an antique Oriental coin inspired Ella Bolster to design a fitting home for it. She used heavy polypropylene cord in a circular motif. *Ella Bolster.*

Here's a design problem of a different sort. A friend of Trudy Nicholson's wanted a macramé setting for her hand-carved ivory pendant from Nepal.

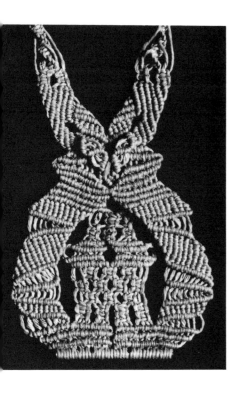

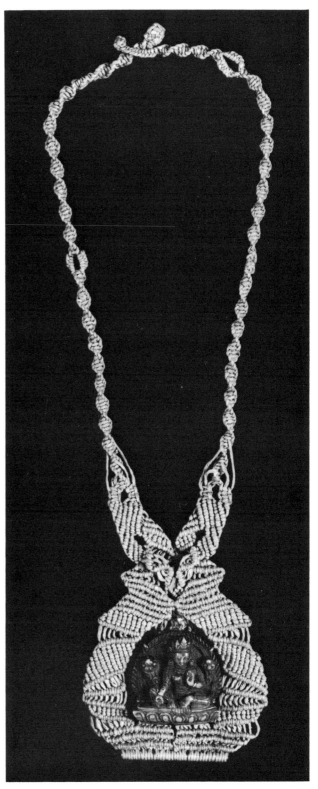

Fig. 128 (top left) This is a hand-carved ivory pendant from Nepal and its owner wanted a macramé setting for it. *Fig. 129 (left)* A comfortable and very suitable home for the Nepalese pendant. The setting is complete in its own right. It has a built-in hook for the ivory pendant to hook on to, and spaces where the pin back will fit. The ivory piece may be taken on or off at will. *Trudy Nicholson.* *Fig. 130 (above)* Macramé setting with ivory pendant. Here's the setting with the pendant in place. *Trudy Nicholson.*

The germ of an idea may come from almost any-
where. My sons gave me this assortment of fishing
gear for Mother's Day. As a fellow knotter, I'm
sure you know that they didn't expect me to use it
for fishing.

Fig. 131   Raw materials for a wall hanging.

Fig. 132   Here's a tentative plan around which
a wall hanging may be built.

Fig. 133 Red, white, and blue flags were the design source for this pillow. Vertical and horizontal double half hitches, were knotted on the face of the pillow, and sometimes on the reverse side, to vary the texture. *Hannelies Penner.*

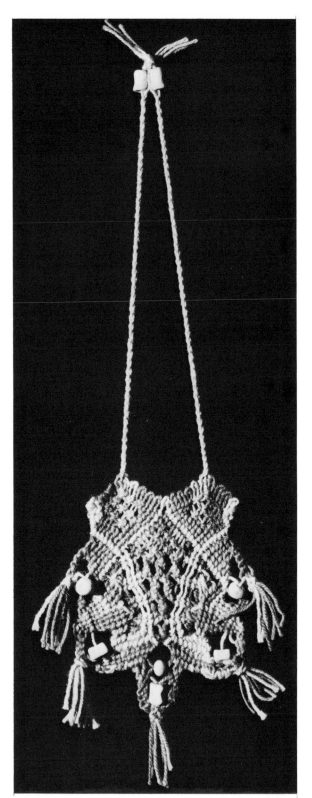

Consider some of these as headings for a wall hanging:

> Ornamental drawer pulls
> Key chain
> Unusual belt buckle
> Bamboo
> Israeli oil lamp
> Toe rings
> Boomerang
> Chopsticks
> Bamboo flute
> Dowels
> Moldings
> Knitting needles
> Rug shuttle
> Plastic bars
> Ceramic pieces
> Turned pieces from discarded furniture
> Hoops (embroidery)
> Clock handles

Fig. 134 (left) Pendant. The design for this pendant is quite original and interesting. The initial inspiration for the design came from Paisley patterns and designs from India. *Hannelies Penner.*   *Fig. 135 (right)* Israeli Oil Lamp. We don't need an oil lamp any more, but won't this make a distinguished heading for a macramé piece!

174

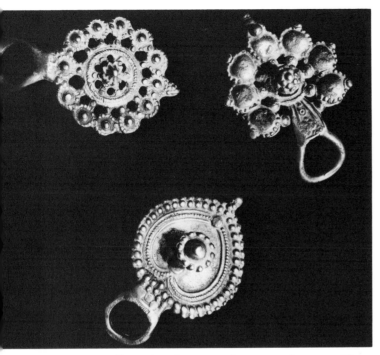

136 Toe Rings. Bells on her fingers—and rings on her toes. These rings from India will complement macramé well.

Once you start looking, you'll probably find design ideas in the most unlikely places and at the most unlikely times—perhaps while feeding peacocks at the zoo or while idly watching shadow patterns on the floor.

ig. 137 While on a scientific trip to the Galápagos Isnds, *Allen Bress* came across is tree cactus. Immediately, e saw the possibilities for acramé designs, and took is picture for us to contemplate.

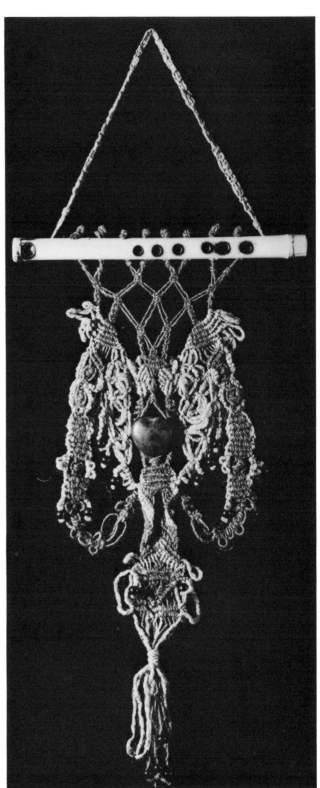

Fig. 138 Hanging. Using a bamboo flute as a top piece, Connie Brown handled a potential design problem very deftly. The flute didn't lend itself to having many cords mounted on it. When a piece of macramé starts with a small number of cords, it is usually narrow at the top and gets wider as it goes along. That's fine if that's the shape you want. If it isn't, however, study Miss Brown's treatment for another idea. *Connie Brown.*

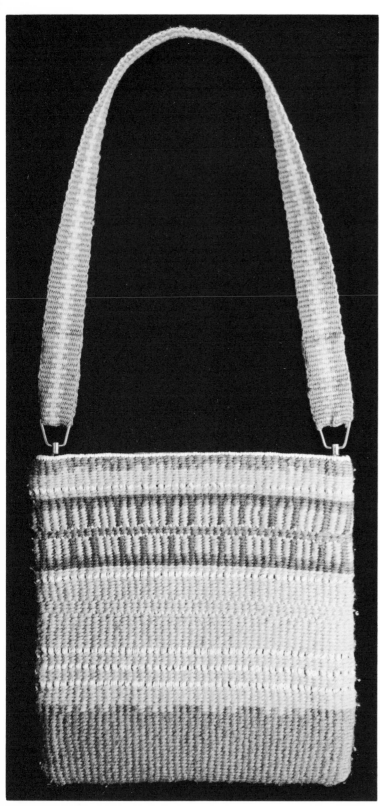

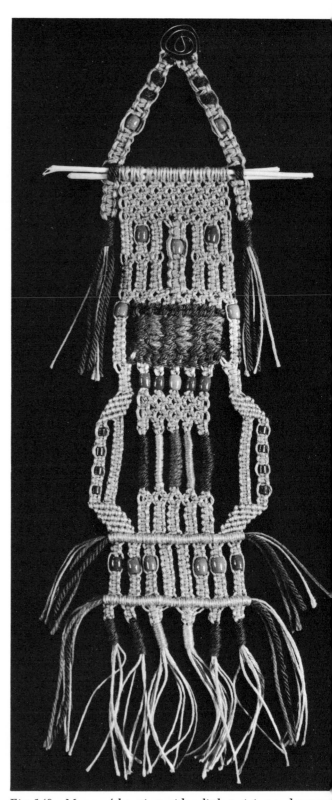

Fig. 139 Twined Purse. This purse was made in my "pre-macramé" days. Just a few overhand knots were sprinkled in with the twining. The warp threads are 10/5 linen; the twining yarns or weft, 3 shades of knitting worsted. *Helene Bress.*

Fig. 140 Macramé hanging with a little twining and wrapp (See also color plate 3.) *Helene Bress.*

6

WIDENING HORIZONS:
unique ways with macramé

The marriage of different techniques often results in unique and pleasing effects. There is nothing new about the following techniques in themselves. Their use with macramé, however, helps to give macramé a new dimension.

TWINING

The art of twining dates back thousands of years. Contemporary weavers most often use twining in making solidly twined fabrics occasionally decorated with a few knots.

If we borrow the twining technique and reverse the proportions to much knotting and just a little twining, the results can be very interesting.

When using macramé alone, the same color or colors are generally carried through from beginning to end. When combining macramé and twining, color can be added in controlled areas. The twining can completely cover the cords you are using for the macramé portion of your piece and you can get clear, unmuddied areas of color.

You can twine with soft yarns and fragile yarns

—yarns that are difficult or impossible to knot with. For example, a touch of fragile, bright red chenille was twined into the three-dimensional Christmas tree pictured in Plate 13. The knotted portion of the tree is done with dark green nylon seine twine. The textural contrast of the yarns is interesting.

And what's more, twining is easy.

HOW TO TWINE

Materials Needed: The cords you twine around are your usual macramé cords. For the twining yarn, all you need is some soft yarn. Knitting yarns, such as knitting worsted, wool or synthetic, and chenille work particularly well. Some rug yarns and some jute are soft enough to pack down well, too. Start with the knitting yarns or chenille, and experiment with other yarns after you're comfortable with this technique.

Let's make a little sample: Cut eight cords—each cord about 16 inches long. These cords are your hard, twisted macramé cords!! Fold the cords in half and mount them onto a mounting cord or small stick. Pin this to your knotting board.

Fig. 141 Close-up of the twined purse showing some of the overhand knots. *Helene Bress.*

Prepare your twining cords in this way: Measure off two yards of soft yarn. Fold the measured yarn in half and pin the center of it to your knotting board. Starting a foot from the center, shorten each strand.

We'll work from left to right first:

Remove your twining yarn from the knotting board and keep it folded over. Hold it in your right hand.

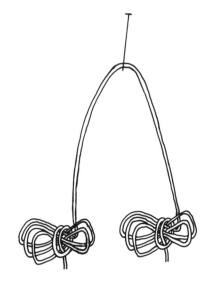

With your left hand, bring the first two cords on the left through the loop of your twining cord.

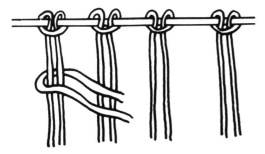

With your right hand, give the twining cord a half twist away from you, clockwise.

With your left hand, bring the next two cords down between the two twining cords.

Now, half twist again with your right hand, clockwise, as you did before.

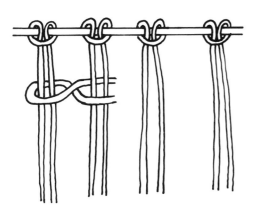

Continue in this manner all across the row. Push the twined cords upward and into place after every few half twists.

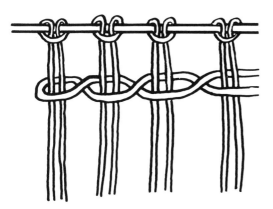

When you reach the end of the row, bring cord "A" (which has just gone *over* the last cords) around and *under* the last two cords. Bring cord "B" (which has just gone *under* the last two cords) around and *over* the last two cords.

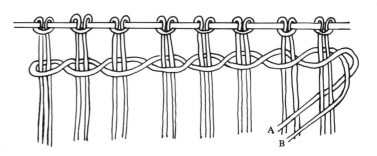

To return from right to left, reverse your hand positions. Hold your twining cords in your left hand and bring the vertical macramé cords down between the twining cords with your right hand. Continue twining the rest of the row.

When you reach the end of the row, reverse direction as in the diagram below.

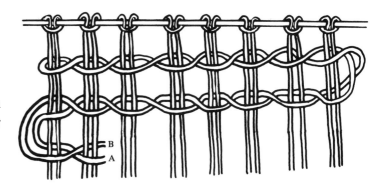

When you run out of yarn or want to change the color, merely knot a new cord to the old twining cord, and see to it that the knot stays on the reverse side. The ends can be woven back into the fabric later.

When I did my first twined purse, the hand positions seemed rather awkward for a while. With a little practice, however, the movements became automatic and smooth.

The method of twining just described produces a solid color area. If you want to use two colors, prepare your twining cord like this:

Measure out one length of one color, and one length of another color.

Shorten each cord and tie the free ends together with an overhand or square knot.

Twine in the same fashion as before. Your colors will come to the surface with every other half twist.

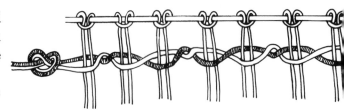

With this information, you should be able to give your macramé pieces a new dimension. There are many more variations to this technique. If twining particularly catches your fancy, you might like to refer to some of the books on this subject listed in the bibliography.

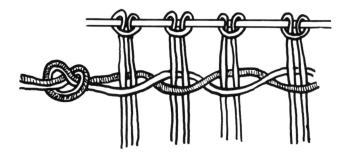

If you want to make a specific design, you can make your colors come to the surface by controlling them like this:

When you want the same color to come to the surface more than one time, give the twining cord a *double twist*. You may need to give the bottom twining cord a little extra tug to completely hide the color you don't want to see. Intricate patterns can be worked out in this way.

WRAPPING

We have discussed the wrapping technique before, but only in reference to ending pieces (see pages 74 and 113). It does make a neat ending, but can also be used decoratively within a piece.

As we have seen, adding new, clear-cut areas of color in macramé is sometimes a problem. One of the nicest things that wrapping can do for you is to allow you to add spots of new color wherever you choose. I think that the little gold linen hanging illustrated in color on page 176 helps to illustrate the point.

The basic knotted portion is all of a deep gold color and it includes some burnt-orange beads. This color scheme was carried one step further with the twined area and again with some wrapping below it.

Groups of cords were wrapped with different colors and textures of yarns, and this added textural interest to the piece. Yarns used for wrapping were gold and orange linen and rusty-orange and deep olive rug wool. Some more knotting, a few more beads, and then the piece was ended with wrapped fringes. The same colors as before were used for the bottom fringe, but in a somewhat different order.

If you need further persuasion to use wrapping within a piece, leaf through Edwina Drobny's pieces in Chapter 7, and see how freely and effectively she uses this technique.

RYA OR GHIORDES KNOT

The Ghiordes knot is a very common knot to rug makers, and one that can add new dimensions to your macramé. It is one of the most widely used knots for making a pile surface, such as long-pile rya rugs and short, clipped flossa rugs. Hand-weavers often use it to create surface texture on purses, pillows, or wall hangings. Knotters can adapt it for their needs, too. Paul Johnson has used it very effectively in the following wall hangings.

As you can see from the pictures, the Ghiordes knot enriches the surface of the knotting with an interesting texture.

Let's do a few Ghiordes knots to see how it works.

Materials needed for the Ghiordes knot: Soft yarns, such as knitting yarns and rug yarns, work well. They can be combined with other yarns such as fine cottons and linen to give interesting effects.

For a sample: Cut six cords, each two feet long. Use any cord you would usually use for macramé projects. Fold them in half and mount them on a knotting cord or stick.

Instructions:
With the first four cords (using two core cords and two knotting cords) make one square knot.

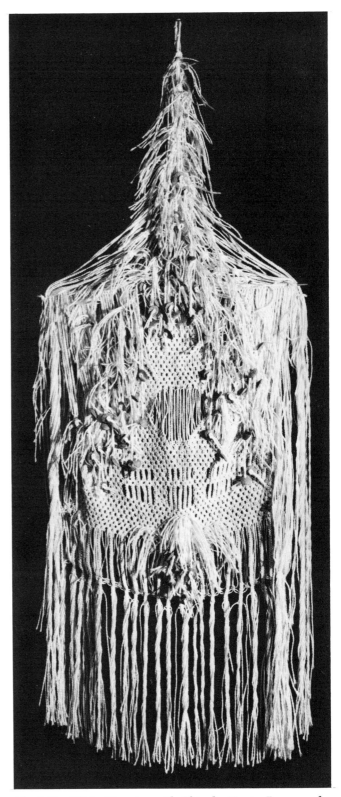

Fig. 142 White Hanging with Ghiordes Knots. Rayon and wool blend yarn. Unglazed stoneware beads made by the artist. 16″ x 39″. *Paul Johnson.*

181

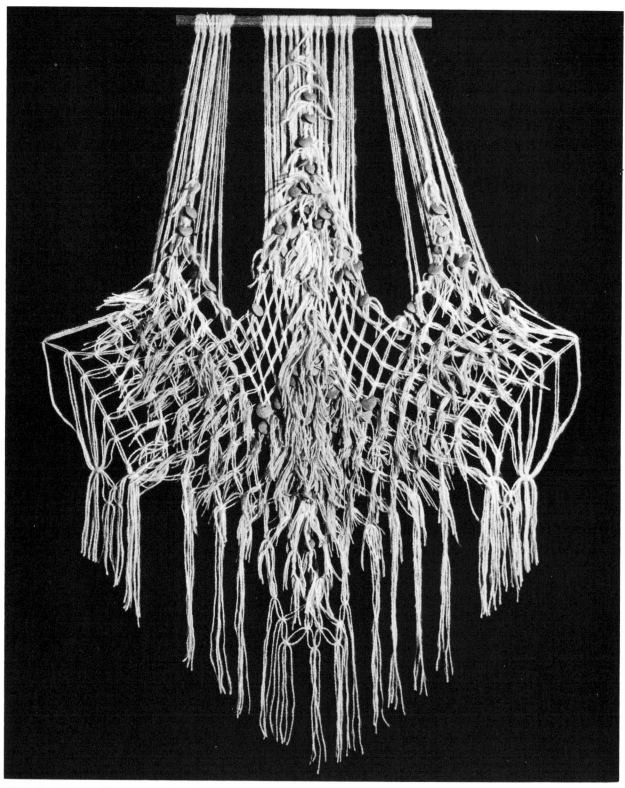

Fig. 143 Orange Hanging with Ghiordes Knots. The materials in this hanging include crewel wool, wool and mohair blend, and unglazed stoneware beads that Paul Johnson made himself. Courtesy *Jane Lawnhurst. Paul Johnson.*

Cut three strands of knitting yarn, each six inches long. Keep them together as if they were just one strand of yarn.

Center the three strands over the two core cords of the square knot.

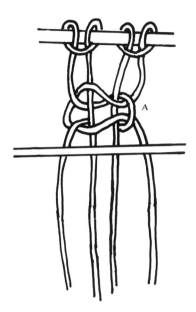

Bring the strands on the left around and under the left-hand core cord.

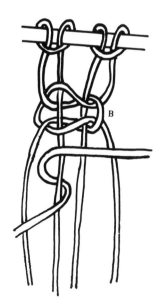

Bring the three strands on the right around and under the right-hand core cord.

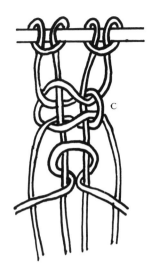

Push the ends up or pin them to your knotting board to keep them out of the way while you do the next step.

Make a square knot directly below the Ghiordes knot. This will hold the Ghiordes knot in place.

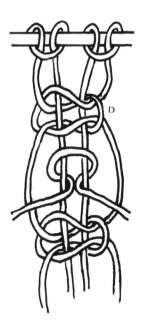

For practice, continue this across the row and then experiment with various combinations and patterns of square knots and Ghiordes knots.

The ends of the Ghiordes knot can be left long, or clipped rather short—or used in a combination of the two. New colors can be added to your macramé piece freely and easily in this way. Ghiordes knots can be clumped together in great quantities or spaced far apart and used sparingly. Most often several strands of yarn are used together to make a Ghiordes knot. These strands can all be of one color and material, or they may be of a few colors and different materials.

This technique is especially suited for use in decorative pieces such as wall hangings and pillows, and perhaps purses and necklaces. With appropriate materials, you could even make a rug!

ENCLOSING AN OBJECT

If an object has a hole in it, or can easily have a hole drilled into it, knotters eye it knowingly, and usually build a macramé piece around it. Unfortunately, there are some beautiful objects in this world that have no hole, and resist having one put into them. Don't despair. Perhaps you can use it by knotting around it.

Here's my first attempt, and it failed. The problem I set out to solve was to enclose a pretty-colored shell disc into a piece of knotting without putting a cord *through* it. I chose navy cord to work with. If you've ever worked with navy cord, you know that although it knots well, it is stiff and has a strong will.

Well, the disc refused to stay lodged where I put it. If the disc were more tapered and the cord a bit more cooperative, the idea might have worked. I put square knots directly above and below the disc, leaving the core cords behind the disc, and the knotting cords in front of it. Good idea, but when it was finished the disc slipped out. I admitted defeat, undid the bottom square knots, slipped a cord through the hole in the top of the disc, and proceeded as before. It held this time, but a little reluctantly. The skips in the cords are long and they don't always stay lined up where I meant them to.

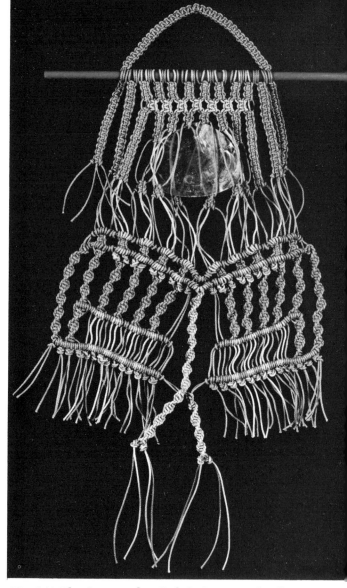

Fig. 144 The Attempt that Failed. Orange and yellow navy co
Helene Bress. (Failure described in text.)

We learn from our mistakes as well as our successes.

It will be impossible to set down the exact directions telling you how to enclose a particular object. I'll put down some starting points, and hints, and hope that with this, and a little of your own ingenuity, you'll be able to cope with problems your own treasures may present.

I've selected a flat, round, enameled disc for this first sample and some heavy cotton cord so that

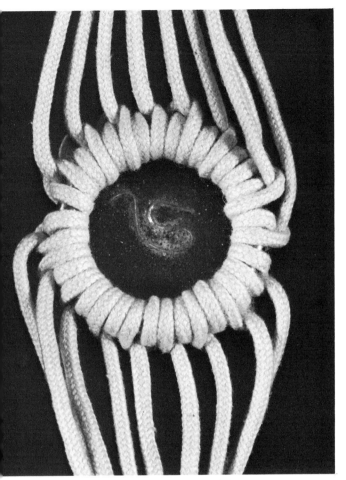

Fig. 145 Front view of Figure 146 below.

you'll be able to follow the knots in the photograph easily. In the hardware store I found a ring that is just slightly smaller than the disc. The disc was set aside temporarily, and the ring pinned to the knotting board. A few cords were folded in half and mounted to the ring with *double half hitches*. PLEASE NOTE CAREFULLY: All the cords were hitched onto the ring with *double half hitches*.

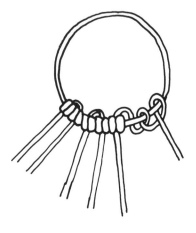

The next cords were worked like this:
The first half was hitched right next to the other cords.
The second half was brought to the opposite side of the ring and hitched onto it there.

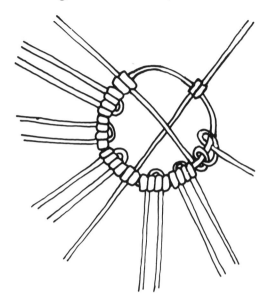

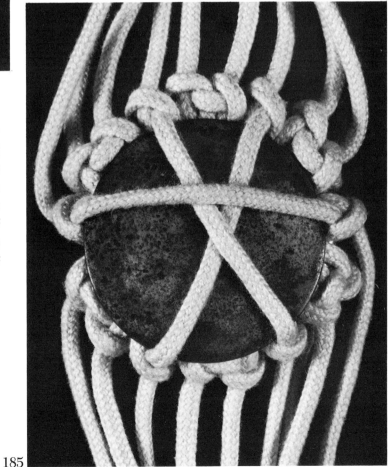

185

Fig. 146 Back view of a flat enameled disc that has been firmly enclosed into a piece of macramé. (Description in text.)

A few more cords were double half hitched onto the ring.

Another pair was then broken up as before. The first half was hitched on alongside the others; the other half was hitched on directly opposite to it.

Then the enameled disc was put into place behind the ring, and under the crossed cords. More cords were hitched on and one more crossover was made on the back of the disc.

The enameled disc is now being held in place quite firmly. The cords can now be used to make a choker, necklace, bracelet, or belt. They can also radiate and be made into a circular piece.

The object could also be worked into a piece that is being worked from the top down. When you reach the point where you want to enclose your object, hitch your ring on as you would hitch on a new holding cord. After a few double half hitches are completed, begin to criss-cross some cords on the back as before.

You can't always find a ring the right size for your object, and a purchased ring may be too thick to be in character with the rest of your piece. Also, you may want to start with a different shape, one which more closely resembles the shape of your object. If you do, you can fashion your own mounting piece out of wire. Copper wire is readily available in hardware stores.

Bend the wire in your hands to the shape you want. Check to be sure that it's slightly smaller than the object you plan to enclose. Overlap the ends of the wire generously and twist them lightly around each other a few times to hold the shape closed. (Pliers might come in handy if you are using a thick wire.) Mount your knotting cords onto this with double half hitches and continue as before.

ENCLOSING A THREE-DIMENSIONAL ITEM

A three-dimensional item can be incorporated into a piece of macramé, too. In this case, you will probably want to be able to see as much of the piece as possible—the sides as well as the top.

Again, you can start with a ring or form a shape out of wire to conform to the shape of your object to be enclosed. Of course, your starting piece will have to be slightly smaller than the piece being enclosed. For a sample, and trial run, I chose a relatively regular seashell, a ring slightly smaller than the top of the shell, and some heavy cotton cord. This will illustrate the technique, and then we'll go on to more complex situations.

Fig. 147 Sample of one method of enclosing a three-dimensional object.

To wrap up this seashell:
Pin the ring to a knotting board.
Mount cords onto the ring with double half hitches.
Make sennits of square knots, or other knots if you prefer, using core cords.

When the sennits are long enough to reach from the top of the shell to the bottom of it, remove the knotting from the board.

Turn it upside down and put the shell in place. Bring the core cords from one of the sennits under the shell, to a sennit on the opposite side.

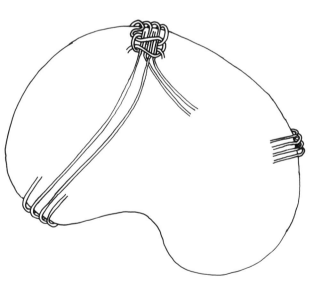

Make a square knot around this cord.

Repeat this procedure several times until the shell is securely locked in.

Continue knotting as desired.

Now that the simpler forms of enclosing are understood, let's discuss enclosing an irregularly shaped object. When you reach this point, you may need to inject some imagination and ingenuity into the situation.

Almost certainly you'll want to shape your own starting piece out of wire. Keep in mind that wire shapes can be worked effectively into any natural crevices or depressions in the piece. Next, you'll need to mount some cords, but because you'll want the sides of your piece to show, you won't want to mount them densely. Well, you can just double half hitch some cords on at intervals around the wire. If you want to cover the wire completely, double half hitch some cords on and where you want a space, yet want to cover the wire, make a third half hitch—and maybe a fourth and fifth—with the same cord.

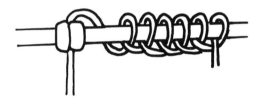

You have covered the wire, yet left a space.

After the cords are mounted, knot in a design, using any knots that please you. When the pattern of knots is long enough to reach from the top of your object to the base of it, take your knotting off your board and turn it upside down. Put your object in place. Now you want to keep this object from falling out. If you have sennits of square knots, you can switch core cords as before and secure it in place this way.

If you have double half hitches, just take a knotting cord from one side as in the earlier sample, bring it across to the other side and use it as an additional knotting cord on this side. Do this as many times as necessary to secure the object in place.

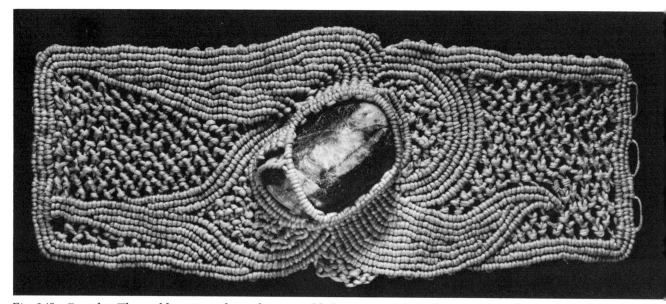

Fig. 148 Bracelet. The problem: to enclose a large, tumbled stone in a piece of macramé so that it would be secure, yet have a great deal of its surface exposed. The solution: this exquisitely designed bracelet. In designing the enclosure, Mary Belle Frey followed the natural markings in the stone. *Mary Belle Frey.*

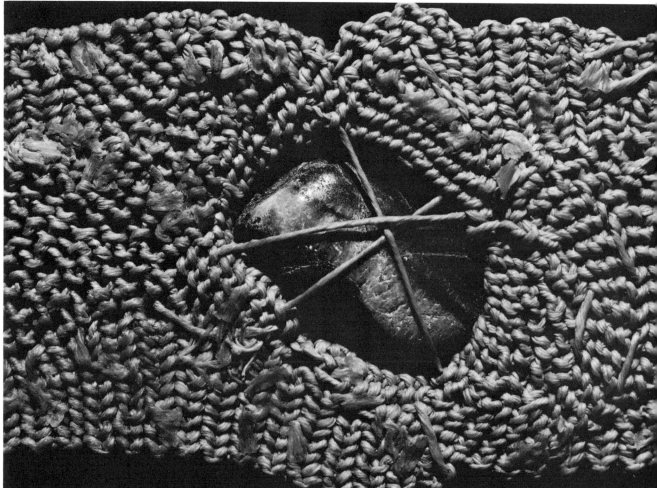

Fig. 149 Close-up of the underside of the bracelet. The waxed linen cord is very strong and these few cross-overs will hold the stone in place. *Mary Belle Frey.*

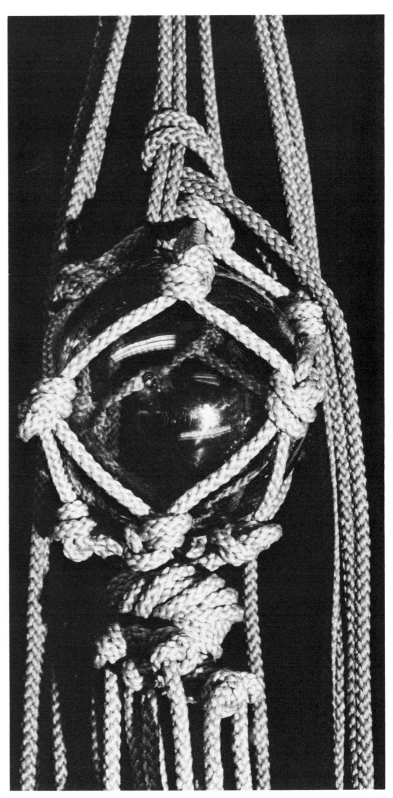

150 (above) Close-up of section of hanging "To Harry." A
ple way to enclose an object. The knotting cords are lodged
e natural crevices of this shell.   *Fig. 151 (right)* Close-
of another section of the wall hanging, "To Harry." This
d, glass float is securely locked in place with overhand knots
rategic places. *Madge Schneider.*

7

ARTISTS AT WORK

Edwina Drobny, Paul Johnson, and Joan Michaels Paque are three talented artists who choose to work with cords and knots. Their work is strong—their style very individualized.

EDWINA DROBNY

Of herself, Edwina Drobny says, "My ideas often grow out of each other. Almost all are emotionally connected with my life and its relation to nature. Natural forms are what I am most concerned with along with a desire to explain myself as a woman.

"I weld light forms, over which I can have control, rather than their controlling me. These forms over which I work are carefully planned in advance—only the overlap work of macramé is left for later discretion. I am not so interested in macramé as an end in itself as I am as a medium with which to sculpt. . . . My influences are a mingling of the so-called primitives—ancient Japan, Africa, and South America being the primary sources of inspiration.

"But all this is somewhat extraneous and stems from a simple need to work with my hands and become physically involved. And if beyond the labor, I am able to say something of my emotions and my politics, I am very pleased."

Fig. 152 "Te Quiero." Linen macramé over steel frame. *Edwina Drobny.*

191

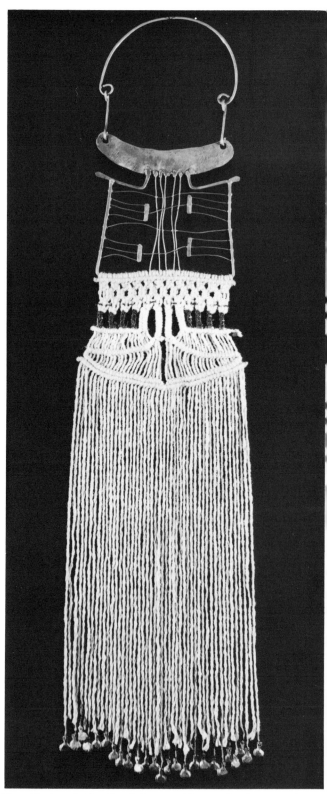

Fig. 153 (top left) Head Piece. Edwina Drobny wearing her linen headdress. *Edwina Drobny.* *Fig. 154 (left)* Head Piece. Back view. Linen. *Edwina Drobny.* *Fig. 155 (above)* Neckfall. Silver, linen, and wool. *Edwina Drobny.*

Fig. 156 (above) Necklace. Linen, wool, pewter, and black onyx.
Edwina Drobny. Fig. 157 (right) Neck Piece. Linen, copper,
bone, wood, and walnuts. Edwina Drobny.

193

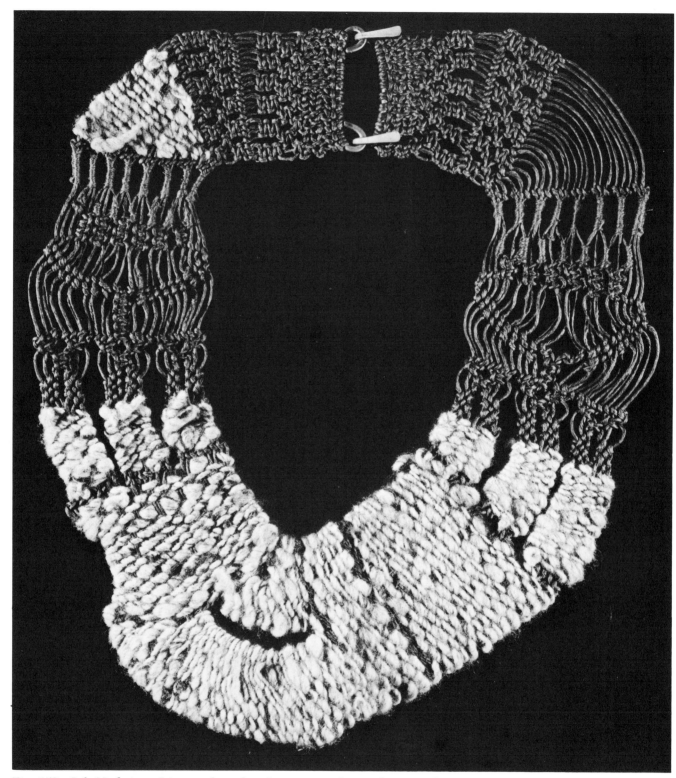

Fig. 158 Soft Neckpiece. Linen and wool with a pewter clasp. *Edwina Drobny.*

Fig. 160 Bib. Linen, wool, and forged pewter. *Edwina Drobny.*

g. 159 Necklace. Linen, wool, red onyx beads, red and purple
sels. *Edwina Drobny.*

195

Fig. 161 Collar. Linen, pewter, and colored onyx. *Edwina Drobny.*

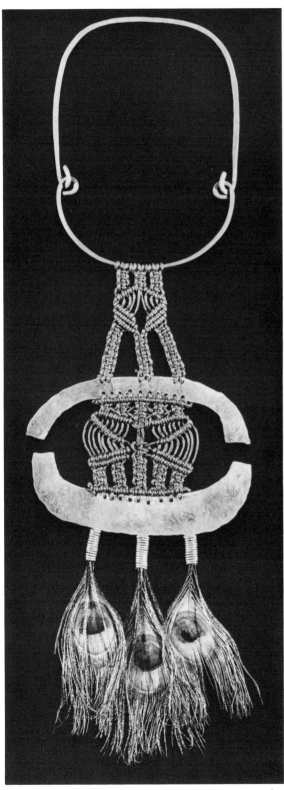

Fig. 162 Necklace. Linen, pewter, and peacock feathers. *Edwina Drobny.*

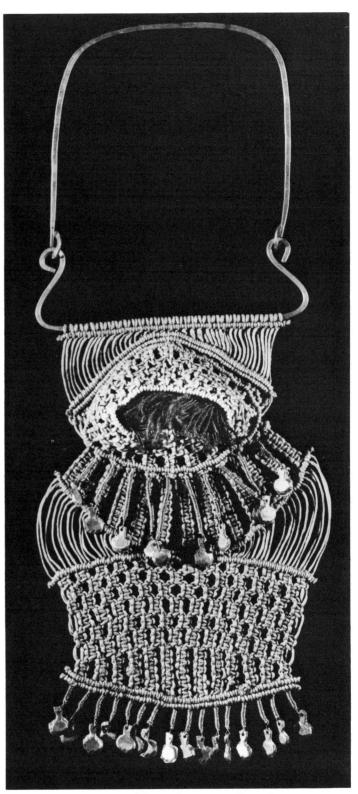

Fig. 163 Necklace. Linen, wool, and cast pewter. *Edwina Drobny.*

Fig. 164 (left) Necklace. Linen, wool, sand dollars, and pewter. *Edwina Drobny.* Fig. 165 (right) Neckpiece. Linen, pewter, and fur. *Edwina Drobny.*

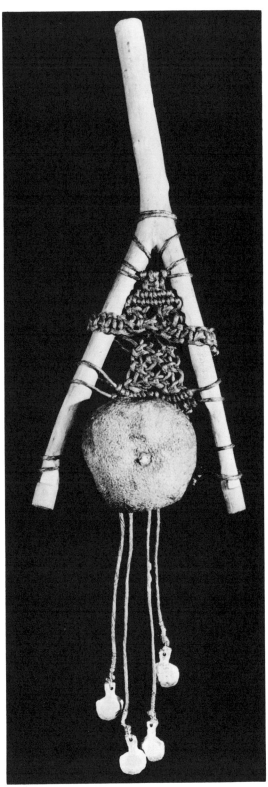

. 166 *(left)*   Neck Sculpture. Brass and linen. *Edwina Drobny.*

Fig. 167 *(right)*   Sling shot.   Wood, linen, cast pewter, and dried tangerine. *Edwina Drobny.*

Fig. 168 (*above*) Earrings. Linen and beads. *Edwina Drob[…]*
Fig. 169 (*left*) Leather Case for Small Etchings. Leather, lin[…]
and wood. *Edwina Drobny.*

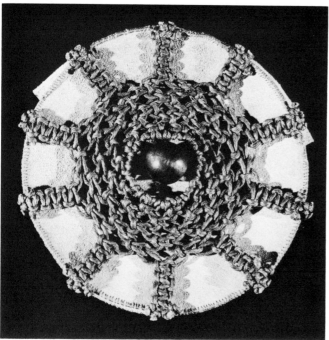

Fig. 170 Earrings. Linen, cast pewter, wishbones. *Edwina Drobny*.

Fig. 171 Table Sculpture. Linen, etching on canvas stretched over steel frame. *Edwina Drobny.*

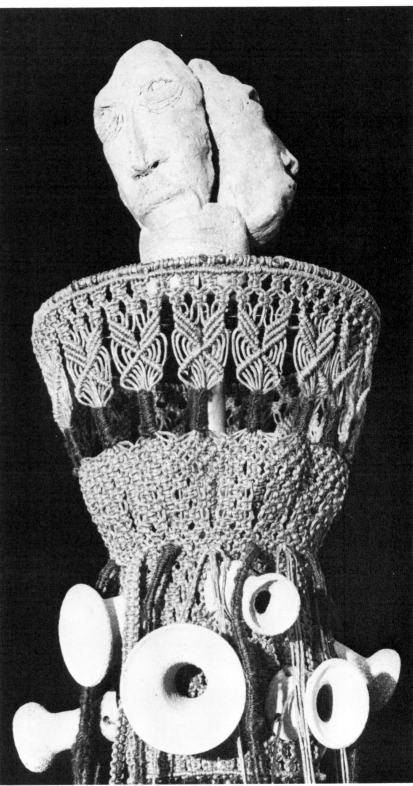

—unfinished. This sunflower, together with many others, will sway in the wind. The first of many. *Edwina* *ght)* Sculpture. "The idea [for this tall sculpture] came from a set of Japanese lacquer figures—the pri- is a descendant of the Indian Goddess Shiva (the one with many faces and arms). The spouts . . . rep- *dwina Drobny.*

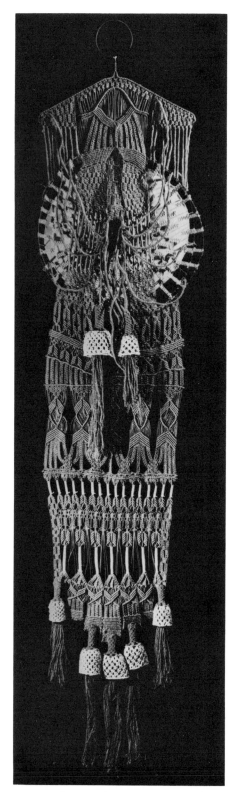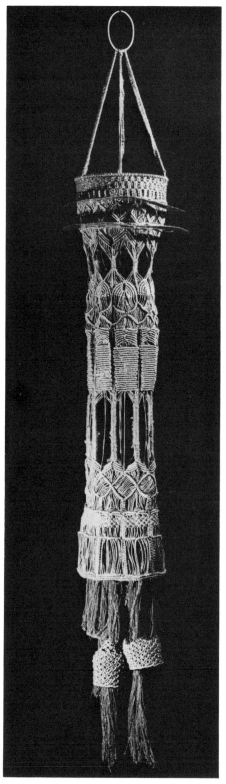

Fig. 174 (left) The Clothes Horse. Macramé over steel frame, painted canvas, and wool. *Edwina Drobny.* *Fig. 175 (right)* Cylinder Sculpture. Linen, wool, and forged pewter. *Edwina Drobny.*

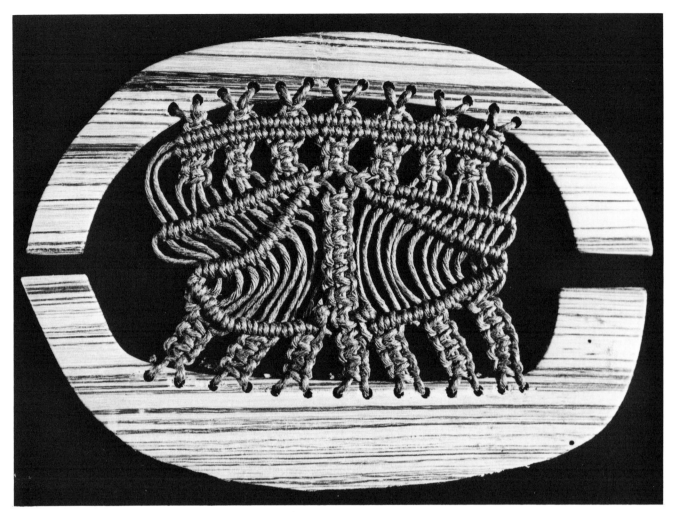

Fig. 176   Object. Zebra wood and linen. *Edwina Drobny.*

Fig. 177   Painting. Painting is nameless because it is "For all women and children who have to suffer the ultimate ugliness of war." *Edwina Drobny.*

PAUL JOHNSON

When Paul Johnson started to do macramé, he felt the macramé he had seen was too boxy looking, and too heavily done. He thought that there was much concentration on the knots and not enough thought to the over-all shape that the pieces took. "I felt that too much macramé formed its own shape without the artists imposing their own ideas. I like a two-way conversation—where macramé knots and I both have our equal say.

"Because of this feeling about heaviness, I have purposely tried many types of fine material [as fine] wools, rayon and wool blends, gold cord, elastic cord, and waxed linen. My favorite material is 3 ply and 6 ply waxed linen because of the crispness of the knots in the waxed cord and the fineness of lines. Also, I like the natural color.

"I have purposely striven to explore the shape macramé could take. They are not necessarily arbitrary shapes but stem from what the knots will allow—with the changes of shapes by adding and cutting out cords.

"Most of my pieces are built in very close monochromatic color schemes. I strive to have the various elements echo each other—such as feathers and beads in closely related colors. . . ."

Paul Johnson finds macramé flexible and spontaneous. "Since there are only the two basic knots, the real fun comes in the variation of using these two elements."

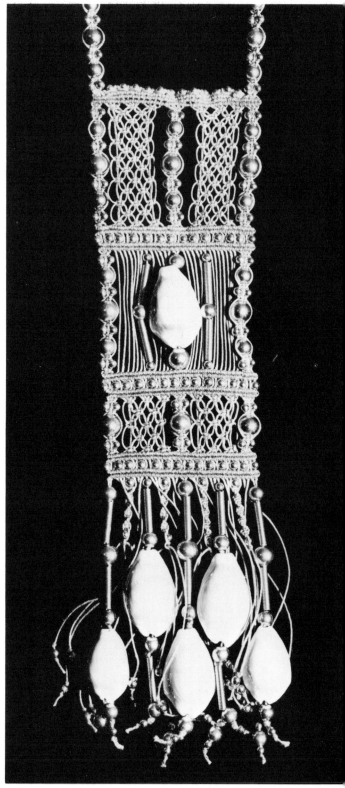

Fig. 178 Money Cowry Necklace. 1971. Waxed linen, gold covered plastic beads, money cowry shells. Shells are held in place tying a double overhand knot, placing glue on it, and pushing into the opening in the back of the shell. *Paul Johnson.*

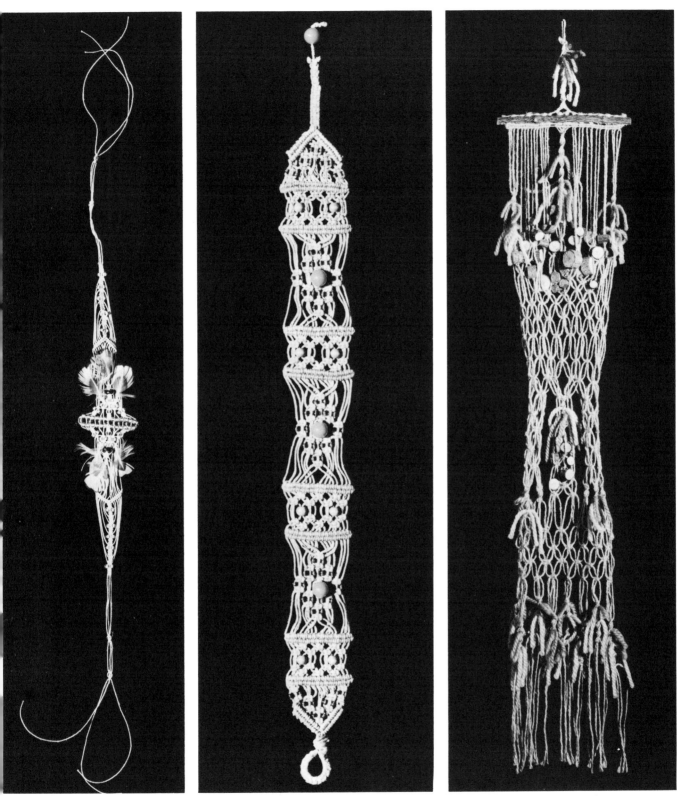

Fig. 179 (left) Choker. 1971. Waxed linen, glass beads, ring neck pheasant feathers. The center row is made by slipping a bead on the knot-bearing cord between each clove hitch (or double half hitch). Owner, *Jennifer Wyckoff. Paul Johnson.*
Fig. 180 (middle) Choker. 1970. Waxed linen, glass, and wooden beads. *Paul Johnson.*   *Fig. 181 (right)* Jute Hanging. 1969. Jute, assorted wools, wood sections cut from native tree branches through which holes are drilled. All alternating square knots. 8″ x 46″. *Paul Johnson.*   207

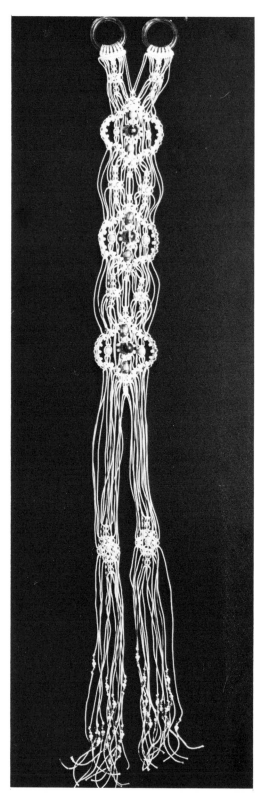 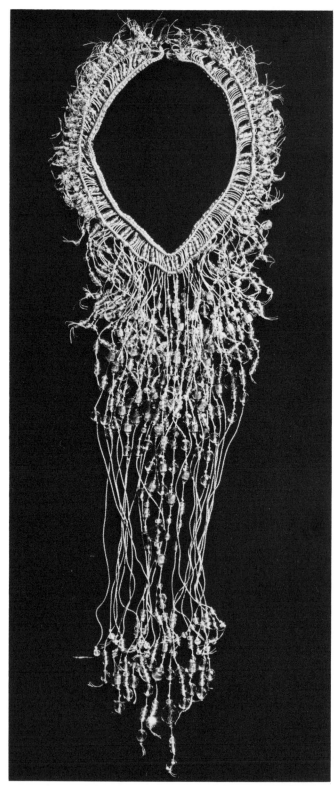

Fig. 182 (left) Belt. The curves in this belt are achieved by making long sennits of square knots which are then pushed up to make them bow out. *Paul Johnson.* *Fig. 183 (right)* Gold-Ambre Long Bib. 1971. Gold corderette. Glass beads, pony, crow and faceted. The long cords in front hang free. Overhand knots hold the beads in place and form a pattern on the cords. 14″ long from the collar down. *Paul Johnson.*

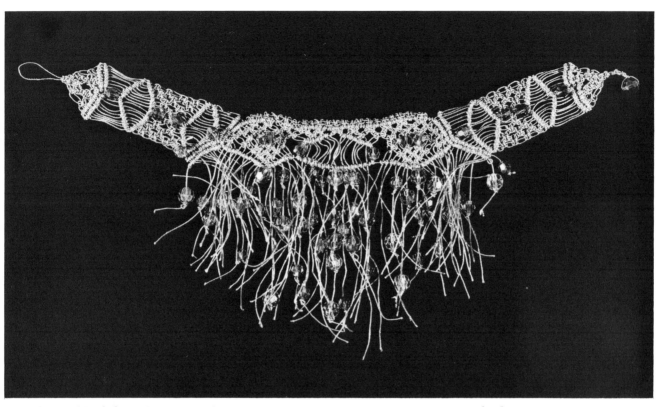

Fig. 184 Gold Choker-Bib. 1970. Gold elastic, blue-faceted aurora borealis beads. *Paul Johnson.*

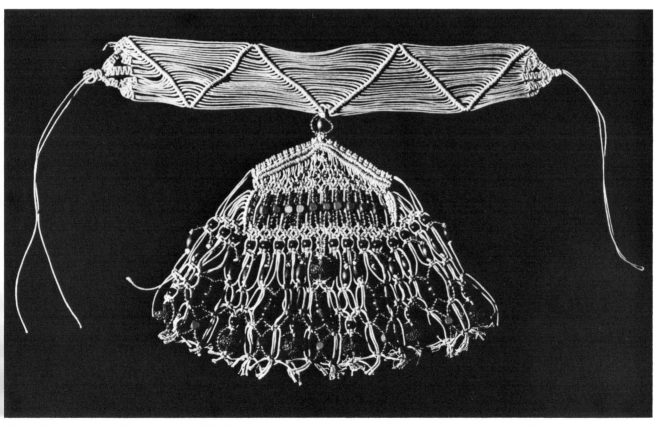

Fig. 185 Pendant and Necklace. 1970. Waxed linen, glass and wooden beads, gold color wire. The pendant is detachable from the choker. It is built on a gold colored wire that is shaped similarly to a miniature hanger. *Paul Johnson.*

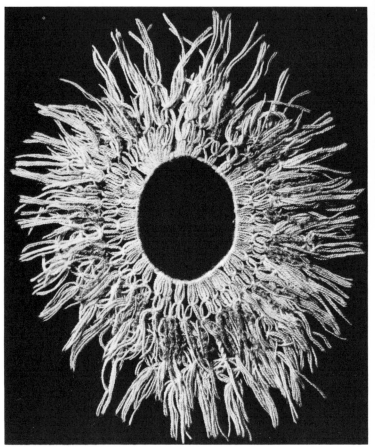

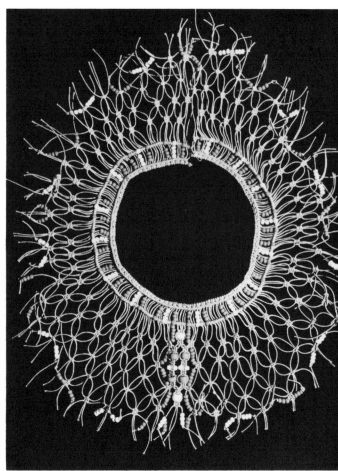

Fig. 186 (left) Red Fuchsia Collar. 1969. Crewel wool, now
purple yarn. 14″ diameter. Owner, *Joan Wyckoff. Paul John*
Fig. 187 (above) Waxed Linen Egyptian Collar. 1971. W
linen. Blue and white opaque pony and crow beads. 14″ diam.
Paul Johnson.

Fig. 188 (left) Champagne Necklace. 1971. Waxed linen. White, champagne, and clear pony beads, assorted faceted glass beads. Hackle and tail feathers from Rhode Island Red Rooster, and Guinea Fowl feathers. *Paul Johnson.* *Fig. 189 (right)* Orange Feathered Bib Necklace. 1971. Waxed linen. Orange and yellow crow beads, jade beads, orange pony beads, hand-dyed duck feathers. *Paul Johnson.*

JOAN MICHAELS PAQUE

The work of Joan Michaels Paque is quite distinctive. Of art, she says, "Art, it seems to me, should simplify. . . . Simplicity, coupled with a willingness to toy with the absurd and only later submitting the stream of ideas to harsh critical judgment results in a widening of creative possibilities. We must also provide an environment in which it is safe and acceptable to err, in which novel juxtapositions of ideas can be freely expressed without fear of failure."

Although there are just two basic knots in macramé, there are many, many more knots that can be used. Joan Michaels Paque freely and creatively uses a wide variety of knots in her work. Her style is crisp, clear, well defined, and rhythmical.

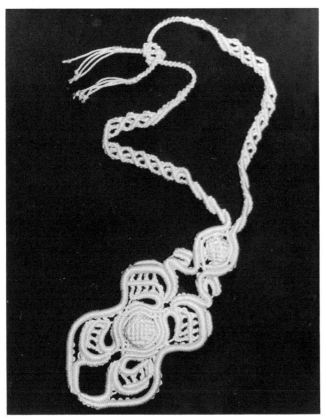

Fig. 190 Macramé Pendant. Nylon. 4″ x 9″ plus tie. *Joan Michaels Paque*. Photo, *Hank Paque*.

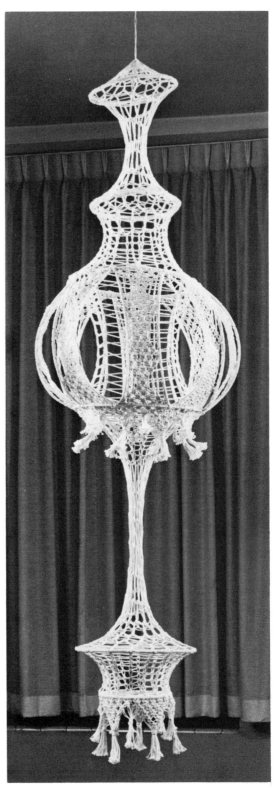

Fig. 191 Space Hanging. "Hoop-looping and macramé." Seine twine. About 5′ long. *Joan Michaels Paque*. Photo, *Jean Picard*.

212

g. 192 (*left*)   Hanging. Macramé and interlooping. Natural Jute. 38″ x 8′. *Joan Michaels Paque*. Photo, *Hank Paque*.
g. 193 (*right*)   Body Piece. This body piece sits on the shoulders and hangs down in front and back. Polished cotton twine.
″ x 28″. *Joan Michaels Paque*. Photo, *Hank Paque*.

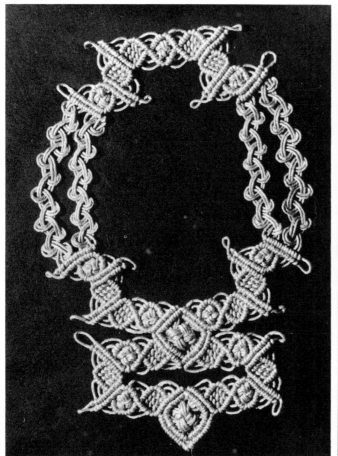

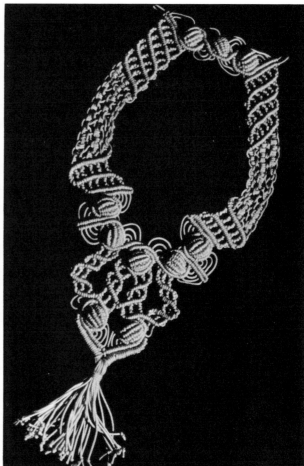

Fig. 194 (top left) Neckpiece. Synthetic fiber. 9″ x 14″. *Joan Michaels Paque.* Photo, Hank Paque. *Fig. 195 (left)* Neckpiece with Wood Beads. Nylon braid. 13″ diameter. *Joan Michaels Paque.* Photo, Hank Paque. *Fig. 196 (top right)* Nylon Braid Neckpiece. *Joan Michaels Paque.* Photo. Hank Paque. *Fig. 197 (above)* Neckpiece. White nylon. 10½″ x 12″. *Joan Michaels Paque.* Photo, Hank Paque.

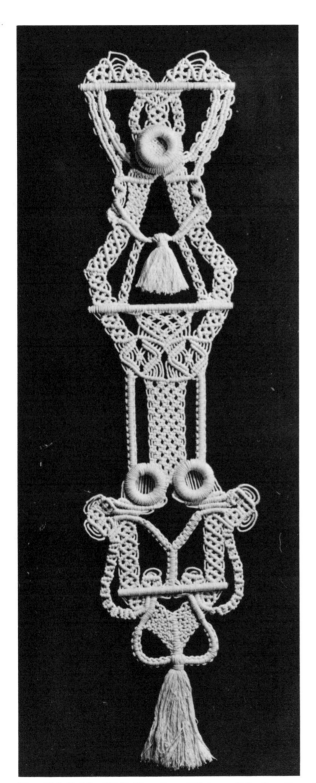
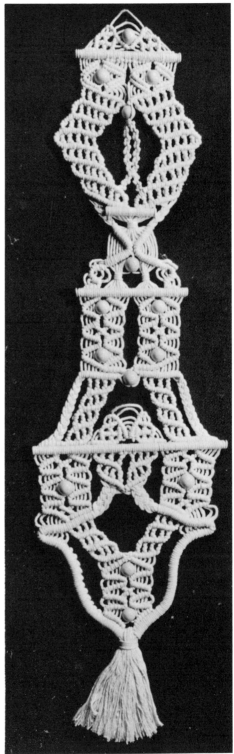

Fig. 198 (left) Wall Hanging. White polished cotton. 11″ x 40″. *Joan Michaels Paque.* Photo, *Hank Paque.*
Fig. 199 (right) Wall Hanging with Beads. White polished cotton. 9¾″ x 36″. *Joan Michaels Paque.* Photo, *Hank Paque.*

215

8

HANG IT ALL

WALL HANGINGS

The creative artist often turns to wall hangings as a means of expression. Restrictions are fewest here and one's imagination can wander far afield.

Fig. 200 Beginning of a Wall Hanging. The triangular shape that Beth Lister started with influenced the general form that this piece is taking. Purple cotton and rayon rug yarn. *Beth Lister.*

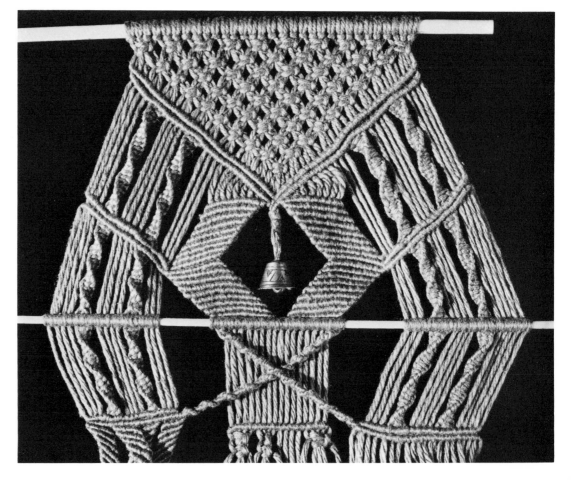

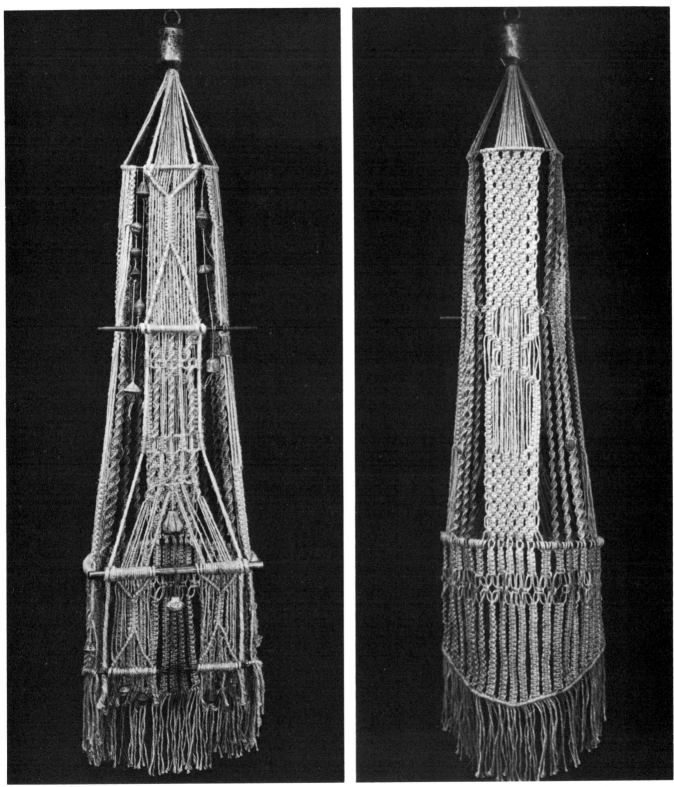

Fig. 201 (left) Serenity. The front of this hanging is flat. The knots are simple and few, the hanging rather open. Marline twine, several weights of jute. 5′ tall. Ceramic beads by *Ebby Malmgren. Helene Bress.* *Fig. 202 (right)* Serenity, back view. The sides and back of this hanging are rounded and the knotting simple, but more concentrated than the front. It is constructed in this way so that when you view the front, the back forms a background that is is not distracting. *Helene Bress.*

217

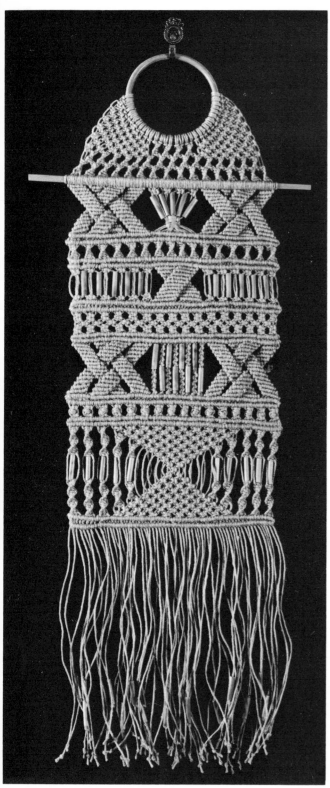

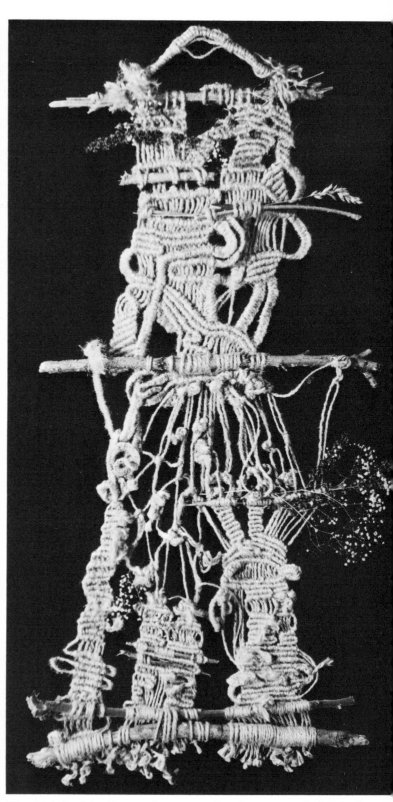

Fig. 203 (left) Meticulously designed and executed wall hanging. Linen, about 10/5. *Ella Bolster*.

Fig. 204 (right) Connie Brown combined twigs and dried plant materials into her fanciful, free wall hanging. *Connie Brown*.

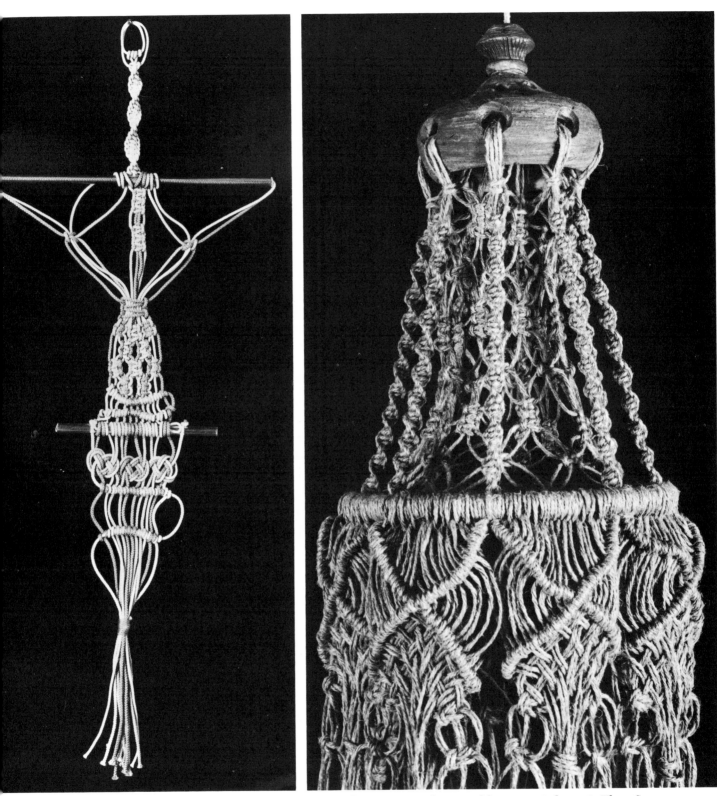

g. 205 (left) The Bright Colored Hanging That Just Grew. This hanging started out in life as a spiral sennit. Then Steven
d the bright idea of adding a hollow plastic bar, some more cords, a few knots . . . *Steven Bress*, when 12 years old.
ig. 206 (right) Close-up of a three-dimensional hanging. Of special interest is the cylindrical form within the outer, open
rcle of spiral sennits. Ceramic heading by *Ebby Malmgren. Sylvia Pocock.*

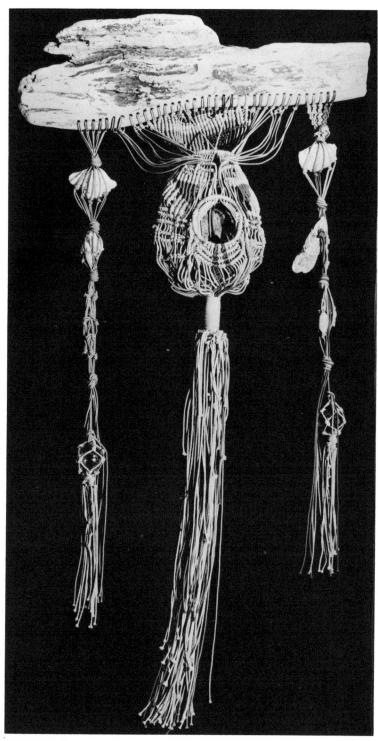

Fig. 207 "To Harry." Madge Schneider's designs grow as she works. She started with a piece of driftwood, some sea shells, glass floats, and polypropylene cord in blues, greens, and brown, and this complex, interesting design evolved. *Madge Schneider.*

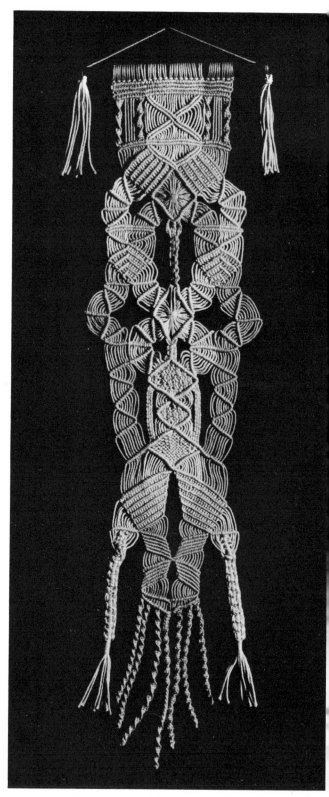

Fig. 208 This is a very dainty piece done in two shades of blue heavyweight crochet cotton. It's very effective hung against a wall or in front of a window with the light coming through the open areas. *Doramay Keasbey.*

220

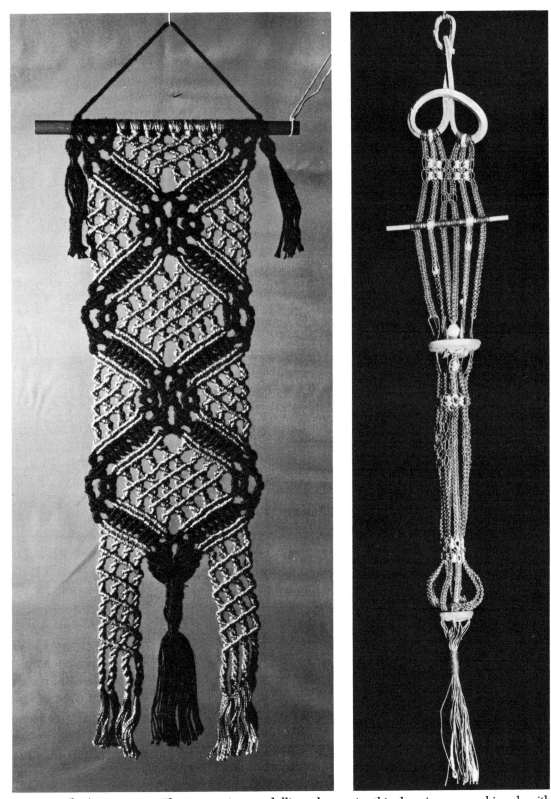

Fig. 209 (left) Hanging. The interesting medallion shapes in this hanging are achieved with double half hitches. Since the black and green rayon yarn is fine, five strands were put together and used as one cord. *Marie Grassi.* *Fig. 210 (right)* Solitude. This hanging starts in two dimensions and adds a third dimension along the way. Black upholsterer's cord, gold linen. About 2′. Ceramic pieces, *Ebby Malmgren. Helene Bress.*

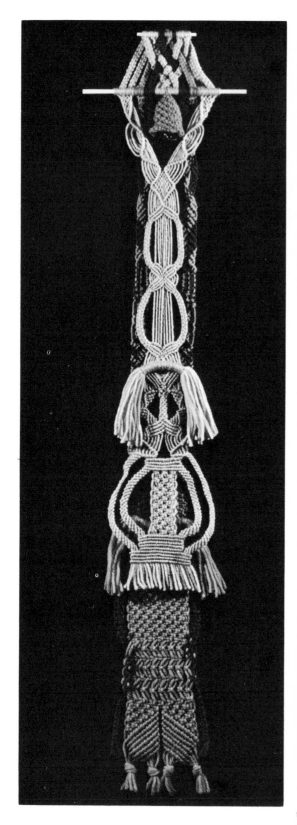

Fig. 211 (left) "Christmas Totem." Made of brilliant colors—red, green and hot pink in two layers. The layers separate at the second dowel, an the top one rests on the lower one. Tapestry wools. *Marjorie Newel*

Fig. 212 (above) Hanging. The colors seem to flow from one area t another in this hanging of many colors. *Augusta Petroff.*

Fig. 213 Airy, open hanging. *Richard Mathews.*

Fig. 214 Large, simple, dramatic hanging. Very heavy jute. 2½′ x 6½′. *Peg Hardy.*

223

Fig. 215 (left) Tall, graceful, three-dimensional hanging. Made of tightly twisted rug yarn. *Marie Grassi.*   *Fig.* 216 *(right)* Close-up of the middle portion of the three-dimensional hanging. The patterns differ on each of the four long tabs. *Marie Grassi.*

Fig. 217 Hanging. Here's one of Richard Mathews's more complex hangings. His double dowel mounting technique adds to the overall effect. *Richard Mathews.*

9

ONCE UPON A TIME

HOW DID IT ALL START?

And at this point, I got all tangled up. I had knotted innumerable projects, had seen the works of hundreds of other contemporary knotters, had seen beautiful old pieces of macramé lace, and now just wanted a few, well-documented facts on the history and development of macramé. My first source book was perfect. It had facts, names, dates, and other pertinent information. The second source book caused all the trouble. It gave different data, but the third and fourth sources quoted from it verbatim. Where did number two get her information? It's hard to say. Who was right? It's hard to say.

To confuse things a bit more, a historian handed me a little, knotted, many-tasseled thing and suggested that it was well worth studying. Very gingerly, I said that the intricate forms were fascinating, but there weren't any square knots, double half hitches, or even overhand knots in it. "Do you consider this macramé?" I asked. My answer was a shrug of his shoulders accompanied by a very pleasant smile.

So—what is macramé?

"Leucothrix mucor, a microscopic . . . algae ties itself into overhand knots in the course of its development, and even sometimes into figure-eight knots and timber hitches."*

Is that macramé? If it is, then macramé may date back farther than the advent of man.

Perhaps you think this is a bit far-fetched. All right, how about this? Apparently the ancient Greeks and Romans believed that Hercules invented the square knot, and they named this knot after him—the Hercules knot. They believed that a Hercules knot had great healing power and they bound their wounds with this knot. Picture a man with ten wounds and each wound bound with the quick-healing Hercules' knot. Is he macramé? Also far-fetched, but how about this? "A Roman bride customarily wore a girdle of wool tied with a Hercules knot..."** Was she wearing a macramé belt?

Whatever your answer, you're not wrong. However, let's advance in time to about the fifteenth century. About that time, macramé, *as we usually think of it today,* seems to have had its beginnings.

* From *Quipus and Witches Knots*, by Cyrus Lawrence (Kansas: University of Kansas Press, 1967).
** *Ibid.*

226

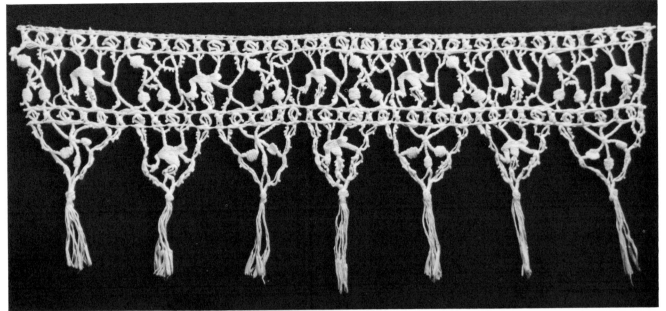

Fig. 218 (above) Fringe with Birds. Linen macramé band with triangular tab edge. The bird and flower motif is worked in double half hitches. Note the similarity between this motif and the bottom section of the design on the page from the pattern book. Courtesy, *Cooper-Hewitt Museum of Decorative Arts and Design, Smithsonian Institution, New York.* Fig. *219 (right)* Photostat of a page from the lace pattern book, *Pretiosa Gemme de Parasole,* Venice MDC (1600). Lace pattern books were popular in the 16th century. Many were reprinted at later dates. Courtesy, *Cooper-Hewitt Museum of Decorative Arts and Design, Smithsonian Institution, New York.* Photos, courtesy, *Cooper-Hewitt Museum.* All other photos in this chapter are by *Allen Bress.*

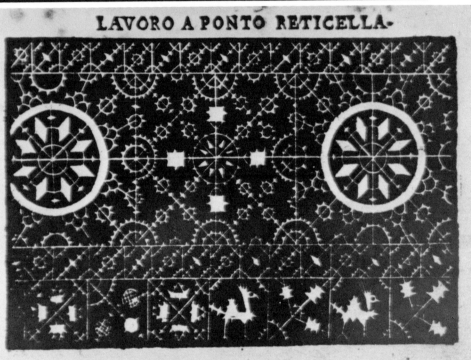

LAVORO A PONTO RETICELLA·

As craftsmen today, we use the term macramé* to designate a type of decorative knotting using square knots and double half hitches as its basic components.

As best we can, let's follow the development of macramé as we have just defined it. The historical sources available to me are all relatively recent, none earlier than 1875, and are often conflicting.

* Macramé. n. a knotted cotton trimming, usually in a geometrical pattern. Also called macramé lace. [< F < It *macramé,* a kind of fringe on hand towels < Turk *makrama* napkin, face towel < Ar *migrama,* embroidered veil]. From the *Random House Dictionary of the English Language,* 1966.

Macramé. n. Coarse lacework made by weaving and knotting cords into a pattern, used as a fringe or trimming for furniture. [French, from Italian *macramè,* from the Turkish makrama, napkin, towel, from Arabic, *miqramah,* striped cloth]. From the *American Heritage Dictionary of the English Language,* 1969.

Very confusing! Any history based on such sources is at best conjectural. Since I enjoy conjecturing as well as the next, I have examined all the pertinent information I could find, and have come to accept the following.

The Sforza Inventory, dated 1493, makes the first mention of a piece of macramé lace. (Inventories of personal possessions such as the Sforza Inventory have often been very fruitful sources of information for historians.) The earliest example we have where macramé lace is pictured is in a painting by Paul Veronese (1528-1588). The picture is of the supper in the house of Simon the Canaanite. The ends of the tablecloth in this painting are ornamented with macramé lace.

When a weaver removes his work from the loom, the warp threads at the beginning and end of the piece must be attended to in one way or another. Often, these ends are cut short and the article is hemmed. If they were left long (see Martha Hoering's mat, p. 249) they could be knotted into a pattern. The earliest form of macramé was done on the fine warp ends of woven fabrics. The patterns formed were fine and were called macramé lace.

Much of the early macramé lace was used for the ornamentation of church vestments and for other ecclesiastical purposes, and was particularly popular in Italy and Spain. This type of lace remained popular from the end of the fifteenth through the seventeenth century.

Fig. 220 Macramé Fringe with Beads. The warp threads of this fine cotton towel or runner were used to make this macramé edge. The knots are minute and, even with a magnifying glass, it is hard to tell whether or not it is macramé lace or lace of a different type. The colored beads are so tiny that at first sight they appear to be embroidered threads. The macramé lace section is 2⅜″ long, and the tassels at the bottom are ½″ high. Courtesy, *Smithsonian Institution, Washington, D.C.*

Fig. 221 (above) Macramé Fringe with Beads. Greatly enlarged close-up of Fig. 220. Courtesy, *Smithsonian Institution*.   Fig. 222 (below) Macramé Lace Insert. This is a delicate, macramé lace insert of fine linen thread and measures about 1⅜″ high and 14″ wide. Perhaps it was used on household linens. Courtesy, *Smithsonian Institution*, Washington, D. C. Photos, *Allen Bress*.

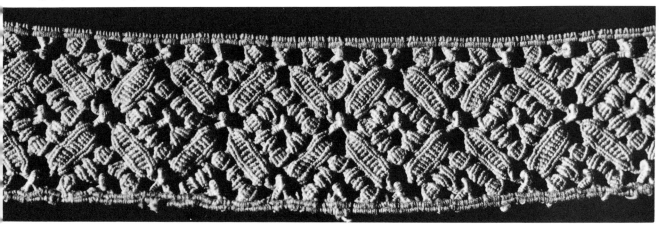

Fig. 223 Macramé Lace. These dainty medallions are made with fine linen thread and are about 3″ high and 1½″ across. Courtesy, *Smithsonian Institution, Washington, D.C.*

Although the making of macramé lace never completely died out, interest must have waned dramatically soon after this.

Little more was written on macramé for about the next 150 years. The technique apparently was rediscovered and revived in the early 1840's and by the 1870's, macramé seems to have become a familiar household word once more. In *The Age of Innocence,* a novel set in the early 1870's, Edith Wharton wrote:

"Mrs. Archer, who had long been a widow, lived with her son and daughter in West 28th St. . . . and the two women . . . in an unclouded harmony of tastes and interests . . . cultivated ferns in Wardian cases, made macramé lace and wool embroidery on linen. . . ."

By the time of Mrs. Wharton's novel, macramé seems to have begun to change its character. Heavier yarns were often used and macramé items, complete unto themselves, were being made.

Although it is not known exactly when the pieces in Figures 224 through 230 were made, it is probable that they were made in the late nineteenth or early twentieth century. The patterns are very similar to those in pattern books published about this time.

Fig. 224 Decorative Linen Piece. This decorative linen piece is 36″ long and 60″ wide. Perhaps it was used to trim a mantel. Courtesy, *Smithsonian Institution, Washington, D.C.*

Fig. 225 (above) The use that this piece was put to is unknown, but often the coarser pieces of macramé were used for mantel and table borders, and other furniture trimmings. This one is made of bast fibers, probably hemp, and is 14½″ high and 17½″ wide. Courtesy, *Smithsonian Institution, Washington, D.C.* *Fig. 226 (below)* Harriet Lynn's grandmother knotted this piece and decorated her tall upright piano with it. It was made in about 1885, following a pattern in a book issued around that time. Courtesy, *Harriet Lynn.*

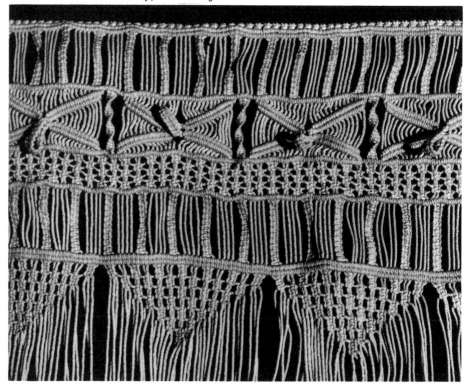

Fig. 227 (top left) Purse. Greta Tobie rescued this purse from an outdoor flea market in New Jersey. The knotting has been done with white seine twine and the fringe has been deliberately unraveled. Gift of *Greta Tobie.* *Fig. 228 (top right)* Purse. Here's a purse that has been in Margie Thurman's family for many years. It is made of paper twine that was much in use in the early 1900's. Courtesy, *Margie Thurman.* *Fig 229 (above)* Mat with Tassels. Paul Johnson found this cotton mat in a flea market in Pennsylvania. Courtesy, *Paul Johnson.*

Fig. 230 Here's a set of step-by-step instructions that someone made for his own edification, or possibly for the edification of others. Courtesy, *Smithsonian Institution, Washington, D.C.*

Shortly after this, interest in macramé declined, with a brief spurt of interest again around World War I. By the late 1920's, very little work was being done in this field.

Macramé might have stayed in the doldrums had not Virginia Harvey become intrigued with this technique.

In studying textiles, Mrs. Harvey had been aware of macramé for many years and had always wanted to learn it. As Curator of the Costume and Textile Study Collections in the School of Home Economics at the University of Washington, she stumbled upon old French book on macramé* while doing some research. She, and several of her colleagues, proceeded to teach themselves the technique.

After much self-teaching, knot tying, and searching for illustrative material, Mrs. Harvey wrote *Macramé: The Art of Creative Knotting* in 1967. This book, together with the many workshops she gave in the United States and Canada, and a trav-

* *Le Macramé* by Thérèse de Dillmont.

Fig. 231 Door Curtain. This is a much used piece of macra It hangs in a doorway in the Levitov home and one walks thro the unknotted part to go from one room to the other. Ma Levitov is quite contemporary but has designed this piece i manner reminiscent of the Victorian era. *Marvin Levitov.*

234

eling macramé exhibition which was shown throughout the United States, caused an instant revival of the craft.

future—or perhaps macramé will evolve into a completely new art form.

In this new era, macramé has been taken a step further. While people are still using macramé in a rather conventional way, many others have gone off in new directions and macramé has become a creative art form. Perhaps the definition of macramé we started with will need revision in the

SAILORS AND MACRAMÉ

Knots have always been the working tool of sailors. It is not surprising then, that in their free time, they used this basic skill for decorative purposes.

Decorative knotting flourished on shipboard in the early nineteenth century. It is not known when sailors took up square knotting (much the same as, if not the same as, macramé), but it is known that in the middle of the nineteenth century both American and British seamen were skilled knotters. The craft declined rapidly with the advent of fast ocean-going ships after the Civil War. Shorter crossings and smaller crews meant that the sailor had little free time to devote to this pastime.

Fig. 232 Here's some "fancy ropework or sailorizing" done by Captain John Shickell of the *Bal Clutha*, which is a full rigger now at the San Francisco Maritime Museum. Courtesy, *Chesapeake Bay Maritime Museum*.

Fig. 233 Strip Sampler. In this photograph some ends are left untrimmed so that construction details can be observed. In strip No. 11 new knot-bearing cords have been added below the angled parts in order to keep the symmetry of the colors. In strip No. 12 the beginning of the contrasting cord is not yet trimmed. (See diagram on page 238.) *Helene Bress.*

10

SPREADING THE WORD

We warned you earlier, macramé is infectious, and once bitten, the disease intensifies to MACRA-MANIA.

We warned you before, you chose to ignore the warning, and now you're highly contagious, ready to spread your mania to other unwarned, unsuspecting souls.

Let's see if we can be of some help.

Exciting things happen when you teach macramé. Often, you start with a timid but hopeful group. They're sure it's going to be very complicated, but are hopeful that they'll learn. With a little guidance, they find that it's not really very complicated after all, and almost immediately they are happily knotting away.

Among the most common words a teacher hears is, "I have no talent," "I can only copy things," "I have no color sense." Certainly some people have more talent than others, but most people have at least some artistic ability. When a teacher successfully encourages his students to reach out and try his wings, it is very gratifying for both student and teacher.

As a teacher, your enthusiasm is contagious; your patience very much appreciated.

Different situations require different methods of approach. Here are a few concrete suggestions.

USING A STRIP SAMPLER

After teaching for a while using the method on pp. 241-245, I became aware of many limitations inherent in its use. In an effort to make the teaching-learning experience a more vibrant and versatile one, I worked out the Strip Sampler method of teaching. As I thought about it, so many possibilities occurred to me that I couldn't wait to make several different kinds of this type of sampler myself—and to spread the word to others.

Here's the first sampler of this kind that I made. The strips were made in the order as numbered in the sketch. As you can see, the strips go from the simple to the more complex one step at a time. Each strip, in order, builds upon the knowledge learned in previous ones.

Some people come to the first class knowing a knot or two, some know none. Some people are quick to learn and work easily with their hands, others are slower. With the Strip Sampler, each can progress at his own speed. More or fewer strips can be made according to the time available and the ability of the individual. It is hoped that everyone will master the basics, but some of these strips are just variations that are fun to know, and not absolutely necessary.

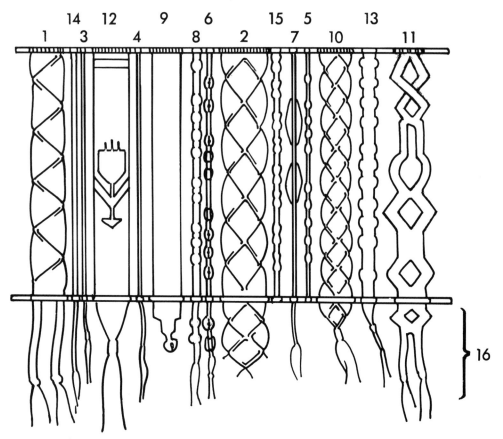

Diagram of Strip Sampler showing the order in which the strips were made.

The strips are done in a variety of materials. This gives students a chance to see what materials are available and how different materials work. The cords used are relatively short and the students prepare them quickly in class.

Colors are used and students see from the very beginning many ways in which color can be used successfully in macramé. The possibilities are endless—and the chances of any two people having identical hangings are quite remote.

Here are the vital statistics for the various strips as shown on my hanging. The space between the dowels is 14″ long. The chart is arranged in the order in which the strips are taught.

Since this sampler will probably be used as a wall hanging, the student also is immediately concerned with color coordination and design. These need not be overwhelming concerns, however, because the strips can be rearranged and some can even be discarded, or repeated for accent, or redone in a more suitable color.

The strips are started in class, but only partially finished there. As soon as the student demonstrates that he can go on independently, he can stop, go on to something else, and finish the strips at home.

238

CHART III   VITAL STATISTICS FOR STRIP SAMPLER HANGING

Strip #	Teaching Point	No. of Colors	No. of Ends	Length of Cords (All cords will be folded in half)
1	Double Half Hitch Horizontal and Oblique	2	8	Main color—3 cords, each 4 yards long Contrasting color—1 cord 4 yards long
2	Diamond, crossing over in center	3	14	Main color—4 cords, each 4 yards long Secondary color—2 cords, each 4 yards long Third color (center)—1 cord 4 yards long
3	Spiral—Half Square Knot, with right cord over left	1	4	Core Cords—1 cord 2 yards long Knotting cord—1 cord 6 yards long
4	Spiral—Half Square Knot, with left cord over right, plus beads. Spiral twirls in opposite direction to #3.	1	4	Core Cords—1 cord 2 yards long Knotting cords—1 cord 6 yards long
5	Whole Square Knot, combines the knots in #3 and #4	1	4	Core Cords—1 cord 2 yards long Knotting Cords—1 cord 4½ yards long
6	Variations with Square Knot, 2 colors, core cord showing, overhand knot and bead combination	2	4	Core Cords (contrasting color) 1 cord 2 yards long Knotting Cord (Main Color) 1 cord 4½ yards long
7	Square Knot with Picot	1	4	Core Cords—1 cord 2 yards long Knotting Cords—1 cord 6 yards long
8	Square Knot with one type of Raised Picot	1	4	Core Cords—1 cord 4 yards long Knotting Cords—1 cord 9 yards long
9	Alternating Square Knots	1	12 or 16	If cords are fine, cut 8 cords 4 yards each If cords are heavy, cut 6 cords 4 yards each
10	Diamonds with various knots in center	1	16	Cut 8 cords, each 4 yards long
11	Angling. Two colors used so that the movement of colors can be observed. No need to copy this pattern exactly.	2	8	First color—cut 2 cords, each 8 yards long Second color—cut 2 cords, each 8 yards long
12	Vertical Half Hitch combined with Horizontal Half Hitch to form a pattern (Cavandoli)	2	12	Main color—6 cords, each 7 yards long Contrasting color—1 cord 13 yards long. This cord is *not* doubled over. If more design area than in here is desired, make this cord longer.

239

Strip #	Teaching Point	No. of Colors	No. of Ends	*Length of Cords* (All cords will be folded in half)

I think that it is important to teach all of the above in a basic course. If time permits, the following can be included as well:

Strip #	Teaching Point	No. of Colors	No. of Ends	Length of Cords
13	Josephine Knot	1	4	2 cords, each 4 yards long
14	Double Chain Knot	2	4	Color #1—1 cord, 4 yards long Color #2—1 cord, 4 yards long
15	Square Knot with colors interchanged	2	4	Color #1—1 cord 4 yards long Color #2—1 cord 4 yards long
16	Endings—various ways to end projects			No new cords are needed—except for short ends to wrap with.

In design, the hanging can be very controlled, very free or anything in-between. The strips can all be the same size as in the first example, or like the diagram on the left.

The strip sampler can be started on a dowel, brass or plastic rod, hoop, flat stick, curtain rod, etc., but the heading should be even and smooth so that the strips can be rearranged if necessary. The endings can be varied, too, but should suit the character of the rest of the piece.

On my personal list of things to do, are samplers of this sort:

An elegant one—with yarns such as rattail, soutache, and gold lamé, and accented with some beads made of porcelain or semi-precious stones.

A tiny one with thin, fine cords.

A big, bulky one of heavy jute, accented with handmade ceramic beads and cork floats.

When using this strip sampler method, I usually have five sessions at weekly intervals and each session lasts two and one-half hours. My classes average four to six people. I start everyone on the first strip together—and watch for problems and questions. When I feel that someone is quite comfortable and confident with the particular knot or technique, I suggest that he finish that strip at home and go on to the second strip. I start him off, still watching for the others. If someone is particularly quick, I give him some of the optional strips or other variations to work on. If someone is particularly slow, I'll have him skip some of the less important variations. In this way, the class progresses from one type of knotting to another at approximately the same time, and the most important procedures are covered by all. The last session is usually reserved for finishing techniques.

At the first session, I have out:

A knotting board and pins for each person.

Scissors.

Dowels or plastic rods.

A yardstick and measuring board.

An assortment of yarns in many colors, usually one type of yarn predominating, however.

The first strip will set the tone for the rest of the sampler.

At the second session, I add some beads to the above collection, and some other types of yarns. I encourage each one to sample various kinds of yarn.

In the remaining sessions, the same materials are generally used.

It's always of great interest to students to see finished macramé pieces, as well as books and periodicals on the subject, lists of suppliers, samples of different yarns, slides and to know about exhibits that may be in town. I try to have these things and information available for students to study at the beginning and end of sessions.

VERTICAL SAMPLER

Here's another type of sampler that can be used as a basis for class sessions.

The same logical one-step-building-upon-the-previous-step order is followed as before. It works well, but is somewhat less versatile than the first one and is more tedious to set up.

When I use this method, I usually have four to five class sessions at weekly intervals and each

Fig. 234 Vertical Sampler.

241

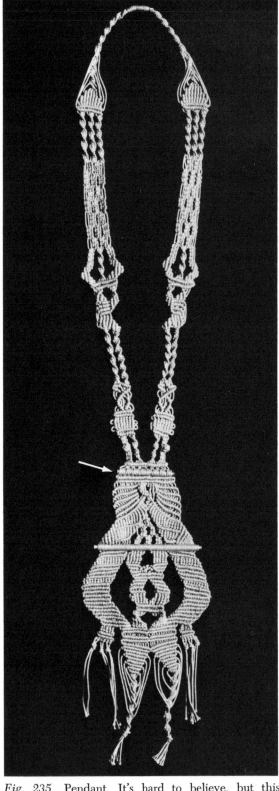

Fig. 235 Pendant. It's hard to believe, but this pendant started out as a class exercise. The arrow points to the starting point. If you turn the picture upside down, you can follow the knotting as it was done. When the back portion was completed, Trudy Nicholson turned it around, as pictured, and knotted the pendant portion adding threads as needed. Only a small portion of this was knotted in class. *Trudy Nicholson.*

session lasts from two to three hours. I keep the classes small, from four to six people.

Before the first class meets, I prepare for it by measuring and cutting the cords for each sampler. I use a different type of yarn and color for each sampler and hope that each person will find a set of cords that appeals to him. Each individual sampler is made in one color with only one type of yarn. In practice, I actually prepare several more packets of cords than there are people in the class, so that there will be more of a choice.

I use the following measurements for my vertical sampler but always run out of cord 1 somewhere along the way. When I do, I take the opportunity to teach splicing methods. If you don't want to run out of cord 1, add *ten yards* to the measurement of that cord.

I start with: 16 cords, each eight yards long. Since these are halved when mounting, I wind up with 32 ends, each four yards long.

If the cords were not prepared in advance, the first session would be taken up by measuring, mounting, and shortening the cords. I feel that this would be a discouraging way to start.

As the students arrive, I have them choose a packet of cords, help them mount the cords on a starting piece, and teach them how to shorten the cords. We all work hard and fast so that everyone will have time to do two rows of horizontal double half hitches and the beginning of a diamond. Before the end of the first session, everyone understands how to form the diamonds. Some have only started the diamonds, others have completed them. Their homework is to complete the first two diamonds and do two more rows of horizontal double half hitches. If they have time, and choose to do so, they may make a second row of diamonds, or any similar pattern, and finish it off with another double row of horizontal double half hitches.

Within these relatively rigid limits, some of the more creative students come up with very interesting variations.

For the second session, I have on hand a good

assortment of beads. I start out by teaching the spiral, or half square knot, and have the students leave groups of cords for the whole square knots and beads. After six of the spirals are completed, I teach the second half of the square knot, and have students select some beads. This is always a very interesting time for both the student and the teacher.

It's the first real opportunity for the student to inject a little of his own personality into his wall hanging. Usually, he sorts through the beads as if they were jewels—jewels he may have, but only a few—and so he must choose carefully. Sometimes this is the very first design experience for the student. How many beads should he choose, what color or colors, and in what order should he use them? I have strong ideas about these, but force myself to offer as few suggestions as possible. It usually pays off well. The student chooses what pleases *him*. He's really added something of his own to the project—and it usually looks well! Students often compare notes at this point, and are excited and inspired by the growth of the work around them.

After this section is completed, another row of double half hitches are done in class if there is time. The principle of the alternating square knot is taught, and the next section is finished at home.

Up to this point, each student has been working with just one type of cord. I feel that it's important for students to try a variety of cords. For the third session I have them put their samplers to one side. I have out an assortment of yarn, and each one chooses something different from what he had been working with. They measure out six or eight cords, each cord two arm-lengths long and then mount them on a chopstick, dowel, or just with pins. I emphasize that this is just for practice, and won't be used for anything, but it often ends up as a necklace, bookmark, or some small piece anyhow.

Using these cords, I teach the raised picot, over-hand knot, show how to add a stick and extra cords, and how to do the vertical half hitch. Some-

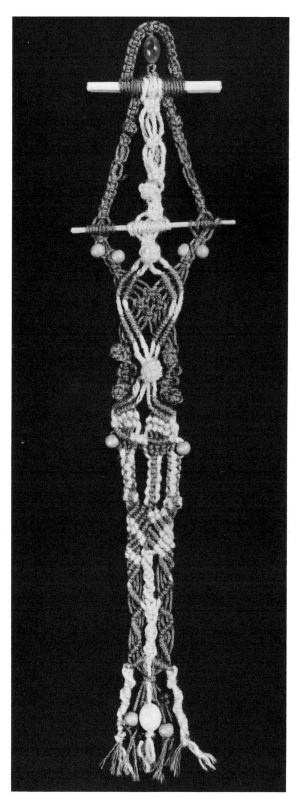

Fig. 236 Practice Sampler-Turned-Hanging. Started at the third class session and finished at home. *Ruth Gainer.*

243

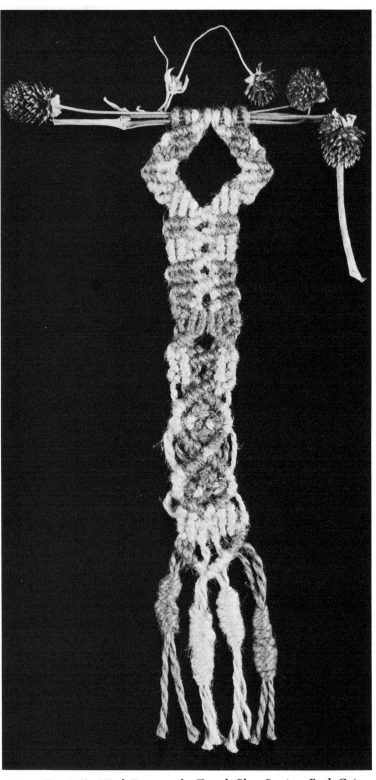

times there's time to teach the Josephine knot. I take extra cords for this.

This new little sampler is done extemporaneously and grows differently with each student. I try to have each person design his own somewhat, yet learn as many new things as possible. If you need to be more orderly than this, you can just follow the order as is shown in the large, pictured sampler. The homework for this session is to transfer the new techniques learned in class to the larger sampler. This may be done exactly like mine, or the student may design it in his own way. I always hope he'll design his own, but some students are still timid about this.

At the fourth session, all samplers are duly admired, questions are answered, and then the samplers are put aside once again. More cords are chosen this time, and two colors are used. I start with:

Two cords of color #1—each four yards long.

Two cords of color #2—each four yards long.

I have the students fold the cords in half and mount them on any small stick, or just with pins. I then teach them how to angle, using double half hitches, and go on to show the combination of horizontal and vertical half hitches and how to bring colors up at will (Cavandoli work). I spend the rest of the session teaching diamonds with filled centers and show how to cross the diamonds. Before the very end, we wrap the bottom cords. The homework is to complete the samplers at home incorporating these new techniques into them.

We're all sorry when a series of classes end, so a few former students formed a Macramé Guild. We meet once a month. I don't see the finished samplers at a formal class session, but do see them at these meetings. It's always a pleasant surprise. Usually, no two are alike, and some have even added their own hanger pieces on top.

Fig. 237 Work Done at the Fourth Class Session. *Ruth Gainer.* Photo, *Seymour Bress.*

g. 238 (left) Some more practice work using the techniques taught in the Fourth Class Session. *Ruth Gainer*. Photo, *Seymour* *ess.*   Fig. 239 (middle) Student Sampler. Here's Ruth Gainer's interpretation of the Vertical Sampler. She added ceramic ads and a ceramic top piece. Ceramic pieces, *Ebby Malmgren. Ruth Gainer*.   Fig. 240 (right) Another variation of the Vertical mpler.

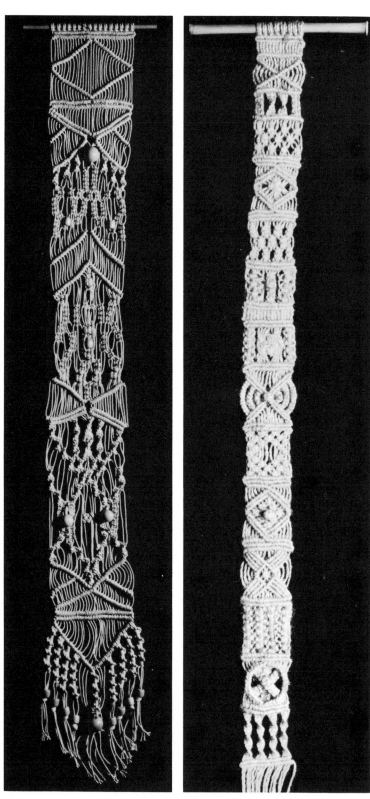

WORKSHOPS

Once the basic knots and techniques are learned, students often enjoy attending workshops geared to one specific topic. Sometimes students suggest topics; sometimes you may have a pet idea you would like to get across. Here are some possibilities:

> Covering a bottle
> Making circular pieces
> Christmas items
> Necklaces
> Purses
> Chokers
> Enclosing an object
> Twining and macramé
> Three-dimensional wall hangings
> More knots—knots that have not
>   been taught in class before
> Design: found objects
> Making lampshades
> Clothing
> Belts

The approach you take will depend upon the particular topic you are working with. For a Christmas workshop, for example, you may want to have all the materials on hand and specific items to copy, whereas for a workshop on design using found objects, each student will probably be asked to bring his own found objects, and the design of the piece will evolve during the workshop.

To me, the amount of knotting accomplished in a workshop is the least important part of the workshop. A workshop is successful if people go home with new ideas, enthusiasm, and eagerness to try new approaches. If you are enthusiastic, know your topic, have some good examples on hand or pictures or slides to show, and have some good ideas stored in your head, you're bound to have a good workshop. Of course, there are some very practical matters that must be included, too, and if these are not taken care of, a workshop can just fall apart.

Fig. 241 (left) Sampler. Marion Roscheck chose to design her sampler from the very beginning. *Marion Roscheck.* *Fig. 242 (right)* A student taught a student. Sampler by Trudy Nicholson's student, *Thais Weibel.*

For example, if you are supplying materials, you need to have enough materials on hand to go around.

SOME THOUGHTS ON A CHRISTMAS WORKSHOP

For a Christmas workshop, several projects could be presented for the participants to interpret. Participants may start one or more projects and finish them at home. Hopefully, their enthusiasm and imagination will be sparked by the workshop and they'll interpret the ideas presented to suit themselves. For this type of workshop, appropriate materials need to be available. These may be supplied by the instructor or the participants could be asked to bring specific items.

MERRY CHRISTMAS!

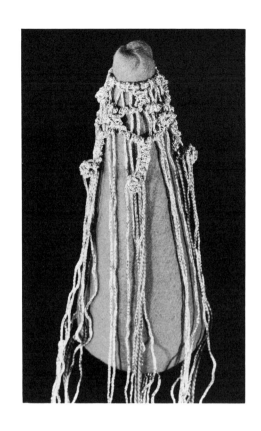

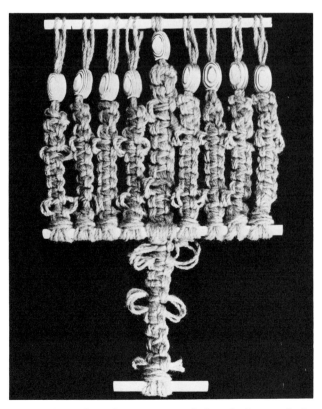

Fig. 243 (left) Wreath. The core of this square knot wreath is a plastic bracelet. Because of the thickness of the bracelet, and because the knotting is so dense, the knotting cords had to be *much* longer than usual. One seven yard cord, folded in half, was used. The bracelet takes the place of core cords. Based on an idea by *Paul Johnson.* *Fig. 244 (top right)* A different type of tree is taking form here. The base is a cone shape—e.g. Styrofoam or an empty cone from yarn. The tree is prettiest when the cone is painted or covered with felt before the knotting is done. *Fig. 245 (right)* Menorah. "But I don't celebrate Christmas," said Aileen Goldman. Here's her menorah, or candle holder, for Hanukkah. *Aileen Goldman.*

11

COMBINING CRAFT TECHNIQUES

As a craftsman grows within his field, he often reaches out toward other crafts as well. Also craftsmen tend to know and associate with other artists and craftsmen. Combining different crafts and arts is a natural outcome of both of these occurrences. Macramé combines well with many different arts—weaving, ceramics, leatherwork, enameling, sculpture, jewelry-making, woodworking, knitting, crocheting, stitchery, and sometimes even painting.

In combination, sometimes the macramé will assume only a utilitarian or decorative role. At other times, the knotting will be the focal point, with the other techniques used as decorative accents, and sometimes there is a complete marriage of the two.

Let's take a look at some pieces which are a combination of knotting and another medium.

WEAVING AND MACRAMÉ

It seems strange to extol the virtues of combining weaving and macramé within one piece as if today we are doing something brand new. Very likely, macramé was first used in this way. Well, this is still a good way to combine the two crafts. The warp threads are the threads that go vertically on a loom. Usually, it was these threads that were used to knot with after a piece was completed. However, weft threads which are woven across the warp, can be used too, as we'll soon see.

Here's a pretty white blouse that Sylvia Hoffman bought in Mexico (Figure 248). The weaver left long weft threads hanging at the sleeve part and long warp threads for the bottom part. When she removed the blouse from the loom, she knotted the long threads into a simple, macramé pattern.

Handweavers will appreciate the ingenious way in which Ella Bolster handled the problem of combining macramé within a woven piece (Figures 249-251).

Another weaver, Jeanne Vernon, handled the problem of combining weaving and macramé in quite a different way. The playful knotting and wrapping is done around warp threads and an added ring (Figure 252).

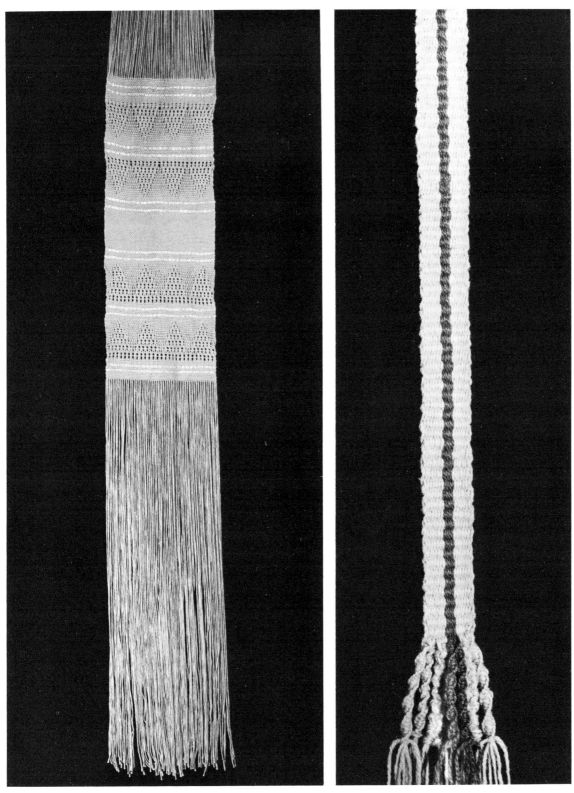

Fig. 246 (left) Handwoven Christmas Runner. Martha Hoering designed and wove this runner with a simple leno "Christmas Tree" pattern. She left long warp ends at the beginning and end of the runner so that they could be knotted—and before Christmas they will be! The macramé-to-be will follow the lines of the leno pattern. 4/4 red cotton for warp and weft. *Martha Hoering.*   *Fig. 247 (right)* Handwoven Inkle Belt. Here's a belt that Dan Bress wove on a narrow inkle loom. He, too, left long warp ends at each end so that they could be knotted. He used green and gold rug wool. *Dan Bress.*

Fig. 248 Handwoven Mexican Blouse. Simple, handwoven cotton blouse, with decorative edgings of macramé on the sleeves and bottom edge. Long weft threads were deliberately woven in and left hanging at the sleeve part and long warp ends left at the bottom so that the knotting could be done. Courtesy, *Sylvia Hoffman.*

Fig. 249 Linen Wall Hanging. Ella Bolster skilfully combined macramé with weaving on a handloom. All the work was done on the loom as she went along. Front and back of this meticulously done hanging is shown so that the astute weaver can decipher the techniques used. *Ella Bolster.*

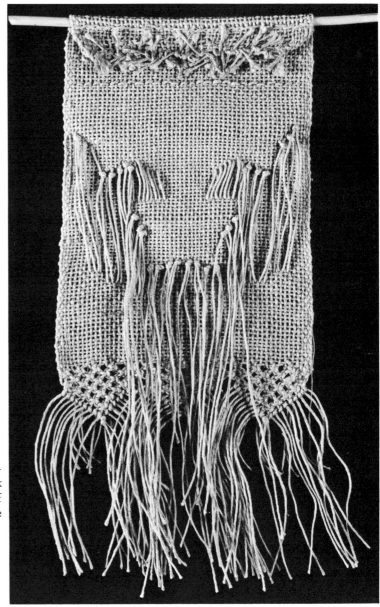

Fig. 250 Back view. Linen Wall Hanging. *Ella Bolster.*

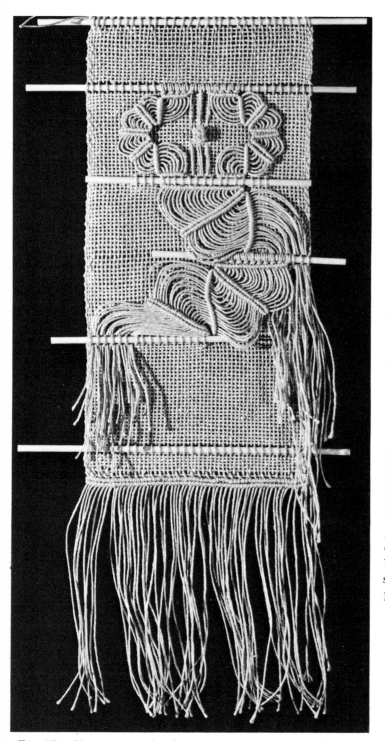

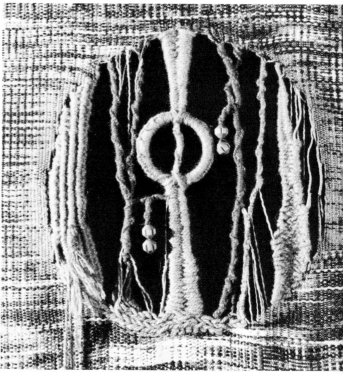

Fig. 252 "Freedom is . . ." Red, White, and Blue Wall Hangin[g]
Close-up of the focal point of a large, woven wall hanging. Jean[ne]
Vernon set several difficult, technical problems for herself, a[nd]
solved them in a light, free way. She did some knotting and wra[p]
ping on the warp threads within this woven piece. *Jeanne Vern[on]*

Fig. 251 Hanging. Another hanging designed and worked by Ella
Bolster combining weaving and macramé on a handloom. A different technique is used this time, and all the technical aspects can
be viewed from the front side. The dowels are both functional and
decorative. 10/5 linen. *Ella Bolster.*

Fig. 253 (left) Handwoven Purse with Macramé Overlay. Dick Malmgren wove this blue tubular purse on a handloom and left old warp threads at the beginning and end of it. He added some extra threads at the bottom to fatten his tassels, and wrapped them with a contrasting color. He turned down the top part and overlaid the purse with an open, lacy pattern. The handle was plotted separately and combines both colors. *Richard Malmgren, M.D.* Photo, *Seymour Bress.*   *Fig. 254 (right)* Ikat Wall Hanging. Using her warp ends, Martha Hoering trimmed her Ikat wall hanging with a short overlay of macramé at the top, and macramé fringe at the bottom. It's a perfect finish for her handsome, handwoven, hand-dyed wall hanging. *Martha Hoering.*

Fig. 255 Pandora's Box. We didn't know Pandora's box was as lovely as this! The top is done in vertical and horizontal double half hitches, and the sides of the box are woven. *Susan Gable Williamson.*

We don't all have the elaborate equipment and weaving skill needed to make some of the previous examples of weaving and macramé combinations. If you like the effect of this combination though, you could try the following:

Buy a piece of fabric, hem it to the size you desire, add threads onto this, and knot the ends. Attractive stoles, runners, and belts are some articles that can be made in this way.

Choose a fabric with a relatively loose weave.

Cut your cords as long as necessary. They will be halved, so account for this in your calculations. (For example, a single cord 24 inches long will become two 12-inch cords when mounted on your fabric.) Insert the cords in the cloth in this manner:

Fold your cord in half.

Ease a crochet hook between some threads in the fabric and hook the cord onto it.

Gently bring the cord through the fabric.

Bring the free ends through the loop, and tighten.

Continue in this way until all your cords are hitched on, and then knot in your pattern.

Martha Hoering will weave on anything from a 50-inch wide, four-harness loom to a loom made of corrugated cardboard. Here's how she set up a simple frame loom to make a woven wall hanging with a macramé fringe. In an art supply store, she bought a canvas stretcher 20 inches wide by 24 inches long. (Buy the size to suit your needs.) To this, she tied a dowel at the top and bottom, as in the diagram. Treating this as if it were a macramé project, she measured, cut cords, and hitched them onto the top dowel. She then lifted up the bottom dowel and double half hitched the cords onto this bar so that the threads between the dowels were even and taut.

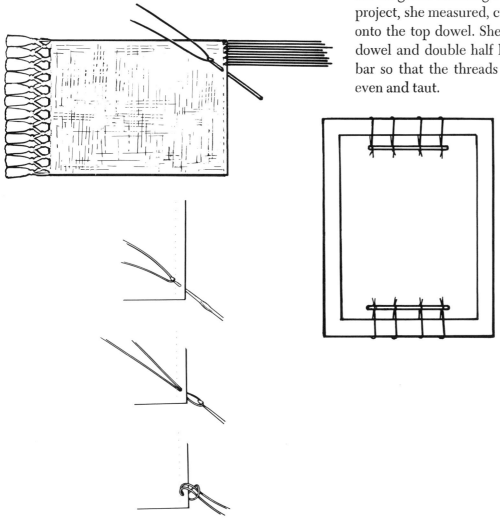

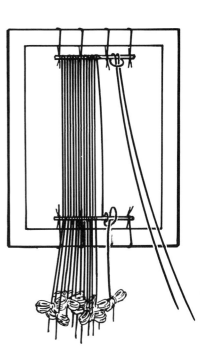

She wove between the two dowels, starting from the bottom dowel and working to the top. I leave the weaving part to your imagination or know-how, and also refer you to the books listed in the bibliography for ideas and methods of weaving with a frame loom.

However, Martha Hoering's method of warping, or setting up the frame loom, is unique and particularly suited for combining the weaving with macramé. When Martha finished the weaving part, she handed the project over to me. I removed the woven hanging from the canvas stretcher, pinned the bottom dowel to my knotting board and then blithely knotted away. I kept reminding myself

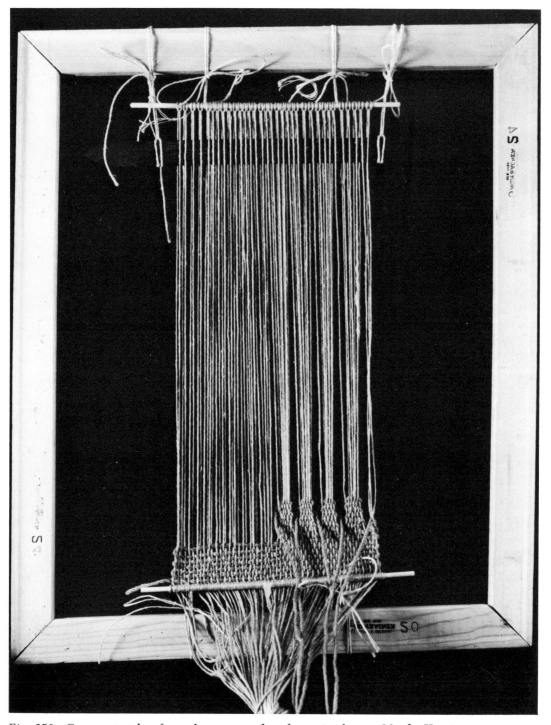

Fig. 256 Canvas stretcher frame loom, warped, and weaving begun. *Martha Hoering.*

that the knotting must be in keeping with the rest of the hanging. The first one (the white and red) (Figure 257) was easy because the end cords were rather short. I had the choice of keeping the pattern very open and very simple, or running out of all the cords. I kept the pattern simple.

The second was a different story. I had long, linen cords and a very long automobile trip. I became very involved with the knotting and perhaps the knotting became too involved!

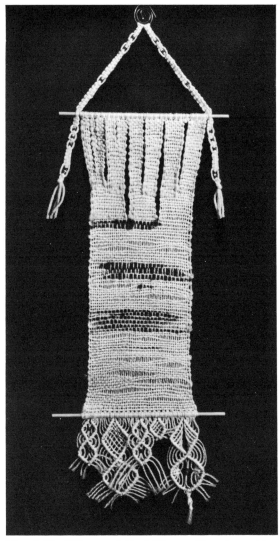

Fig. 257 White and Red Woven Hanging with Macramé. Woven by *Martha Hoering* on a canvas stretcher frame loom. Macramé by *Helene Bress*. (See text for description.)

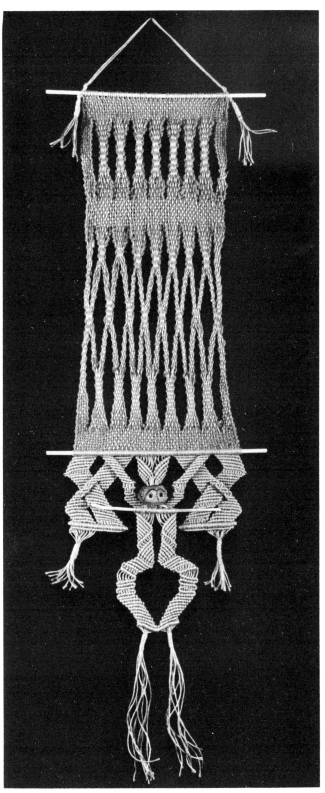

Fig. 258 The combined effort of three good friends. Weaving on a canvas stretcher frame loom. *Martha Hoering*. Macramé by *Helene Bress*. Ceramic bead, *Ebby Malmgren*. (More in text.)

257

CERAMICS AND MACRAMÉ

Ceramics and macramé work beautifully together. Ebby Malmgren is a skilled potter always ready to experiment. The idea of combining ceramics and macramé appeals to her greatly. Sometimes she makes ceramic pieces and does the macramé herself; other times she creates the pottery and leaves the knotting to others. Here are a few samples of the pottery she creates with macramé in mind.

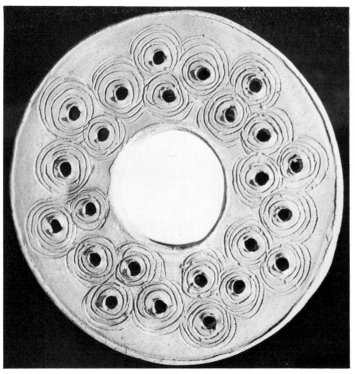

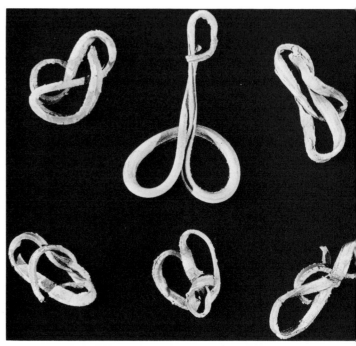

Fig. 259 (above) Mirror Blank. A knotter's delight—large holes abound! This mirror blank could be used in many, many different ways. *Ebby Malmgren.* Fig. 260 (top right) More Ceramic Pieces. The top middle piece was used in the hanging on page 221. *Ebby Malmgren.* Fig. 261 (right) Ceramic Pieces. Some ceramic pieces intended for use with macramé. The larger ones may become the starting point for someone's three-dimensional wall hanging, the smaller ones used as beads for decorative accents. *Ebby Malmgren.*

Fig. 262 Candle Holders. Ceramic candle holders with knotted hangers of tarred marline twine. *Ebby Malmgren.*

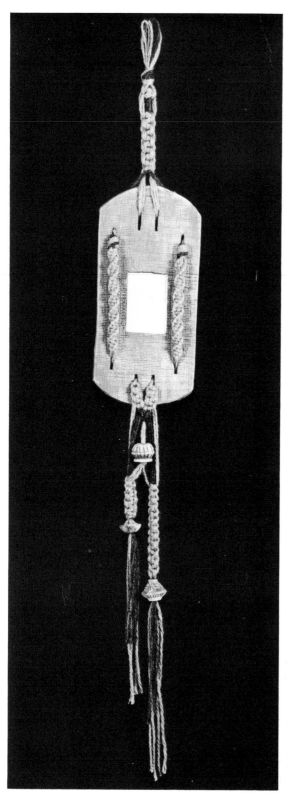

Here's one way that enameling and macramé have been successfully combined. This was a family project. Melissa Diamanti designed macramé panels for a fire screen around tiles her family had enameled. Her father soldered wires onto the back of the tiles so that they could be securely attached to the knotting (Figure 264).

Fig. 263 Clay Mirror with Macramé. Ebby Malmgren made this ceramic mirror blank, and incised a few slits into it. Just a touch of macramé and a few of Ebby's handmade beads were added to it. *Ebby Malmgren, Helene Bress.*

OTHER ART FORMS AND MACRAMÉ

Other art forms lend themselves well to combining them with macramé. Edwina Drobny does a superb job of combining handwrought metalwork with macramé to make especially handsome jewelry. She also creates her own armatures of steel on which she uses macramé. Her work is featured in Chapter 7, pages 190-205.

Fig. 264 (left) One panel of a Fire Screen. This is the first of a series of panels to be used as a fire screen. The macramé and enameling blend well together. Macramé, *Melissa Diamanti.* Enameling, *the Diamanti Family.*   *Fig. 265 (right)* Crochet and Macramé. Crochet, ceramics, and macramé combine freely and imaginatively in this neckpiece by the mother-daughter team, Lucille Cooper and her daughter, Cathy Cooper. Mrs. Cooper does the ceramic work, and Cathy, the crochet and macramé. The work of one interweaves beautifully with the work of the other. Ceramic piece, *Lucille Cooper.* Crochet and macramé, *Cathy Cooper.*

Fig. 266 Swamp Moss. Painting, stitchery, and macramé—it takes imagination to combine the three successfully. Madge Schneider has done it here. The painting is in pastel tones, is highlighted with stitchery and "framed" with macramé, top and bottom. Acrylic on unprimed canvas. *Madge Schneider.* Photo, *Seymour Bress.*

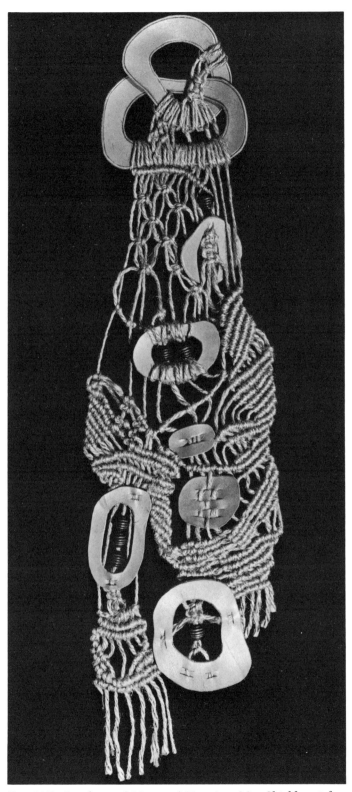

Fig. 267 Leather and Macramé Hanging. May Shields cut free form shapes out of leather and designed this jute wall hanging around them. Again, they look as if they were made for each other—and they were! *May Shields.*

263

Fig. 268 Don't look to Madge Schneider to separate media. This time she's dressed up her wire sculpture giraffe with a knotted jute bridle and saddle! *Madge Schneider.*

Bibliography

MACRAMÉ TECHNIQUES

Anchor Manual of Needlework, 3rd ed. Newton Centre, Mass.:
    Charles T. Branford Company, 1968.
de Dillmont, Thérèse, *Encyclopedia of Needlework.* Mulhouse,
    France, D.M.C., n.d.
Harvey, Virginia I., *Macramé: The Art of Creative Knotting.* New
    York: Van Nostrand Reinhold Company, 1967.
Nuova Enciclopedia Dei Lavori Femminili. Milan, Italy: Edizione
    Mani di Fata, n.d.
Paque, Joan Michaels, *Visual Instructional Macramé.* Privately
    printed, 1971.
Phillips, Mary Walker, *Step by Step Macramé.* New York: Golden
    Press, 1970.
West, Virginia M., *Finishing Touches for the Handweaver.* Newton
    Centre, Mass.: Charles T. Branford Company, 1968.

TWINING

Birrell, Verla, *The Textile Arts.* New York: Harper & Row, 1959.
Harvey, Virginia I., and Tidball, Harriet, *Weft Twining.* Lansing,
    Mich.: Shuttle Craft Guild, 1969.
Spencer, Elsie H., and Orwoll, Joanne, *Twining,* vol. 4-65. Shelby,
    N.C.: 1965.

FOR IDEAS ON FRAME LOOM WEAVING

Wilson, Jean, *Weaving Is for Anyone.* New York: Von Nostrand
    Reinhold Company, 1967.
Znamierowski, Nell, *Step by Step Weaving.* New York: Golden
    Press, 1967.

HISTORICAL

Ashley, Clifford W., *Ashley Book of Knots*. New York: Doubleday & Company, 1944.

Caulfield, S. F. A., and Saward, Blanche C., *Dictionary of Needlework*, 2nd ed. London: L. Upcott Gill, 1885.

di Brazza, Cora A. Slocomb, *A Guide to Old and New Lace in Italy Exhibited at Chicago, 1893*. Chicago: W. B. Conkey Company, 1893.

Groves, Sylvia, *The History of Needlework Tools and Accessories*, 2nd ed. New York: Hamlyn House, 1968.

Jackson, Mrs. F. Neville, *A History of Hand Made Lace*. New York: Scribners, 1900.

Jourdain, M., *History of Lace*. England: B. T. Batsford, 1908.

Lawrence, Cyrus, *Quipus and Witches' Knots*. Kansas: University of Kansas Press, 1967.

Lowes, Emily Leigh, *Chats on Old Lace and Needlework*. London: T. Fisher Unwin, 1908.

May, Florence Lewis, *Hispanic Lace and Lace Making*. New York: Hispanic Society of America, 1939.

Palliser, Fanny Bury, *History of Lace*. London: Sampson Low, 1875.

Ricci, Elisa, *Old Italian Lace*, vol. 1. Philadelphia: J. B. Lippincott, 1913.

Schuette, Marie, "Technique and Origin of Lace—History of Lace," *Ciba Review* (April 1949), No. 73, Basle, Switzerland.

Wharton, Edith, *The Age of Innocence*. New York: D. Appleton & Company, 1920.

Suppliers

These are dealers who are equipped to fill mail orders. You might also check your telephone directory for local suppliers, such as craft stores, hardware stores, upholstery shops, and marine supply stores.

Craft Yarns of Rhode Island
   603 Mineral Spring Ave.
   Pawtucket, R.I. 02862
	wide selection of macramé yarns

Frederick J. Fawcett, Inc.
   129 South St.
   Boston, Mass. 02111
	linen yarns

P. C. Herwig Co.
   264 Clinton St.
   Brooklyn, N.Y. 11201
	wide selection of macramé yarns

Macramé & Weaving Supply Co.
   63 E. Adams St.
   Chicago, Ill. 60603
	wide selection of macramé yarns

The Unicorn
   Box 645
   Rockville, Md. 20851
	macramé supplies and a wide selection of craft books

Yarn Depot
   545 Sutter
   San Francisco, Cal. 94102
	wide selection of macramé yarns

Index of Subjects

271

Index of Artists